A Cognitive Behavioural Therapy Programme for Problem Gambling

Namrata Raylu has been involved in a number of research activities in the area of addictive behaviours over the last 12 years and has published in the problem gambling area. Currently, she works as a research collaborator at the Psychology Department, University of Queensland and as a clinical psychologist in private practice.

Tian Po Oei has published widely in the areas of substance, anxiety and mood disorders and processes of change in psychotherapy, especially CBT in Asian cultures. Currently, he holds a personal Chair in Clinical Psychology at the University of Queensland and is the Director of the CBT Unit at Toowong Private Hospital.

This book is a treatment manual providing guidance for therapists treating clients with gambling addictions.

In this book the authors use a cognitive behavioural approach and provide a session by session guide for overcoming problem gambling. Essential topics covered include:

- assessment and psychoeducation
- cognitive behavioural strategies to stabilize gambling
- identifying and challenging thinking errors
- relaxation and imaginal exposure
- problem solving and goal setting
- managing negative emotions
- relapse prevention: maintaining a balanced lifestyle and coping with high-risk situations

A Cognitive Behavioural Therapy Programme for Problem Gambling supplies detailed information to help the therapist and client understand gambling behaviours, as well as practical advice on techniques that can be used with the client to change these behaviours.

This practical guide includes handouts and exercises that can be downloaded by purchasers of the print edition. It will provide helpful guidance for addiction counsellors and therapists worldwide.

A Cognitive Behavioural Therapy Programme for Problem Gambling

Therapist Manual

NAMRATA RAYLU AND TIAN PO OEI

Routledge
Taylor & Francis Group

LONDON AND NEW YORK

First published 2010 by Routledge
27 Church Road, Hove, East Sussex BN3 2FA

Simultaneously published in the USA and Canada
by Routledge
270 Madison Avenue, New York, NY 10016

Routledge is an imprint of the Taylor & Francis Group, an Informa business

Copyright © 2010 Namrata Raylu and Tian Po Oei

Typeset in Stone Serif by Garfield Morgan, Swansea, West Glamorgan
Printed and bound in Great Britain by TJ International, Padstow, Cornwall
Cover design by Andy Ward

This publication has been produced with paper manufactured to strict
environmental standards and with pulp derived from sustainable forests.

British Library Cataloguing in Publication Data
A catalogue record for this book is available from the British Library

Library of Congress Cataloging-in-Publication Data
Raylu, Namrata.
  A cognitive behavioural therapy programme for problem gambling:
therapist manual / Namrata Raylu & Tian Po Oei.
       p. cm.
  Includes bibliographical references.
  ISBN 978-0-415-54816-8 (pbk.)
  1. Compulsive gambling–Treatment. 2. Compulsive gamblers–
Rehabilitation. 3. Cognitive therapy. I. Oei, Tian Po. II. Title.
  RC569.5.G35R39 2010
  616.85'227–dc22
                                                        2009049336

ISBN: 978-0-415-54816-8 (pbk only)

Contents

Figures and tables

Figures

Tables

Preface

The journey of this book started more than 10 years ago. At that time, the efficacy of cognitive behaviour therapy (CBT) in treating anxiety and mood disorders was well established. However, the efficacy of CBT in treating problem gambling was still unclear. In addition, due to changes in government policies and social factors gambling, in particular casino and electronic machine gambling were legalized and thus, widely accessible to the public in general. Thus, problem gambling and in particular the treatment of problem gambling became an important issue.

Professor Oei is one of the earlier researchers examining the efficacy of CBT for the treatment of addictive behaviours, in particular alcohol addiction (Jackson & Oei, 1978; Oei & Jackson 1980; 1982; 1984). When Dr. Raylu arrived at the University of Queensland in 1999, the journey of this book began. We decided to collaborate. Since both of us were using CBT for addictive behaviours, it was natural for us to find an efficient CBT programme for problem gambling.

The CBT treatment programme provided in this book largely reflects the findings of a comprehensive literature review of the factors associated with the development, maintenance and treatment literature (originally published as Raylu & Oei, 2002 and updated in Chapter 2) and a literature review of the treatment of problem gambling (also provided in Chapter 2).

This CBT treatment programme consists of ten core and three elective sessions. The first two sessions involve assessment, psychoeducation and teaching clients self-management strategies to stabilize their gambling behaviours. The other eight core sessions teach coping skills and strategies to help clients deal with the factors that may be maintaining their gambling and to prevent relapses. The three non-core sessions aim to assist clients in dealing with financial difficulties experienced because of gambling and to deal with issues relating to interpersonal relationships, especially with significant others. It also aims to teach significant others strategies to cope/deal with the client's behaviours and hence assist with achieving and maintaining a change in the client's gambling behaviours.

The manual is written for professional health workers with some background training in health and social sciences as well as some knowledge of CBT. Therapists with more knowledge of the gambling/problem gambling literature may find some sessions too detailed (e.g. the assessment and education sessions). We decided that such detail would ensure that therapists from a wide range of backgrounds would feel comfortable using this manual to work with a client with problem gambling. We are fully aware that no one single treatment approach can help everyone experiencing gambling problems and that therapists must play an important role integrating and treating factors that are relevant to the clients. Thus, the treatment programme detailed in this book needs to be used just as a guide. Therapists need to keep in mind that each client is different and has different needs. Thus, therapists can vary the duration, frequency and distribution of the sessions depending on the needs of clients. As long as the major points are covered the therapists own natural presentation style is encouraged.

This book would not have been possible without the involvement of many postgraduate clinical psychology students and staff at the School of Psychology, the University of Queensland who helped field test the treatment programme for several years. We would like to thank them for their contributions, in particular Dr. Leanne Casey who helped in coordinating and supervising some of the postgraduate clinical students. The treatment programme has benefited from their comments and their dedication.

We would like to thank the Queensland Office of Gaming Regulation for providing several research grants for the field testing of this treatment programme. In addition, the School of Psychology and the University of Queensland provided generous facilities and administrative support. IN addition, the School of Psychology and the University of Queensland provided generous facilities and administrative support.

Although many people and organizations contributed to the outcome of this book, the statements do not necessarily represent or reflect the views of the University of Queensland, the Queensland Office of Gaming Regulation or the Queensland Government. We take full responsibility for any shortcomings of this book.

The journey for this book has been a long but very rewarding one. We have learned from our postgraduate students, the clients who participated in the field testing and the difficulties of this long journey. We feel that this journey had made both of us better practising clinical psychologists and researchers. Similarly, it is our sincere hope that you, the therapists, may find this book useful and helpful in treating your clients with gambling problems. Our final wish is that clients with gambling problems benefit from this book.

Namrata Raylu
Tian Po S Oei

Overview

1.1 PROGRAMME CONTENT AND GOALS

This manual focuses on providing treatment to individuals experiencing gambling problems. The programme has a cognitive behavioural treatment (CBT) approach. It supports the role of basic conditioning principles in the development and maintenance of problem and pathological gambling. It also emphasizes that an individual's thinking (e.g. the way things are interpreted) affects the individual's behaviour. It highlights the importance of changing distorted beliefs/thoughts and behaviours in reducing the frequency and severity of gambling. It provides practical information to help understand the development and maintenance of problem gambling. It also provides a range of coping skills/strategies to help change dysfunctional gambling behaviours and issues associated with it.

The treatment programme provided in this manual largely reflects the findings of a comprehensive literature review of (1) the factors implicated in playing a role in the development and maintenance of problem gambling, and (2) the treatment of problem gambling. This review can be found in Chapter 2. Please note that some of the material in this review was originally published in *Clinical Psychology Review* (i.e. Raylu & Oei, 2002).

Presently, behavioural, cognitive and combined CBT have the most outcome research and appear to be the most effective psychotherapy in treating gambling problems (Grant & Potenza, 2007; Toneatto & Ladouceur, 2003; Toneatto & Millar, 2004). Several controlled studies (Ladouceur & Sylvain, 1999; Petry et al., 2006; Sylvain, Ladouceur, & Boisvert, 1997) have shown CBT to be an effective treatment for gambling problems. Behavioural and CBT appear to have several advantages such as being cost-effective, having long-term benefits and allowing for booster sessions.

A substantial part of the treatment programme aims to assist the client to deal with factors that maintain gambling problems and thus, are responsible for lapses or relapses. Thus, it teaches the client a range of alternative cognitive behavioural coping (includes social and life) skills. It assumes these skills are important in reducing/stopping problem behaviours and maintaining the treatment gains in the long term. The treatment programme also has two additional CBT components highlighted by the literature review in Chapter 2 as important techniques in treating problem gambling. First, relapse prevention strategies have not only been used in the treatment of substance disorders (Rawson & Obert, 2002; Witkiewitz & Marlatt, 2009), they have been shown to be an effective treatment for problem gambling (Echeburúa, Fernández-Montalvo, & Báez, 1999; 2000). Teaching the client techniques to maintain therapeutic gains and minimize relapse in the future (i.e. when the client leaves the programme) is very important for long-term success/recovery (Echeburúa et al., 2000). If the client has techniques to help them identify and cope with difficult high-risk situations that can lead to a lapse or relapse, he/she is more likely to avoid further gambling behaviours. Second, numerous CBT studies of problem gamblers (Milton, Crino, Hunt, & Prosser, 2002; Wulfert, Blanchard, Freidenberg, & Martell, 2006; Wulfert, Blanchard, & Martell, 2003) have shown that motivational interviewing strategies can improve compliance with the treatment programmes. These studies are discussed in more detail in Chapter 2. Thus, the treatment programme described in this book also supports this additional component in treating problem gamblers.

There are four parts to the programme.

⊙ The aim of the first part is to assess the client's problems and needs. It also aims to use psychoeducation (e.g. for recognition of problem gambling behaviours and monitoring their own gambling patterns) as well as motivational interviewing techniques to encourage the client to change dysfunctional behaviours and their attitudes to functional ones.

⊙ The second phase aims to provide the client with basic cognitive and behavioural self-management/coping strategies to help stabilize excessive gambling. It also aims to provide the client with strategies to cope with the urges to gamble as well as basic cognitive and behavioural strategies to minimize negative consequences in case lapses occur. It also encourages/teaches life skills such as engagement in physical exercise, as well as pleasurable and/or relaxation activities. The general aim of this second phase is to assist the client to successfully stop or control gambling (i.e. stabilize gambling) and increase motivation and their sense of efficacy in relation to successfully completing the programme.

⊙ The third part of the programme teaches the client a range of coping skills to help maintain positive changes made in relation to his/her gambling behaviours as well as other areas in his/her life. The client needs to become aware of (and how to deal with) the thoughts, feelings and physical sensations associated with maintaining gambling behaviours (Sharpe, 1998). This includes teaching the client techniques to challenge dysfunctional thinking and deal with negative emotions. Relaxation training and imaginal exposure techniques will help the client control and habituate to the high levels of arousal that are often experienced in the presence of gambling triggers or gambling urges. Skills to self-manage negative emotions (e.g. depression, anxiety and anger) as well as stress are also included. Problem-solving and goal-setting skills training will be beneficial to the client as the ability to consider the long-term consequences of actions and delay immediate gratification is often lacking among problem gamblers.

⊙ Finally, the fourth phase of treatment aims to teach the client strategies to maintain therapeutic gains and minimize relapse in the future via relapse prevention strategies (i.e. identifying and coping with high-risk situations that can lead to gambling).

1.2 STRUCTURE OF THE PROGRAMME AND SESSIONS

The programme is composed of ten core sessions and three elective sessions. Session one involves completing a thorough assessment of the client's problems in order to devise a case formulation as well as an individualized treatment plan. Assessment of the client's motivation towards treatment is essential at this point. Motivational interviewing techniques can help increase the client's commitment to change. Session two involves providing the client with psychoeducation on gambling-related problems, and teaching the client some skills (both behavioural and cognitive skills) to help stabilize gambling. Session three includes helping the client identify gambling-specific thinking errors that encourage the client to continue gambling despite significant losses. Session four involves teaching the client to challenge these gambling-specific thinking errors. Session five involves teaching the client to identify and challenge other gambling-related thinking errors. These include thinking errors regarding the client's perceptions of gambling behaviour, consequences of the gambling problems, etc. Session six involves relaxation and imaginal exposure training. Session seven focuses on problem-solving and goals-setting skills training. Session eight explores the negative emotions that are common among problem gamblers including guilt, anger and provides the client with strategies to effectively deal with such negative emotions. The last two sessions aim to maximize treatment gains and reduce relapse in the future. Session nine involves discussing with the client the importance of a balanced lifestyle and encouraging the client to identify areas in his/her life that require changes and set goals to achieve these changes. The last session helps the client deal with anxieties about leaving the programme and teaches the client how to cope with high-risk situations that can lead to gambling.

There are three elective sessions. The first elective session involves teaching the client strategies to improve his/her interpersonal relationships. It assumes that some problem gamblers might benefit from basic social communication and assertiveness skills training. The second elective session involves helping the client to deal with financial difficulties experienced because of gambling (e.g. getting out of debt, budgeting). The last elective session is specially designed for significant others. It involves discussing/assessing the impact of the client's and his/her significant other's behaviours on each other. It also aims to educate significant others about the nature of problem gambling and factors involved in the development and maintenance of the problem. It also teaches significant others strategies to improve the client's readiness for change, assist the client through recovery and cope with the negative consequences of the client's behaviours. The ideal time to deliver any of these sessions is in the third part of the programme. Furthermore, each elective session can be covered over a number of sessions.

These skills are taught in the elective sessions for a number of reasons. First, problem gamblers present with financial difficulties to differing degrees depending on their income levels, socioeconomic status, etc. Not all problem gamblers are actually in debt when presenting for treatment. Furthermore, many problem gamblers that do present with debts require financial counselling due to the vast extent of financial problems. Thus, only those problem gamblers with minor debt problems would benefit from this elective session. Similarly, problem gamblers present to treatment with varying degrees of relationship problems with their significant others. Some clients will require more intensive relationship counselling to address their relationship problems. Also, there are differences in the degree to which clients are involved with various significant others in their lives as well as the degree to which the significant others are affected by the client's gambling. Thus, not all problem gamblers presenting for treatment will find these three elective sessions of benefit. The therapist therefore needs to assess whether a client will benefit from these sessions or require more extensive counselling in these specific areas (i.e. relationship or financial counselling).

Figure 1.1 is a flow chart of the programme structure.

1.3 GUIDELINES ON USING THE TREATMENT PROGRAMME

As no single recovery programme can help everyone experiencing gambling problems, the treatment programme detailed in this manual is just a guide. A thorough assessment and an individualized treatment plan

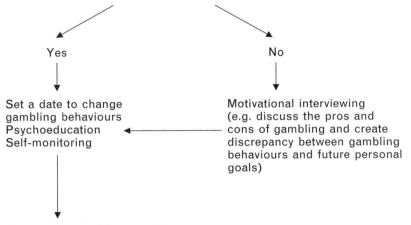

Assessment (including assessment of the motivation to change – Is there a commitment to change?)

Yes   No

Set a date to change
gambling behaviours   Motivational interviewing
Psychoeducation   (e.g. discuss the pros and
Self-monitoring   cons of gambling and create
                               discrepancy between gambling
                               behaviours and future personal
                               goals)

Strategies to stabilize gambling
– Environmental/stimulus control
– Changing contingencies of reinforcement and
  punishment via contingency contracting
– Strategies to cope with urges
– Self-instructional training

Strategies to maintain abstinence/control
(Dealing with maintenance factors)
– Identifying and challenging negative/dysfunctional
  cognitions
– Relaxation techniques
– Imaginal exposure
– Strategies to cope with negative emotions
– Problem-solving skills training
– Goal-setting skills training
– Interpersonal skills training (including assertiveness,
  social and communications skills)
– Budgeting, debt reduction strategies

Strategies to prevent relapse
– Balanced lifestyle (including establishing support
  networks)
– Identifying and coping with high-risk situations

Figure 1.1 Flow chart of the programme structure

are important for each client. Problem gamblers often present with a multitude of problems including anxiety and depressive disorders. This manual is only useful for clients who present with a gambling problem as the main issue of concern.

This manual can be used to treat problem gamblers experiencing problems with different forms of gambling (e.g. table gambling, machine gambling, sports gambling, horse race gambling or Internet gambling). Furthermore, those individuals that want to abstain from gambling as well as those that prefer to just control their gambling can benefit from the treatment programme.

The manual was written for professional health workers with some background training in health and social sciences as well as some knowledge in CBT. Therapists with more knowledge of the gambling/problem gambling literature may find some sessions too detailed (e.g. the assessment and education sessions). We decided that such detail would ensure that CBT-trained therapists from a wide range of backgrounds would feel comfortable in working with a client with problem gambling.

The CBT programme can also be used as an adjunct to other therapies available. There are a wide range of practical skills and techniques (e.g. relaxation exercises as well as identifying and challenging negative/dysfunctional thinking) described in this manual. One or a number of these techniques can be combined with non-CBT interventions (e.g. psychodynamic therapy or pharmacotherapy). Many multimodal treatment inpatient and outpatient studies (Taber, McCormick, Russo, Adkins, & Ramirez, 1987; Russo, Taber, McCormick, & Ramirez, 1984) that have incorporated CBT as a component of their treatment programmes have reported positive results.

CBT can enhance the efficacy of other treatment approaches with problem gamblers. Recently Ravindran et al. (2006) demonstrated that pharmacological therapy (paroxetine) in conjunction with CBT may be superior to either treatment used alone. The individuals in the combined treatment group had significantly less gambling behaviours at post-treatment compared with those only taking paroxetine. The researchers suggested that CBT was most likely to be an effective form of treatment for problem gambling. However, the addition of paroxetine to the CBT may benefit a subgroup of problem gamblers.

Therapists need to keep in mind that each client is different and has different needs. Thus, the duration, frequency and distribution of the sessions are only a suggestion, and could vary depending on the client. Some sessions are one and half hours long, whereas others are only an hour long. Significant others could be included in none of the sessions, only some of the sessions or all the sessions. The therapist can combine or mix certain sessions (e.g. sessions relating to identifying and challenging cognitions). Depending on the client's needs, certain strategies/skills discussed in the latter sessions can be covered in earlier sessions (e.g. relaxation training for anxious individuals). The therapist can also cover a particular session topic over a number of sessions (e.g. Session two in Chapter 4 that provides psychoeducation and discusses strategies to stabilize gambling) depending on the client's needs. Mixing of Session one and two is especially advised. At the end of the first session (i.e. assessment interview), it would be beneficial to the client to briefly discuss some strategies to control gambling (discussed in Chapter 4) so that the client can start putting in place some strategies to control his/her gambling. Even a small degree of success might lead the client to feel a sense of achievement and improve the client's motivation to continue treatment. Consequently, session one (assessment interview) could be conducted over the first two sessions. Similarly, Session two (self-management strategies to control gambling) could also be conducted over the first two sessions.

Prior to the sessions, the therapist is encouraged to read relevant sections of the manual and ensure the main points of each session are covered. Photocopying information for the client or relevant monitoring sheets before the start of some of the sessions is required.

Client information handouts are included at the end of most sessions. Client handouts summarize the main points and main techniques learnt in those sessions. Thus, the client should be encouraged to buy a folder to collect these notes, as the notes will be useful to the client even after the programme has completed.

Sessions usually begin with a review of the skills taught in the preceding session and the home exercises. Therapists need to discuss reasons for non-compliance (if necessary) with home exercises to ensure they complete the subsequent exercises. The therapist can use contingencies other than social praise or disapproval to enhance compliance with the home exercise tasks (Kadden et al., 1995). Appendix A contains some guidelines for home exercises. Prior to introducing new material there is a discussion of the aims and rationale of the sessions.

Therapists need to take care not to give the client the impression that they are concerned about following a strict agenda. As long as the major points are covered the therapists' own natural presentation style is encouraged. It is also important that therapists do not spend significant portions of the sessions lecturing to the client.

For long lasting changes it is vital that therapists model the strategies appropriately and provide the client with constructive feedback. The client should be encouraged to actively participate in recovery and to problem solve, role-play (behavioural rehearsal) and complete home exercises that enable the client to apply the skills learnt outside the therapy sessions. Appendix A and B outline some guidelines for home exercises and role-plays/behavioural rehearsals respectively.

Review of the problem gambling treatment literature

2.1 INTRODUCTION

Pathological gambling is a progressive and chronic disorder that is characterized by an unrelenting failure to resist impulses to gamble, and where this 'maladaptive behavior disrupts, or damages personal, family, or vocational pursuits' (American Psychiatric Association, 1994, p. 615). Research studies report that the prevalence of pathological gambling in the population is between 1 and 2 per cent (Shaffer, Hall, & Vander Bilt, 1997; Stucki & Rihs-Middel, 2007). However, estimates of prevalence rates for pathological gambling, internationally range from 0.8 to 5 per cent (Molde et al., 2004). The prevalence of problem gambling (that is, those experiencing gambling problems to a lesser degree than required by the Diagnostic Statistic Manual IV (DSM–IV) criteria as well as those meeting the criteria) exceed these figures.

The legalization of gambling has had an impact on the growth of the gambling industry due to the increase in the variety, availability and accessibility of games (Productivity Commission Report, 1999). This greater accessibility to gambling has led to an increase in the amount of money individuals spend on gambling, the number of individuals who would be classified as 'regular gamblers', and subsequently, an increase in the number of people experiencing gambling problems (Campbell & Lester, 1999; Dickson-Gillespie, Rugle, Rosenthal, & Fong, 2008; Jacques, Ladouceur, & Ferland, 2000).

Problem gambling has gained much attention as a result of the many negative social consequences it has on gamblers, their significant others and on society in general. Some of the common social consequences of problem gambling include its negative impact on gamblers' physical and mental health and performance in vocational situations (Productivity Commission Report, 1999). Financial hardship (via debts and asset losses) may lead to legal consequences, such as bankruptcy, loans or criminal acts to gain money (Grant, Schreiber, Odlaug, & Kim, 2010; Ladouceur, Boisvert, Pepin, Loranger, & Sylvain, 1994). Interpersonal problems between gamblers and their significant others include domestic violence, relationship breakdown, neglect of family and a negative impact on the physical and mental health of family members (Kalischuk, Nowatzki, Cardwell, Klein, & Solowoniuk, 2006; Korman, Collins, Dutton, Dhayananthan, Littman-Sharp, & Skinner, 2008). Problem gambling also has a negative impact on society, by its association with increased crime committed by some gamblers and the financial costs associated with treatment (Productivity Commission Report, 1999).

Considering the many negative impacts associated with problem gambling it is important that successful treatment programmes are available to those experiencing such problems. This chapter provides an overview of the status of treatment for such individuals by examining the literature on problem gambling and its treatment. To achieve this, PsycINFO and Medline databases (all years up to August, 2009) were reviewed. The current review aims to provide:

- a summary of the factors associated with the development and maintenance of problem gambling;
- a summary of the current treatments for problem gambling;
- evidence for the efficacy of CBT for problem gambling;
- the rationale and evidence of the effectiveness of the CBT programme contained in this book.

2.2 FACTORS IMPLICATED IN PLAYING A ROLE IN THE DEVELOPMENT AND MAINTENANCE OF PROBLEM GAMBLING

Several factors have been identified in the literature as being 'motivations' for gambling. These include participating in gambling activities as a way to:

- demonstrate one's worth;
- get approval and social acceptance from others;
- rebel;
- relieve difficult and painful events/emotions (e.g. anger, depression, frustration and anxiety);
- win;
- be sociable;
- beat the odds;
- experience excitement;
- reduce boredom;
- pass time and have fun (Raylu & Oei, 2002).

Although no single motivator has consistently been identified a range of variables has been implicated in explaining the development and maintenance of problem gambling. These factors include familial, individual and sociological factors. Each of these will be outlined below.

2.2.1 Familial factors

Studies have supported both environmental (e.g. the role of social learning) and genetic factors as risks for problem gambling (Oei & Raylu, 2003; 2004; Scherrer, Xian, Shah, Volberg, Slutske, & Eisen, 2005; Xian, Scherrer, Slutske, Shah, Volberg, & Eisen, 2007). Social learning theory posits that individuals learn, model and maintain behaviours that are observable and are reinforced. Thus, family members as well as friends can often act as models for gambling behaviour. Several studies have reported that problem gamblers are more likely than non-problem gamblers to report having relatives, especially parents, with gambling problems (Grant & Kim, 2001; Black, Monahan, Temkit, & Shaw, 2006; Black, Moyer, & Schlosser, 2003).

There is also evidence of a genetic transmission of problem gambling (e.g. Shah, Eisen, Xian, & Potenza, 2005; Winters & Rich, 1998). Genetics could explain 40–54 per cent of the variance in risk of developing gambling problems (Eisen et al., 1998; 2001). Williams and Potenza (2008) summarized a number of genetic mechanisms that may underlie susceptibility to problem gambling. These included the serotonin transporter gene (Perez de Castro, Ibáñez, Saiz-Ruiz, & Fernandez-Piqueras, 1999), DNA polymorphisms in Monoamine oxidases A genes (Ibáñez, Perez de Castro, Fernandez-Piqueras, Blanco, & Saiz-Ruiz, 2000), and dopamine 1, 2, and 4 receptor genes (Comings et al., 1996; da Silva Lobo et al., 2007; Perez de Castro, Ibáñez, Torres, Saiz-Ruiz, & Fernandez-Piqueras, 1997).

2.2.2 Individual factors

Several individual factors have been implicated in the development and maintenance of problem gambling. These include personality, cognitions, psychological states and biology/biochemistry. These are discussed below.

2.2.2.1 Personality

Problem gamblers differ from non-gamblers in some personality traits. Although a number of personality traits have been assessed among problem gamblers, impulsivity and sensation seeking have been studied the most. Impulsivity (i.e. the tendency to act before forethought) is currently the personality trait most strongly related to problem gambling. Impulsivity has been found to consistently predict problem gambling (e.g. Myrseth, Pallesen, Molde, Johnsen, & Lorvik, 2009).

Problem gamblers score higher on measures of impulsivity or dimensions of impulsivity, as compared with non-gamblers, recreational gamblers and/or low-frequency gamblers (Bagby, Vachon, Bulmash, Toneatto, Quilty, & Costa, 2007; Carlton & Manowitz, 1994; Loxton, Nguyen, Casey, & Dawe, 2008; Steel & Blaszczynski, 1998). Impulsivity has also been related to treatment drop out (Leblond, Ladouceur, & Blaszczynski, 2003), severity of problem gambling (Steel & Blaszczynski, 1996) and poor response to treatment (Maccallum, Blaszczynski, Ladouceur, & Nower, 2007).

Some researchers have also identified sensation seeking as a risk factor for developing problem gambling (Ledgerwood & Petry, 2006; Slutske, Caspi, Moffitt, & Poulton, 2005). However, other researchers have not found this connection (Coventry & Constable, 1999; Clarke, 2004). Some other studies have indicated that sensation seeking may be a factor for only certain types of problem gamblers. These include younger gamblers (Powell, Hardoon, Derevensky, & Gupta, 1999), those that play certain games (e.g. gamblers that participate in casino or illegal gambling) (Coventry & Brown, 1993; Dickerson, 1993) and gamblers that are not in treatment (Blanco, Orensanz-Munoz, Blanco-Jerez, & Saiz-Ruiz, 1996).

It is possible that sensation seeking and impulsivity operate at two separate stages of problem gambling. Sensation seeking may motivate some gamblers (especially young ones) to participate in different forms of gambling, whereas impulsivity may drive them to continue gambling despite heavy or continuous losses (Zuckerman, 1999).

Sensation seeking is also related to the arousal hypothesis of gambling, which suggests that rather than the money, it is the excitement of playing that acts as a reward for problem gamblers (Anderson & Brown, 1984). Dickerson (1984) suggested that there is a range of stimuli in gambling situations (e.g. spinning wheels at roulette tables, croupier's calls in casinos, lights and sounds of gambling machines and placing bets in table games) that act as reinforcers by producing excitement and arousal. There is a great deal of empirical evidence suggesting that regular gamblers become aroused while gambling, where arousal is assessed via heart rate measurements, self-reports or questionnaires (Raylu & Oei, 2002). Furthermore, this arousal effect has been found for a number of games (Raylu & Oei, 2002).

Considering the number of personality traits associated with problem gambling, it is not surprising that problem gamblers often present with comorbid personality disorders. Blaszczynski and Steel (1998) found that 93 per cent of the problem gamblers in a treatment programme for gambling problems met the diagnostic criteria for at least one personality disorder and there was an average of 4.6 personality disorders per gambler. Some researchers have found high rates of cluster 'B' personality disorders (i.e. personality disorder types that appear to be dramatic, emotional and erratic such as antisocial, borderline, histrionic and narcissistic personality disorders) that were linked to high impulsivity and affective instability among problem gamblers (Bagby, Vachon, Bulmash, & Quilty, 2008; Blaszczynski & Steel, 1998; Fernández-Montalvo & Echeburúa, 2004). However, others have found high rates of cluster 'A' (i.e. personality disorders marked by odd, eccentric behaviours) or cluster 'C' personality disorders (i.e. personality disorders marked by anxious and fearful behaviours) among problem gamblers (Black & Moyer, 1998; Specker, Carlson, Edmonson, Johnson, & Marcotte, 1996). However, Bagby et al. (2007) noted that the particular personality disorders found among problem gamblers depended on the measuring instrument used.

2.2.2.2 Cognitions

Evidence suggests that irrational and negative thoughts play a significant role in the development and maintenance of problem gambling (Gaboury & Ladouceur, 1989; Oei, Lin, & Raylu, 2007a; 2008; Raylu & Oei, 2004b; Zuckerman, 1999), as well as relapse (Hodgins & El-Guebaly, 2004). That is, the gambler holds a set of false beliefs about gambling that helps to maintain gambling despite heavy/continuous losses. These include believing that they can directly or indirectly influence gambling outcomes, believing that they can correctly predict the outcomes, and making false interpretations about gambling outcomes (Toneatto, 1999). A number of studies have reported high rates of these kinds of beliefs among regular gamblers and problem gamblers as compared with non-problem gamblers. Also, these findings have been replicated under several different conditions including: frequent or infrequent wins; limited or unlimited stakes; regular or occasional gamblings; and in a variety of games (Raylu & Oei, 2002).

Several factors have been found to influence gambling cognitions. The more a gambling situation contains factors of choice (e.g. having the opportunity to choose your number/colour in a roulette game), famili-arity (e.g. having a favourite gambling machine) and involvement (e.g.

being able to throw your own dice in a game of craps), the more it creates an illusion of control (Langer, 1975). Furthermore, games that require or are perceived to require skill (e.g. horse race, cards or sports gambling) are more likely to produce impaired control and encourage continued gambling despite losses than those that are perceived to require luck such as lotteries (Dickerson, 1993; Langer, 1975; Toneatto, Blitz-Miller, Calderwood, Dragonetti, & Tsanos, 1997). Dickerson (1993) suggested that there might be different psychological processes causing impaired control in different forms of gambling because different games vary across dimensions. Some games are continuous in nature (e.g. inconsiderable time between bet and outcome) such as gaming machines, whereas others are discontinuous in nature (e.g. considerable time between bet and outcome) such as lotteries. Games that are continuous in nature are more likely to produce impaired control and consequently encourage gamblers to continue gambling despite losses. Games that have high frequency and immediacy of pay out (e.g. gambling machines) are more appealing for gamblers, because the instant gratification and excitement/arousal experienced is greater than for games that have low frequency and delayed payment (e.g. lotteries). Walker (1992) reported that machine gamblers have higher levels of irrational thinking associated with problematic gambling, as compared with gamblers that play other games. Other factors found to act as significant factors associated with impaired control for problem gamblers include alcohol (Baron & Dickerson, 1999; Kyngdon & Dickerson, 1999), stress (Friedland, Keinan, & Regev, 1992) and difficult emotions such as depression (Dickerson, 1993).

Studies have also suggested that a gambler's cognitions may work together with physiological factors, such as bodily arousal, to help explain the maintenance of problem gambling (Griffiths, 1991; Ladouceur, Sévigny, Blaszczynski, O'Connor, & Lavoie, 2003; Oei, Lin, & Raylu, 2007a; 2007b; Raylu & Oei, 2004c). The expectancy of winning money rather than playing the game affects arousal (Ladouceur, Sylvain, Boutin, Lachance, Doucet, & Leblond, 2003). When a gambler nearly wins, he or she gets physiologically aroused and the gambler's cognitions suggest that he/she is not constantly losing but constantly 'nearly winning' and, thus, this stimulates further play (Griffiths, 1991).

2.2.2.3 *Negative psychological states*

Negative psychological states such as anxiety, depression and stress have frequently been linked to the initiation and maintenance of gambling (Coman, Burrows, & Evans, 1997; Friedland et al., 1992; Henry, 1996; Oei,

Lin, & Raylu, 2008), high severity of gambling problems (Oei & Raylu, 2009) as well as gambling relapse (Hodgins & El-Guebaly, 2004). However, it is still not known whether such negative moods are a result or a cause of problem gambling.

Suicide attempts are also very common among problem gamblers (Blaszczynski & Farrell, 1998; Ledgerwood, Steinberg, Wu, & Potenza, 2005; Newman & Thompson, 2007). Suicide attempt rates range from 12 to 24 per cent among this population (Raylu & Oei, 2002). Suicide among problem gamblers has been linked to greater severity of gambling problems (Hodgins, Mansley, & Thygesen, 2006), debt (Blaszczynski & Farrell, 1998; Yip, Yang, Ip, Law, & Watson, 2007), mental health and substance misuse problems (Blaszczynski & Farrell, 1998; Hodgins et al., 2006), relationship problems (Blaszczynski & Farrell, 1998; Maccallum & Blaszczynksi, 2003) and illegal behaviours (Maccallum & Blaszczynksi, 2003).

Several studies have suggested that the presence of other psychological problems may either increase the chances of an individual developing problem gambling or aid in the maintenance of gambling problems (Langenbucher, Bavly, Labouvie, Sanjuan, & Martin, 2001; Maccallam & Blaszczynski, 2002; Specker et al., 1996). Specker et al. (1996) investigated psychiatric problems among problem gamblers seeking outpatient treatment for gambling, and found high lifetime rates of Axis I (92 per cent) but not Axis II (25 per cent) diagnoses in problem gamblers as compared with controls. Gambling problems are often associated with other comorbid psychological problems such as substance use problems, affective and anxiety disorders, personality disorders, attention-deficit hyperactivity disorder (ADHD) and other impulse control disorders (Black & Moyer, 1998; Brewer, Grant & Potenza, 2008; Iancu, Lowengrub, Dembinsky, Kotler, & Dannon, 2008; Petry, Stinson, & Grant, 2005).

2.2.2.4 Biology/biochemistry

Although research in this area is still in its infancy, several biochemistry/biological factors have been linked to problem gambling, including frontal lobe deficits, chemical imbalances/dysfunctional neurotransmitter systems and physiological arousal (Iancu et al., 2008; Raylu & Oei, 2002). Current theories of the neuropathology of problem gambling implicate pathways in the brain related to motivation, reward, memory, learning, control, decision-making and impulsivity (Iancu et al., 2008).

A number of studies have demonstrated deficits/lesions in specific parts of the brain that are related to problem gambling. Some studies have suggested the involvement of frontal lobe damage in the pathophysiology of problem gambling after finding deficits in decision-making and tasks of inhibitory control among problem gamblers (Cavedini, Riboldi, Keller, D'Annucci, & Bellodi, 2002; Kalechstein, Fong, Rosenthal, Davis, Vanyo, & Newton, 2007; Marazziti et al., 2008a; Roca, Torralva, Lopez, Cetkovich, Clark, & Manes, 2008). These studies suggest that executive functioning impairment may play a role in the development of problem gambling. Reuter, Raedler, Rose, Hand, Gläscher, and Büchel (2005) found that prefrontal activation was negatively related to severity of gambling problems. Goldstein, Manowitz, Nora, Swartzburg and Carlton (1985) found that gamblers performed worse than controls on order attention measures and were more likely to report childhood behaviours consistent with attention deficits. This suggested that problem gamblers might be distinguished by problems with attention that are similar to those suggested for ADHD. These findings also support studies that have reported increased rates of ADHD symptoms among problem gamblers (Rugle & Melamed, 1993).

The problem gambling literature has also shown that problem gamblers may have chemical imbalances/dysfunctional neurotransmitter systems. A number of studies have shown dysfunction in the serotonergic system among problem gamblers (e.g. Blanco et al., 1996; Ibáñez et al., 2000; Marazziti et al., 2008b; Perez de Castro et al., 1999). These studies demonstrate evidence of reduced serotonergic activity with possible postsynaptive hypersensitivity of serotonin receptors in problem gamblers (Blanco, Ibáñez, Saiz-Ruiz, Blanco-Jerez, & Nunes, 2000). Serotonin dysfunction is linked to behavioural initiation, disinhibition and poor impulse control (Hollander, Buchalter, & DeCaria, 2000), which is related to the onset of the vicious gambling cycle and difficulty in stopping gambling (Raylu & Oei, 2002).

Evidence also suggests that problem gamblers may have a disturbance of the central noradrenergic system in the brain (Bergh, Eklund, Soedersten, & Nordin, 1997; DeCaria, Hollander, Nora, Stein, Simeon, & Cohen, 1997; Roy et al., 1988). Noradrenaline has been linked with arousal and impulse control (Siever, 1987). These studies suggest that the noradrenergic system plays a possible role in explaining selective attention among problem gamblers and is related to greater arousal (perhaps related to sensation seeking), 'readiness for gambling' or risk taking among these individuals (Blanco et al., 2000).

Evidence regarding dopamine suggests that problem gamblers may have a hyperactivity of the dopaminergic pathways, which are associated with both positive and negative rewards/reinforcement (Bergh et al., 1997;

Blanco et al., 2000). Individuals whose genetic or environmental situation leads to low or insufficient dopamine in the reward system of the brain are prone to anxiety, cravings and not being well. In order to replace these feelings gamblers may engage in activities that momentarily overcome this scarcity (Sunderwirth & Milkman, 1991). Increased activity of the dopaminergic pathways could be related to positive reinforcement (e.g. increased arousal) that the gambler receives for gambling. Increased activity of the dopaminergic pathways may also be related to negative rewards as increased gambling may produce a withdrawal state that is reflected in increases in brain stimulation reward thresholds similar to those for opiate withdrawals (Bergh et al., 1997). This may produce the behavioural (e.g. anxiety) and cognitive symptoms (e.g. irrational thinking) of withdrawal from gambling in problem gamblers.

Physiological studies that have looked at heart rate measures have suggested increased arousal among problem gamblers (Anderson & Brown, 1984; Leary & Dickerson, 1985). There is also biological evidence that supports the role of increased arousal among people with gambling problems. Plasma endorphins (a group of peptides found in the brain and pituitary) have been implicated in 'mood disturbances associated with psychological states and in addictive processes, the latter through their reward transmitting properties in accordance with operant and classical conditioning principles' (Blaszczynski, Winters, & McConaghy, 1986, p. 3). Thus, it may be that development and maintenance of gambling is related to endorphin activity. Manowitz, Amorosa, Goldstein and Carlton (1993) found that plasma levels of uric acid increased over time during gambling, indicating that an increase in uric acid levels may be related to the psychological activation (arousal or activity level) that occurs during gambling.

2.2.3 Sociological factors

A number of sociological factors have been found to be related to gambling. Although problem gamblers are a very varied group, higher rates of gambling occur among some groups, including unemployed individuals as well as individuals with low socioeconomic status and low education levels (Raylu & Oei, 2002). Significant gender difference have also been found in gambling behaviours, the presence of comorbid problems and problems presented for treatment, as well as with treatment outcomes (Crisp et al., 2000; Dannon et al., 2006; Welte, Barnes, Wieczorek, Tidwell, & Parker, 2002). Dickson, Derevensky and Gupta (2008) assessed risk and protective factors among 2179 adolescents (aged 11–19) and found that lower levels of connectedness to the school (i.e. belief that they belong, are respected and cared for at school) and to the family, were related to problem gambling. Culture has also been found to be an important factor in the development and maintenance of problem gambling (Raylu & Oei, 2004a; Oei & Raylu, 2007). Some cultural groups may be more exposed to gambling opportunities than other cultural groups and consequently have higher rates of problem gambling (Loo, Raylu, & Oei, 2008; Raylu & Oei, 2004a; Oei & Raylu, 2010).

A number of other sociological factors that have been linked to problem gambling include living in disadvantaged neighbourhoods (Welte, Wieczorek, Barnes, & Tidwell, 2006) and the presence of family problems (Hardoon, Gupta, & Derevensky, 2004). Low levels of monitoring/ supervision by parents (Vachon, Vitaro, Wanner, & Tremblay, 2004; Vitaro, Brendgen, Ladouceur, & Tremblay, 2001) and inadequate disciplinary practices (Vachon et al., 2004) in childhood have also been linked to problem gambling. There is also evidence to suggest an association between increased availability/accessibility to gambling and increased gambling prevalence rates (Ladouceur, Jacques, Ferland, & Giroux, 1999; Productivity Commission Report, 1999).

2.3 OVERVIEW OF THE PROBLEM GAMBLING TREATMENT LITERATURE

A number of treatment approaches have been used to treat problem gambling including various forms of pharmacotherapy and psychotherapy.

2.3.1 Pharmacotherapy

Current pharmacological treatments for problem gambling include a range of approaches such as selective serotonin reuptake inhibitors (SSRIs), opioid receptor antagonists, mood stabilizers/anticonvulsants, and bupropion (Iancu et al., 2008).

2.3.1.1 SSRIs

A number of double blind studies assessing the efficacy of SSRIs (e.g. fluvoxamine, paroxetine or sertraline) in the treatment of problem gambling have shown mixed results (Iancu et al., 2008). Some of these studies have shown that SSRIs are successful in reducing gambling urges and behaviours (Hollander, DeCaria, Finkell, Begaz, Wong, & Cartwright, 2000; Kim, Grant, Adson, Shin, & Zaninelli, 2002), whereas others have not (Blanco, Petkova, Ibáñez, & Saiz-Ruiz, 2002; Grant et al., 2003; Saiz-Ruiz et al., 2005). Researchers using open label studies assessing the efficacy of SSRIs (e.g. escitalopram and citalopram) (Black, Shaw, Forbush, & Allen, 2007; Grant & Potenza, 2006; Zimmerman, Breen, & Posternak, 2002) have shown that these drugs can reduce gambling urges and behaviours as well as some comorbid symptoms such as anxiety. In an 8-week open label trial, Pallanti, Rossi, Sood and Hollander (2002) showed that oral nefazodone (an antidepressant) could reduce gambling urges and behaviour as well as improve mood.

2.3.1.2 Opioid receptor antagonists

Naltrexone is an opioid receptor antagonist that is often used to decrease cravings in opiate and alcohol users. Considering that problem gambling and substance disorders may share some traits researchers have used naltrexone to treat problem gamblers (Iancu et al., 2008). Naltrexone has shown more consistent efficacy compared with SSRIs in reducing gambling urges and excitement relating to gambling (Kim & Grant, 2001; Kim, Grant, Adson, & Shin, 2001). Naltrexone does not usually result in intolerable side effects (Korn & Shaffer, 2004).

Grant and his colleagues (2006) conducted a 16-week double blind randomized placebo controlled study with 207 problem gamblers to assess the effectiveness of a long-acting opioid receptor antagonist, Nalmefene, in the treatment of pathological gambling. They reported that Nalmefene decreased the severity of problem gambling. Low doses (25 mg/day) resulted in few adverse events. However, higher doses (50 mg/day and 100 mg/day) resulted in intolerable side effects including nausea, dizziness and insomnia.

2.3.1.3 Mood stabilizers/anticonvulsants

Mood stabilizers may target impulsive behaviour associated with problem gambling. Moskowitz (1980) reported that the use of lithium carbonate in three pathological gamblers with bipolar disorder in an open label study resulted in abstinence of gambling behaviours as well as the cessation of mania symptoms. Hollander, Pallanti, Allen, Sood and Rossi (2005) found that sustained release lithium carbonate reduced gambling behaviours, urges, severity as well as mania symptoms among 40 pathological gamblers with comorbid bipolar disorder in a 10-week double blind, randomized, placebo controlled study.

A handful of studies have also assessed the efficacy of anticonvulsants (which often have mood stabilizing properties) in treating problem gambling. Topiramate, an anticonvulsant that has been used successfully with other impulsive disorders, was useful for the treatment of problem gambling (Dannon, Lowengrub, Gonopolski, Musin, & Kotler, 2005a). Black, Shaw, and Allen (2008) assessed the efficacy of an extended release carbamazepine (an anticonvulsant and mood stabilizing drug used mainly in the treatment of epilepsy and bipolar disorder) in the treatment of eight non-depressed pathological gamblers in a 10-week open trial. They found that extended release carbamazepine was effective in improving gambling behaviours and urges. However, a number of subjects dropped out because of the side effects (including drowsiness and diarrhea).

Pallanti, Quercioli, Sood and Hollander (2002) compared the effectiveness of lithium (n=23) and valproate (n=19) (an anticonvulsant) in the treatment of 42 non-bipolar pathological gamblers in a 14-week randomized single blind study and found that both were effective in treating problem gambling.

Fong, Kalechstein, Bernhard, Rosenthal and Rugle (2008) conducted a 7-week double blind, placebo controlled trial of olanzapine (an atypical antipsychotic drug that can reduce impulsivity in other psychiatric problems) to treat 21 pathological gamblers with a problem with video poker. All participants showed reduced levels of gambling urges, gambling behaviour, as well as mood and anxiety symptoms.

2.3.1.4 Bupropion

Slow release bupropion, an antidepressant, is a selective reuptake inhibitor of dopamine and noradrenaline that is often used to manage nicotine withdrawal and urges. Bupropion (slow release) stimulates brain systems that play a role in urges and the enjoyment of problem gambling (Iancu et al., 2008). Studies have also shown that bupropion can reduce gambling behaviour (Black, 2004; Dannon, Lowengrub, Musin, Gonopolski, & Kotler, 2005b; Donald et al., 2007).

2.3.1.5 Comparisons

Only a handful of studies have compared different pharmacotherapies in treating gambling problems. Dannon and colleagues (2005a) compared the efficacy of a 12-week course of topiramate (n=15) versus fluvoxamine (n=16) in the treatment of 31 male problem gamblers. The individuals in the topiramate group showed significant improvements in gambling behaviour at post-treatment, whereas the fluvoxamine group did not. Dannon et al. (2005b) compared the efficacy of a 12-week course of sustained-release bupropion (n=17) and naltrexone (n=19) in the treatment of problem gambling in 36 male pathological gamblers. Both drugs appeared to be equally effective in reducing gambling behaviours. Pallesen et al. (2007) conducted a quantitative review of 130 pharma-cological treatment studies of gambling problems and found no significant differences in treatment outcomes between antidepressants, opiate antagonists and mood stabilizers.

2.3.1.6 Summary

Pharmacotherapy appears to be an adequate treatment for problem gambling. Pallesen et al.'s (2007) meta-analyses showed that at post-treatment, pharmacotherapy was more effective than no treatment or placebo control treatment. However, researchers in this area have suggested that pharmacotherapy may be more useful for clients with comorbid problems such as impulsivity and mood disorders (Fong, Kalechstein, Bernhard, Rosenthal, & Rugle, 2008; Iancu et al., 2008). The best choice of drug to be used appears to depend on the comorbid psychopathology (Dell'Osso, Allen, & Hollander, 2005). These phama-cotherapeutic studies report a number of limitations that affect general-izability of the findings. These include small sample sizes, non-replication of findings, high drop-out rates, overrepresentation of males, large vari-ances in the extent of placebo response from trial to trial and exclusion of participants with comorbid problems (Brewer et al., 2008; Iancu et al., 2008; Grant, Kim, & Potenza, 2008; Pallesen et al., 2007).

2.3.2 Psychological treatment

A range of psychological treatments explored including psychodynamic/analytic therapy, multimodal approaches, Gamblers Anonymous, cogni-tive, behavioural and combined CBT. These treatment approaches will be reviewed next. The CBT problem gambling literature will be reviewed in more detail to present a rationale for the CBT programme outlined in this book. Other psychological treatments for problem gambling that have not all been evaluated but are mentioned in the literature include family/marital therapy, supportive therapy, eye movement desensitization and reprocessing, hypnosis, biofeedback and acupuncture (Korn & Shaffer, 2004). Since these treatment approaches have not been assessed for effectiveness in the gambling literature and not widely viewed as the treatment of choice for problem gambling, they would not be reviewed here.

2.3.2.1 Psychodynamic/analytic therapy

There appear to be three major aspects to the psychoanalytic theory of problem gambling. These include gambling being 'an unconscious substitute for pregenital libidinal and aggressive outlets associated with Oedipal conflicts', a desire 'for punishment in reaction to the guilt', and a means for recurrent 'reenactments, but not resolutions, of the conflict' (Allcock, 1986, p. 262). Psychodynamic/analytic treatments concentrate on dealing with narcissistic personality characteristics and related defence mechanisms. It attempts to provide insight into the underlying source and meaning of individuals' emotions and behaviours.

Several individual case studies have reported the use of psychoanalysis in the formulation and treatment of problem gamblers (Galdston, 1960; Greenson, 1948; Harris, 1964; Lindner, 1950). The success rates for gamblers treated psychoanalytically are generally poor (Greenberg, 1980). Bergler's (1957) study (the only study to present outcomes for a group of psychoanalytically treated problem gamblers) showed an effectiveness rate (i.e. achieved abstinence, addressed core conflicts and stopped self-destructive behaviours) of 75 per cent. However, this rate was based on only 30 per cent of the total group seeking treatment (disregarding individuals who dropped out). Follow-up data for this study was not available.

In general, most of the studies in the gambling literature that have used psychodynamic/analytic therapy with problem gamblers are case studies and did not include control groups. Furthermore, large methodological flaws in these studies including selection bias, absence of acceptable outcome criteria and limited follow-up data, undermine these findings (Allcock, 1986). However, considering that psychoanalytic therapy can be long in duration it might be beneficial for problem gamblers with comorbid personality disorders (Korn & Shaffer, 2004). Furthermore, considering the evidence of high rates of childhood sexual and physical trauma among problem gamblers (e.g. Kausch, Rugle, & Rowland, 2006) psychodynamic/analytic therapy may hold some promise in treating this group.

2.3.2.2 Multimodal treatment

Multimodal treatment approaches with problem gamblers have been assessed in both inpatient and outpatient settings. These treatments include 12-step approaches, psychoeducation, CBT, marital or family therapy, relapse prevention, financial counselling, psychodynamic therapy. These multimodal treatment programmes found that 55–71 per cent of patients followed up 6–24 months after discharge from treatment reported abstinence from gambling (Lesieur & Blume, 1991; Russo et al., 1984; Schwarz & Lindner, 1992; Taber, McCormick, Russo, Adkins, & Ramirez, 1987). Some of these inpatient studies showed that abstinence was also associated with improvement in psychosocial functioning (Lesieur & Blume, 1991; Taber et al., 1987). Major limitations of these studies were that the samples consisted of predominantly males and treatment was conducted in inpatient settings (Petry, 2003).

Stinchfield and Winters (1996) evaluated the efficacy of six multimodal outpatient treatment programmes (n=1342) for problem gambling in Minnesota. Individuals that completed treatment showed significant improvements in gambling behaviours and also psychosocial problems at post-treatment and 1-year follow up. The study showed that 43 and 42 per cent of individuals had reported abstinence at 6- and 12-month follow up respectively. Furthermore, 29 and 24 per cent of individuals reported gambling less than once a month at 6- and 12-month follow up respectively. In 2001 Stinchfield and Winters presented outcome findings for four out of the six multimodal outpatient treatment programmes (n=568) originally assessed in their 1996 study. Two of the programmes were not included as they had distinctly different treatment methods compared with the other four programmes. The multimodal treatment included a 12-step treatment approach, individual, group and family therapy, education and financial counselling. Twenty-eight per cent and 18 per cent of the participants who were followed up reported abstinence at 6 and 12 months after discharge, respectively. Twenty per cent and 18 per cent of participants reported gambling less than once a month at 6 and 12 months after discharge respectively. Nearly half the participants significantly improved their gambling frequency at 6-month follow up. Significant improvements from pre-treatment to follow up were also found in gambling frequency, gambling problem severity scores, amount gambled, number of friends who gamble, psychosocial problems and number of financial problems. Limitations of the study included a large drop-out rate at 12-month follow up, the lack of a non-treatment control group and client self-report.

Due to the wide variety of treatment components used in combination in a multimodal treatment programme it is hard to determine how effective each specific treatment component is. In addition, since these treatments were done in naturalistic settings no comparison groups were used.

2.3.2.3 Gamblers Anonymous

Gamblers Anonymous is a 12-step self-help support group for individuals experiencing gambling problems. Currently, there is a lack of studies testing the efficacy of Gamblers Anonymous (Oei & Gordon, 2008). Early studies have shown that Gamblers Anonymous tend to have high drop-out rates (70–90 per cent) (Rosecrance, 1988; Stewart & Brown, 1988). Stewart and Brown (1988) followed 20 Gamblers Anonymous members and found that nine never returned after the first meeting (Stewart & Brown, 1988). Furthermore, Gamblers Anonymous tends to be beneficial for only some gamblers. Stewart and Brown (1988) reported that only 7 and 8 per cent of the Gamblers Anonymous members reported abstinence 1 and 2 years after first commencing the meetings, respectively (Stewart & Brown, 1988).

However, studies of multimodal treatments (e.g. Russo et al., 1984; Taber et al., 1987) that have included attendance at Gamblers Anonymous meetings suggest that attendance at such support groups improves treatment outcomes. Taber et al.'s (1987) study of inpatient problem gamblers that received multimodal treatments found that 74 per cent of the individuals that reported attending at least three Gamblers Anonymous meetings in the previous month were abstinent. However, only 42 per cent of non-abstinent gamblers reported such meeting attendance. Petry (2003) assessed previous Gamblers Anonymous attendance among 342 treatment-seeking problem gamblers presenting to professional gambling treatment programmes. They found that those that attended Gamblers Anonymous meetings in the past were more likely to be abstinent (48 per cent) than those that did not (36 per cent) 2 months after commencing a CBT programme. Furthermore, the number of Gamblers Anonymous meetings attended as well as the number of treatment sessions completed since commencing treatment was positively related to abstinence from gambling (Petry, 2003). Individuals that attended Gamblers Anonymous meetings as well as engaging in multimodal/professional treatments were more likely to abstain from gambling than those that only relied on multimodal/professional treatments. However, conclusions that attendance at Gamblers Anonymous decreased problem gambling behaviours cannot be drawn as the study was not a randomized trial (Petry, 2003).

In a randomized control study Petry et al. (2006) compared attendance at Gamblers Anonymous meetings, attendance at Gamblers Anonymous plus using a CBT workbook, and attendance at Gamblers Anonymous plus having eight sessions of individual face-to-face CBT with a therapist in 231 problem gamblers. They found that although individuals in all groups showed reduced gambling, individuals that completed the eight sessions of CBT in addition to attending Gamblers Anonymous meetings showed more reduced gambling than those that only attended Gamblers Anonymous meetings.

2.3.2.4 Behavioural therapy

Behavioural theories of problem gambling postulate that gambling is a learned behaviour achieved via a process of reinforcement. Several reinforcers have been identified including monetary gain (Custer, 1982; Moran, 1970), arousal or excitement (Brown, 1986) and avoidance of negative psychological states (Blaszczynski et al., 1986; McConaghy, Armstrong, Blaszczynski, & Allcock, 1988).

Behavioural treatment studies provide some of the most comprehensive treatment literature on problem gambling. Early behavioural treatments based on learning principles (i.e. behaviour modification) have involved aversion therapy using physical or imaginal stimuli (Barker & Miller, 1968; Goorney, 1968; Seager, 1970) in order to decrease positive reinforcement related to the gambling and increase negative reinforcement (Petry, 2002). Subsequent behavioural treatments to treat problem gambling that were reported in the literature included controlled gambling/behavioural counselling (Dickerson & Weeks, 1979; Rankin, 1982), positive reinforcement of gambling abstinence and contingency contracting (Cotler, 1971), paradoxical intention (Victor & Krug, 1967), covert sensitization (Bannister, 1977; Cotler, 1971) and systematic desensitization (Kraft, 1970). However, most of these studies had small sample sizes and lacked comparison groups (Brewer et al., 2008).

Several behavioural approaches have been assessed with larger sample sizes. McConaghy, Armstrong, Blaszczynski and Allcock (1983) randomly allocated 20 individuals to either aversion therapy or imaginal desensitization. Those in the imaginal group compared with those in the aversion group reported fewer gambling urges and behaviours and showed lower state anxiety at the 1-month follow up. They also reported lower state and trait anxieties at 1-year follow up. McConaghy and colleagues (1988) conducted a controlled randomized trial investigating the effectiveness of imaginal desensitization (n=10) compared with imaginal relaxation (n=10). Both groups showed significant reductions in state anxiety at 1-month follow up and trait anxiety at the 1-year follow up. Those with lower anxieties in both groups showed reduction in gambling. McConaghy, Blaszczynski and Frankova (1991) randomly allocated 120 problem gamblers to either imaginal desensitization (n=60) or to other behavioural procedures (i.e. imaginal relaxation (n=20), aversion therapy (n=20), brief *in vivo* exposure (n=10) and prolonged *in vivo* exposure (n=10)). Sixty-three participants were contacted at 2 and 9-year follow ups. Twenty-six out of the 33 individuals who completed imaginal desensitization reported reduction in gambling or abstinence from gambling compared with 16 out of the 30 individuals that completed the other behavioural treatment approaches.

More recent behaviour therapy studies have evaluated the effectiveness of exposure therapy in treating problem gambling. Echeburúa et al., (2000) investigated the effectiveness of stimulus control and exposure with response prevention in two formats (group versus individual) compared with a no treatment control group using 69 (60 males and 9 females) treatment-seeking slot machine problem gamblers. They found that the treatment group (in both formats) had greater success rates (two or less episodes of mild gambling) than the control group. This is supported by a number of single case studies demonstrating the benefits of using stimulus control and exposure with response prevention in treating problem gambling (Amor & Echeburúa, 2002; Echeburúa & Fernández-Montalvo, 2002). Symes and Nicki (1997) found that cue exposure and response prevention led to significant reductions in gambling behaviour and urges in two probable pathological gamblers.

Self-exclusion is a behavioural treatment often used with other forms of therapy rather than in isolation. It involves gamblers voluntarily prohibiting themselves from entering selected gambling institute(s). Ladouceur, Jacques, Giroux, Ferland and Leblond (2000) assessed the characteristics of 220 gamblers who self-excluded from a casino in Canada. Although most of the participants reported being confident that self-exclusion would prevent them from entering the casino, only a third of the participants (30 per cent) abstained from gambling. Thirty-six per cent of participants reported going into the casino an average of six times while still on the programme. Furthermore, nearly half had reported gambling on other games. O'Neil and colleagues (2003) found that of the 933 gamblers that had self-excluded from various gambling institutes in Australia between 1996 and 2002 15 per cent were found to have entered the prohibited gambling institutes on average 3.2 times per person. However, due to methodological problems the generalizability of these findings are limited (Blaszczynski, Ladouceur, & Nower, 2007). Ladouceur, Sylvain, and Gosselin (2007) conducted a 2-year follow-up study assessing the effectiveness of self-exclusion among 161 participants. All participants reported a decrease in their gambling urges and an increase in their perception of control at follow ups. A reduction in the negative consequences of gambling (e.g. negative mood and employment-related problems) and problem gambling behaviours were also reported. More recently, Tremblay, Boutin, and Ladouceur (2008) assessed the benefits of an updated self-exclusion programme among 116 participants. This programme included 'an initial voluntary evaluation, phone support, and a mandatory meeting' at the end of their self-exclusion period (p. 505). Improvements in time and amount spent on gambling, negative results of gambling, problem gambling behaviours and psychological distress were noticed post-treatment compared with pre-treatment. These studies showed that although the available evidence is limited, self-exclusion programmes can be effective for some programme gamblers.

Although behavioural treatments of problem gambling show significant improvements they do have a number of methodological shortcomings. Most of these treatment studies (especially earlier ones) have small sample sizes, limited follow-up periods and do not involve comparisons with other treatments. They have unspecified or poorly operationalized dependent variables/criteria for successful outcome or treatment objectives (Allcock, 1986). There is also usually a lack of controlled comparisons of one treatment with another or with a placebo procedure, or combinations of several techniques are used concurrently so that identification of the active component is impossible (Blaszczynski & Silove, 1995).

In recent times, behavioural treatments have been combined with cognitive therapy (see subsequent sections) to treat problem gambling. Consequently, there are not a lot of recent studies assessing just behavioural treatments for problem gambling in the literature.

2.3.2.5 Cognitive therapy

Cognitive theories of problem gambling suggest that irrational thoughts related to an individual's ability to control and predict gambling outcomes underly the development and maintenance of gambling problem. Cognitive therapy of problem gambling involves explaining/educating clients about the notion of randomness and chance as well as the concept of irrationality. It also involves helping clients to identify and restructure irrational cognitions (i.e. erroneous perceptions about the notion of randomness and betting systems, superstitious beliefs related to gambling,

memory bias and errors related to attribution and causality) and formu-
lating rational cognitions (Korn & Shaffer, 2004).

The first study that provided evidence for the efficacy of using cognitive
therapy in treating problem gambling presented findings from four male
video poker players (Ladouceur, Sylvain, Duval, & Gaboury, 1989). Subsequently, Gaboury and Ladouceur (1990) presented a study that evaluated
the effectiveness of cognitive restructuring in 60 roulette players. They
found that the treatment group significantly decreased their irrational
verbalizations, risk-taking behaviours and increased their rational verbalizations. Ladouceur, Sylvain, Letarte, Giroux and Jacques (1998) assessed
the effectiveness of cognitive restructuring in five pathological gamblers.
Four of the pathological gamblers reported a reduction in gambling urges
and gambling behaviour as well as an increase in their perception of
control. Post-test results were maintained at 6-month follow up.

Ladouceur et al. (2001) completed a randomized controlled trial where
66 gamblers were allocated to either the cognitive therapy (n=35) or a
waiting list control group (n=29). Results showed that at post-test, individuals in the treatment group met fewer diagnostic criteria, showed less
desire to gamble, reported higher perception of control over their gambling, reported higher perceived self-efficacy (confidence), gambled less
frequently, and spent less money. These improvements were generally
maintained at 6- and 12-month follow ups. Recently, Ladouceur, Sylvain,
Boutin, Lachance, Doucet and Leblond (2003) assessed the effectiveness
of a group cognitive treatment for problem gambling (n=34) compared
with a waiting list control group (n=24). Post-test results showed that 88
per cent of the treated subjects no longer met the DSM–IV criteria for
problem gambling, compared with only 20 per cent in the control group.
Therapeutic gains were maintained at 6-, 12- and 24-month follow ups.

As with behavioural treatments in recent times cognitive therapy is not
usually delivered separately but rather combined with behavioural
therapy (see next section) to treat problem gambling.

2.3.2.6 Cognitive behavioural treatment

Cognitive behavioural theories of problem gambling combine the cognitive and behavioural theories mentioned in the two previous sections.
They also often attribute poor coping skills as playing a role in the
development and maintenance of problem gambling. There are a number
of cognitive behavioural models of problem gambling in the gambling
literature (e.g. Blaszczynski & Nower, 2002; Raylu & Oei, 2009; Sharpe,
2002; Sharpe & Tarrier, 1993).

CBT focuses on altering dysfunctional thoughts and behaviours that are maintaining the problem. CBT approaches involve a number of therapeutic techniques including cognitive therapy, *in vivo* exposure, imaginal desensitization, relapse prevention, problem solving, and social/coping skills training (Tavares, Zilberman, & El-Guebaly, 2003). The earliest studies to use both cognitive and behavioural techniques to treat problem gambling with positive outcomes were reported using single case studies (Bannister, 1977; Toneatto & Sobell, 1990). These studies found that participation in CBT improved the severity and frequency of gambling as well as gambling urges. Bujold, Ladouceur, Sylvain and Boisvert (1994) evaluated the efficacy of a CBT programme (interventions included cognitive therapy, problem solving and relapse prevention) with three male pathological gamblers. At treatment cessation, all participants reported being abstinent from gambling, as well as increases in their perceptions of control over gambling, and reductions in their perceptions of the severity of their gambling problems. The improvements were maintained at 9-month follow up. Arribas and Martinez (1991) assessed the efficacy of a CBT programme (cognitive therapy, relapse prevention, stimulus control and response prevention, family therapy and exposure therapy) with four pathological gamblers. Improvement was reported for all participants post-treatment.

Most of these earlier CBT studies with problem gamblers had small sample sizes, no random assignment, no control group and predominantly male samples. Subsequent studies tested the efficacy of CBT against waiting list control groups or pre-treatment results. Sylvain and colleagues (1997) randomly assigned 29 problem gamblers to either a waiting list control group or to a CBT programme (consisting of cognitive therapy, problem-solving training, social skills training and relapse prevention). These researchers found that treatment was associated not only with a reduction in the frequency of gambling episodes and amount of money spent gambling, but also increases in perceived control over gambling. Furthermore, 6- and 12-month follow up showed that improvements were maintained in 85 per cent of the treated subjects. Ladouceur and Sylvain (1999) also examined the efficacy of a CBT programme for problem gamblers. Gamblers were randomly assigned to a treatment group or a waiting list control group. The treatment included the same four components as the Sylvain et al. (1997) study. The results demonstrated significant changes on all outcome measures (including the frequency of gambling and the desire to gamble, as well as an increase in their perception of control and perceived self-efficacy) in the treatment group. Analysis of data from 6- and 12-month follow ups revealed maintenance of therapeutic gains.

Echeburúa, Báez, and Fernández-Montalvo (1996) compared the effectiveness of distinct components of CBT in 64 problem gamblers. Participants were randomized to one of four treatment groups. These included individual stimulus control and *in vivo* exposure with response prevention; group cognitive restructuring; a combination of the two; and a waiting list control group. Individual stimulus control and exposure with response prevention was better than the combined treatment, which did not differ in outcomes from the group cognitive therapy or control group. Clients in the individual therapy group reported significantly less interference of gambling in their daily lives than the control group. Each of the experimental groups showed a significant reduction in depression in contrast to the control group. The differences between individual (75 per cent) and group therapy (62.5 per cent) with relation to success (i.e. abstinence or one to two gambling episodes not exceeding the amount gambled in a week prior to treatment) at a 6-month follow up were not significant.

Most of the studies assessing CBT for problem gambling have used individual formats. Jiménez-Murcia et al. (2007) assessed the effectiveness of a 16-session manualized outpatient group CBT programme in 290 problem gamblers. They reported that nearly three-quarters of their participants were abstinent at post-treatment, and this was the case for nearly 80 per cent of participants at 6-month follow up. Dowling, Smith and Thomas (2007) compared the effectiveness of a 12-session CBT programme delivered in either a group or individual format to 56 females with electronic gaming machine gambling problems. Participants were randomly allocated to a waiting list control group, a group CBT group, or an individual CBT group. They found that, in general, the treatment outcomes of both treatment groups were similar. However, those in the group treatment group did not produce better treatment outcomes in relation to state anxiety and self-esteem as compared with the control group. Furthermore, at 6-month follow up more individuals in the group CBT group (i.e. 40 per cent) than the individual group (i.e. 8 per cent) still met the DSM−IV diagnostic criteria for pathological gambling.

A handful of researchers have also compared CBT for problem gambling and attendance at Gamblers Anonymous meetings and found conflicting outcomes. As discussed earlier, Petry and colleagues (2006) found that those in the individual CBT group reduced their gambling more than those in the Gamblers Anonymous alone group. This study also found that those in the individual CBT group showed a greater reduction in psychosocial symptoms and maintenance of therapeutic gains at 6- and 12-month follow up than the other groups. Toneatto and Dragonetti

(2008) compared eight sessions of CBT (n=65) and eight sessions of Gamblers Anonymous meetings (n=61). At 12-month follow up, there were no significant differences between the two groups on gambling variables such as frequency, abstinence rates and amounts bet.

There is also evidence that CBT can enhance the efficacy of other treatment approaches. Recent evidence demonstrated that pharmacological therapy in conjunction with CBT might be superior to either treatment used alone. Ravindran et al. (2006) compared the efficacy of three treatments for pathological gambling in a 16-week prospective study. The three groups were paroxetine alone (n=12), CBT plus paroxetine (n=10) and CBT plus placebo (n=12). Nineteen participants completed the treatment. Individuals in the combined CBT plus paroxetine group showed the fastest reduction in gambling symptoms (assessed by the Gambling Symptom Assessment Scale; Kim et al., 2001) as compared with the other two groups. Furthermore, the individuals in the combined CBT and paroxetine group had significantly less gambling behaviours at post-treatment compared with the paroxetine only group. The researchers suggested that CBT was most likely to be an effective form of treatment for problem gambling. However, the addition of paroxetine to the CBT may benefit a subgroup of problem gamblers.

Several authors have pointed out that problem gamblers tend to have poor motivation for therapy as indicated by high drop-out and relapse rates (Bolen & Boyd, 1968; Greenberg, 1980). Consequently, a number of studies have assessed techniques to improve motivation and compliance with treatment in conjunction with the CBT to improve treatment outcomes. Wulfert et al. (2006) assessed the efficacy of a treatment programme that consisted of CBT and motivational enhancement treatment among nine severe pathological gamblers (most were horse race bettors) that sought treatment at a community treatment centre. The drop-out rate in the treatment group was significantly lower than the control group, which consisted of 12 gamblers who received treatment as usual in the same centre. Participants in the treatment group also reported significant improvements in gambling behaviours and lifestyle. Milton et al. (2002) randomly allocated 40 pathological gamblers at a university outpatient gambling treatment clinic (29 males and 11 females) to either CBT alone (psychoeducation, cognitive restructuring, problem solving and relapse prevention) or to CBT that included treatments designed to increase motivation and compliance (i.e. attendance at all treatment sessions). Treatments designed to increase motivation and compliance included providing reinforcement via encouragement and praise at various stages of recruitment and treatment, sending letters confirming some of the appointments, providing participants with assessment results, contacting participants after the first missed session and emphasizing the positive impact of attendance on treatment outcomes at assessment. Participants were also required to complete a decisional balance sheet between each session. Throughout the treatment, participants were assisted in identifying and eliminating barriers to change using problem-solving skills and their ability to successfully complete treatment was reinforced. The researchers found that significantly fewer individuals dropped out of the CBT group that included motivational treatments that improved treatment compliance at post-treatment than the CBT alone group (35 versus 65 per cent). However, there was no difference in the treatment outcomes in relation to meeting the Structured Clinical Interview for Pathological Gambling (Anjoul, Milton, & Roberts, 2000; Walker, Milton, & Anjoul, 1999; Walker et al., 1999) criteria for pathological gambling, percentage of income gambled and South Oaks Gambling Screen (SOGS; Lesieur & Blume, 1987) scores between the two treatment groups at 9-month follow up.

Hodgins, Currie and El-Guebaly (2001) randomly allocated 121 individuals into three groups: a waiting list control group; a group who received a motivational enhancement telephone treatment plus CBT self-help workbook that consisted of goal-setting skills training, coping techniques and relapse prevention in the mail; and a CBT self-help workbook only group. Results showed that those that received the motivational enhancement telephone treatment plus CBT self-help workbook had better treatment outcomes than those that received the workbook alone at 3- and 6-month follow up. At 12-month follow up the group difference was significant for only those with less severe gambling problems. Hodgins, Currie, El-Guebaly and Peden (2004) conducted a 2-year follow up of the participants in the two treatment groups from the Hodgins et al. (2001) study. Fifty-two participants successfully completed the 2-year follow up. They reported that the difference between the two treatment groups in relation to the number of participants reporting an abstinence period of 6 months was not significant. However, participants who received the motivational telephone treatment plus the CBT self-help workbook reported gambling fewer days, losing less money and had lower problem gambling scores (assessed by the SOGS) than the participants in the CBT workbook only group.

Recently, Oei, Raylu and Casey (in press) compared the CBT programme contained in this book in both individual and group formats. Participants (n=102) were volunteer pathological gamblers who were recruited by means of media release, by Internet links from various search engines and via advertisements placed on various health websites, and newspapers. All participants were classified as pathological gamblers (i.e. had DSM−IV and SOGS scores greater than five). Although most of the participants reported playing with gambling machines, the sample consisted of gamblers experiencing problems with various forms of gambling.

Participants were randomly allocated to complete the CBT programme contained in this book in either an individual format (n=51) (i.e. one to one with a therapist) or in a group setting (n=51). Both the individual and groups sessions were delivered over a 6-week period. Individual sessions were 1−1½ hours long in duration and were delivered two sessions weekly. Group sessions were 2½ hours long in duration and were delivered once a week. All therapists were registered intern psychologists (i.e. had completed 4 years of a psychology degree and were undergoing postgraduate training/supervision in the field of clinical psychology). A range of dependent variables assessed the success of the CBT programme. This included the frequency and amount gambled as well as gambling correlates such as gambling urges (via the Gambling Urge Scale; Raylu & Oei, 2004c), gambling cognitions (via the Gambling Related Cognitions Scale; Raylu & Oei, 2004b), psychological states (via the Depression Anxiety Stress Scale − 21; Lovibond & Lovibond, 1995), quality of life (via the Quality of Life Inventory; Frisch, 1994), satisfaction with life (via the Satisfaction with Life Questionnaire; Diener, Emmons, Larsen, & Griffin, 1985) and alcohol use (via the Alcohol Use Disorders Identification Test; Saunders, Aasland, Babor, de la Puente, & Grant, 1993). A total of 28 of the 102 participants were randomly selected to a 6-week waiting list control group prior to receiving the allocated treatment. Their progress was assessed at post-treatment and at six-month follow up via mail.

Thirty-five participants in the individual treatment condition and 29 in the group treatment condition completed the programme. At post-treatment, there were significant improvements (compared with pre-treatment scores) in the frequency of gambling, amount of money spent on gambling, gambling related thinking errors, gambling urges, satisfaction with life, quality of life, alcohol consumption as well as depression, anxiety and stress levels for both the treatment conditions. However, there were no significant differences between pre-treatment scores and post-treatment scores for any of the measured dependent variables for the waitlist control condition. Therapeutic gains for gambling correlates were generally maintained at six-month follow-up. Effect sizes for both the treatment conditions were found to be generally higher than those found for the waitlist control condition. For more details of this study, please refer to Oei et al., (in press).

2.4 SUMMARY OF THE PROBLEM GAMBLING TREATMENT LITERATURE AND RATIONALE FOR THE CBT PROGRAMME CONTAINED IN THIS BOOK

In general, the literature indicates that problem gambling can be treated successfully (Echeburúa, 2005; Gooding & Tarrier, 2009; Raylu & Oei, 2002; 2004a). Pharmacological approaches look promising but may be more beneficial for problem gamblers with comorbid depression or high impulsivity (Echeburúa, 2005). Numerous researchers who have reviewed the problem gambling treatment literature agree that behavioural, cognitive and especially CBT interventions appear to have the most treatment outcome literature and appear to be the most effective in the treatment of problem gambling (Toneatto & Millar, 2004; Toneatto & Ladouceur, 2003; Oei & Raylu, 2007; Oei, Raylu & Grace, 2008). Pallesen, Mitsem, Kvale, Johnsen and Molde (2005) conducted a meta-analysis of 37 studies to assess the efficacy of psychological treatments for problem gambling. Psychological treatments were significantly more effective than no treatment at post-treatment and follow up (average 17 months). Korn and Shaffer (2004) reviewed the problem gambling psychological treatment literature and suggested that the therapies that have the most robust evidence in treating problem gambling appear to be behaviour therapy and CBT. Unlike the studies that have assessed the efficacy of other therapeutic approaches in treating problem gambling, studies assessing the efficacy of behaviour therapy and CBT have often been randomized control trials with reasonable sample sizes and follow-up periods (usually 6–12 month follow-up periods). According to Korn and Shaffer's (2004) review, the therapeutic approach that has the next most robust evidence in treating problem gambling is relapse prevention. Relapse prevention is a therapeutic technique located within a CBT model (Marlatt & Donovan, 2005). Korn and Shaffer (2004) also reported that there is very weak evidence for some other therapies used to treat problem gambling including psychodynamic, 12-step, self-exclusion and aversion therapy. Either there is an absence of studies assessing these latter therapeutic approaches or the studies that do exist contain methodological limitations including weak designs, short follow-up periods, small samples and lack of control or comparison groups.

Behavioural, cognitive and CBT also appear to have several advantages over other forms of treatment. First, as CBT is very structured, it can be delivered in a number of formats (Raylu, Oei, & Loo, 2008). This includes via face-to-face contact (e.g. Oei et al., in press), the computer, the Internet or self-help books (e.g. Oei, Raylu, & Grace, 2008). Second, CBT tends to short term compared with other types of psychological therapy (e.g. psychodynamic therapy). Third, CBT's properties including it being short term, active and focused allows it to be more cost-effective than other forms of treatment. Fourth, as CBT focuses on building new skills and strengthening skill deficits it decreases the risk of relapsing. Fifth, unlike medications that are useful only as long as they are taken, CBT provides long lasting and practical skills that individuals can apply on · their own to cope for the rest of their lives.

Thus, considering the evidence of the efficacy of CBT in treating problem gambling and the advantages of using this approach, a book containing a CBT programme to treat problem gamblers is logical. Thus, the following chapters in this book will take the CBT approach to treat problem gambling. It is presented in a manual format to help mental health workers to use the book as a tool for the treatment of problem gamblers.

Session one: Assessment

Session content and goals

3.1 Discuss aim and rationale of the session
3.2 Conduct an assessment
3.3 Devise a case formulation and treatment plan
3.4 Provide treatment rationale and plan
3.5 Introduce home exercises

3.1 DISCUSS AIM AND RATIONALE OF THE SESSION

3.1.1 Aim

The aim of this session is to obtain enough information about the client to develop an individualized case formulation and treatment plan. It also aims to assess the client's goals, strengths and weaknesses. Before treatment begins the client can also be provided with a treatment rationale and plan.

3.1.2 Rationale

Assessment involves interviewing, taking a history as well as administering psychological tests (Masters, Burish, Hollon, & Rimm, 1987). Assessment and accurate diagnosis is very important in designing and implementing an effective treatment programme (i.e. one with good treatment outcomes that meet the client's needs and maintains treatment gains). Assessment also provides the chance for you and your client to build rapport. Assessment results enable you to give your client feedback that will help him/her to develop an alternative view of his/her situation. In addition, ongoing assessment will help you and your client to monitor progress towards treatment goals.

Providing a treatment rationale and brief treatment plan can help the client to get a clear idea about how the treatment will proceed.

Therapists with more knowledge of the gambling/problem gambling literature may find this section too detailed. Assessing all the variables in such detail is not necessary for all clients. We decided that such detail would ensure that CBT-trained therapists from a wide range of backgrounds would feel comfortable in assessing the client. Furthermore, assessment of the client needs to be ongoing and interventions altered as necessary (Marlatt, 1988).

3.2 CONDUCT AN ASSESSMENT

The assessment interview aims to elicit a great deal of information about the nature of the client's problems, current functioning, background and motivation towards treatment. The interview will enable therapists to complete a case formulation of the client's problems and a treatment plan. There are four specific components of the assessment. These are as follows:

- rapport building;
- to assess the nature of presenting problems and other relevant information in order to devise a case formulation and treatment plan;
- to assess the client's motivation to change and increase motivation through motivational interviewing techniques;
- to assess the goals and expectations of treatment.

Questionnaires can be used to collect additional information on various aspects of the client's gambling problems or associated problems. For example, the South Oaks Gambling Screen (Lesieur & Blume, 1987) could be used to assess the extent of problem gambling. The Gambling Related Cognitions Scale (Raylu & Oei, 2004b) could be used to assess gambling cognitions. The Gambling Urge Scale (Raylu & Oei, 2004c) could be used to assess gambling urges. The Depression Anxiety and Stress Scale (Lovibond & Lovibond, 1995) could be used to assess the client's mood states.

3.2.1 Rapport building

Rapport building is a vital part of treatment where the therapist builds trust with the client. Before you start the assessment interview, introduce yourself to the client briefly. Then explain to the client the purpose of this first meeting, which is to get to know the client and to get an idea of the client's gambling patterns and resulting problems (i.e. the aim and the rationale of this session). The initial interview should be informal but allow the collection of necessary information about the client. You may begin the interview with an open question such as, 'Please state in your own words, the nature of your gambling.'

3.2.2 Assess the nature of presenting problems and other relevant information to devise a case formulation and treatment plan

In order to devise a case formulation and treatment plan, you need to assess the five Ps. That is, assessing the client's:

⊙ presenting problems – nature of the current dysfunctional behaviours (i.e. the main presenting problem as well as other related problems);
⊙ predisposing factors – factors that may have made the client vulnerable to develop the current dysfunctional behaviours;
⊙ precipitating factors – factors associated with the acquisition of the current dysfunctional behaviours;
⊙ perpetuating factors – factors that may be maintaining the current dysfunctional behaviours;
⊙ prognostic factors – factors influencing recovery and treatment effectiveness.

Information obtained on the five Ps allows a therapist to discover the antecedents and consequences of the client's gambling behaviours, examine the acquisition of these behaviours as well as what is currently maintaining the behaviours. It also tells the therapist why a client gambles and continues to gamble despite continuous losses. It allows the therapist to devise a treatment plan specifically suited to the client's concerns and needs.

During this initial interview, you will also need to obtain other relevant information about the client such as contact details, age, gender, living conditions, occupation, marital status, educational attainment.

3.2.2.1 Presenting problems

This involves assessing the nature of the client's main presenting problem (the gambling problem) as well as other problems the client is experiencing. Obtain information on the nature, frequency, duration and intensity of the gambling problems. This can include using the DSM–IV-TR (American Psychiatric Association, 2000) to determine whether the client meets the diagnostic criteria for pathological gambling. In summary, a pathological gambler meets five or more of the DSM–IV-TR criteria.

- Preoccupation with gambling (e.g. thinking of ways to get money to gamble or strategies to win).
- Gambling with increasing amounts of money in order to achieve the desired excitement.
- Repeated unsuccessful efforts to control or stop gambling.
- Getting restless or irritable when attempting to control or stop gambling.
- Gambling to escape from problems or negative moods.
- Continuing gambling despite losses to recoup money lost.
- Lying to others to hide gambling behaviours or consequences of gambling (e.g. lost money).
- Committing illegal acts (e.g. theft) to finance gambling or gambling debts.
- Risking or losing significant opportunities (e.g. relationships and jobs) due to gambling.
- Borrowing money to finance gambling or gambling debts.

When assessing problem gambling behaviours try to collect detailed information on the following:

- Current gambling – frequency of gambling; amount spent gambling; forms of gambling (gaming machines, horse race gambling, sports betting etc.); current triggers of gambling; chasing behaviour.

- History of gambling – time and circumstances surrounding the initiation of gambling; duration of gambling; pattern of gambling in the past (e.g. frequency and amount spent); previous triggers of gambling; past attempts to stop gambling (including reasons for trying to stop/reduce gambling, strategies used, outcomes and consequences of outcomes, periods of abstinence/controlled use, reasons for lapse/relapses, chasing behaviour, etc.).

- Treatment seeking – reasons for seeking treatment now; experiences and outcomes with previous treatment(s).

Other problems the client might be presenting with also need to be assessed. Some of these could include the following:

- Relationship problems – is the client experiencing relationship difficulties with any of his/her significant others due to gambling? Is the client in the process of separating/divorcing from his/her partner? Has the client lost significant relationships due to gambling?

- Family problems – assess any familial problems including presence of domestic violence, child abuse, interpersonal conflicts, neglect of family, etc.

- Financial problems – is the client in debt? To whom does the client owe money? Has the client filed or are they thinking about filing for bankruptcy? What is the client's borrowing status due to gambling?

◉ Occupational problems – is the client unemployed? Is the client experiencing problems in the work environment? Has the client recently lost his job? Is the client absent from work a lot due to gambling?

◉ Legal problems – assess the nature of any unlawful act(s); any upcoming court dates and the most likely outcome(s); outcomes and the consequences of previous lawful acts.

◉ Physical health problems – problem gamblers could suffer from a range of physical problems including chronic headaches, breathing difficulties, backache, insomnia, chest pains, cardiovascular illness, obesity and numbness in the limbs. Therapists need to assess presence of any physical health problems and investigate whether these symptoms were consequences of the client's gambling problems or led to gambling in the first instance.

◉ Mental health/emotional problems – problem gamblers often present with comorbid mental health/emotional problems such as depression, anxiety, stress, low self-esteem, substance misuse, grief, etc. Therapists need to assess the presence of any mental health/emotional problems and investigate whether these symptoms are consequences of the client's gambling problems or led to gambling in the first instance.

◉ Suicide – refer to Appendix C for information on assessing and managing a suicidal client. Suicidal ideation is likely to be present if you hear statements such as these from a client.

  – 'I can't take it anymore, I have tried everything.'
  – 'I have caused my family a lot of pain. They would be better off without me.'
  – 'I will never get better. What is the use.'
  – 'I don't deserve a better life as I have caused too much pain.'

◉ Housing problems – what is the client's current living arrangements? Is the client currently homeless or about to be homeless?

3.2.2.2 Predisposing factors

These involve variables that make someone vulnerable to develop gambling problems. Some of these variables are listed below; for more information on these variables including original studies that assessed them in problem gamblers see our review paper (Raylu & Oei, 2002) and the review in Chapter 2.

◉ Familial gambling – several studies have shown a link between familial gambling and problem gambling. There is evidence for a modelling effect (e.g. most adolescents who gamble tend to gamble with family or friends). Cultural beliefs and values that favour gambling can also predispose one to gamble. Some individuals may have a genetic predisposition to develop gambling problems. Particular inherited biologically related characteristics (e.g. impaired impulse control or increased sensitivity to endorphin-based stimulation) may make some individuals more susceptible to maladaptive gambling patterns.

- Big win(s) in the early stages of gambling.
- Parental history of chemical dependence and/other other mental health problems.
- History of abuse (sexual, physical and verbal).
- Childhood death of parent or unrelated grief.
- Low levels of school and family connectedness during childhood.
- Low levels of monitoring/supervision by parents, inadequate disciplinary practices, and presence of family problems during childhood.
- Personality – certain personality factors have been associated with pathological gambling including impulsivity, sensation seeking (especially for casino gambling, gambling machines and illegal gambling), neuroticism and psychoticism.

3.2.2.3 Precipitating factors

These involve variables that encourage one to begin gambling excessively and thus, develop a gambling problem. To enquire about this you could find out when (and why) the client began gambling as well as when gambling started becoming a problem. Possible precipitants of gambling are listed below. For more information on these variables including the original studies that assessed them in problem gamblers, see our review paper (Raylu & Oei, 2002) and the review in Chapter 2.

- Stress/traumatic event.
- Negative mood states (e.g. anger, depression, frustration, loneliness and anxiety).
- Lack of stimulation – boredom, life dissatisfaction, lack of hobby or interest.
- Financial reasons – to win money (e.g. to relieve a financial crisis, to get rich, to buy a certain item or to be recognized as a worthwhile and respected individual). This may especially be true for individuals from low socioeconomic backgrounds or immigrants.
- Peer or family pressure to gamble.
- To have social interaction.
- Substance use/misuse.
- Sociocultural variables – certain sociocultural variables such as recent changes in milieu (e.g. migration, intergenerational conflicts in the family and work changes).
- Relationship problems – changes in social/interpersonal relationships such as separation, divorce, deaths, etc.

3.2.2.4 Perpetuating factors

These involve variables that are currently maintaining the client's gambling. Some of these variables are described below. For more information on these variables including original studies that assessed them in problem gamblers, see our review paper (Raylu & Oei, 2002) and the review in Chapter 2.

⊙ Manipulative behaviours – problem gamblers often use manipulative behaviours in order to continue gambling despite losses and negative reactions from family and friends. Some of these include:

- lying about their gambling;
- giving excuses to explain loss of money (e.g. wallet being lost/stolen, errors in pay, unexpected expenses);
- giving excuses to explain long absences (e.g. overtime at work, missing the bus, car broken down);
- blaming family members for their gambling behaviours, arguments or losses;
- having mail directed to a post office box.

⊙ Distorted cognitions – continued gambling despite significant and consecutive losses have been associated with the existence of faulty thinking regarding chances of winning or skill in winning (i.e. their special ability to beat the gambling odds). Toneatto (1999) completed a review of the gambling specific thinking errors that are common among problem gamblers (see Chapter 5 for more information on these gambling specific thinking errors). Other general distorted cognitions may also exist regarding recovery, perceptions of their gambling behaviour, consequences of their gambling problems, etc. (see Chapter 7 for more detailed information on these cognitions).

⊙ Mental health – problem gamblers can experience several health consequences including physical and psychological/emotional health problems that can exacerbate current gambling problems. Negative emotions such as depression, anxiety, guilt, shame and anger can lead some individuals to begin gambling. For other individuals these negative emotions are a result of a loss in gambling or the feelings of letting significant others down. Problem gamblers often continue gambling to avoid dealing with these negative emotions. Continued gambling often just exacerbates these negative emotions thus, forming a vicious cycle.

   Some problem gamblers may continue gambling to cope with other psychological disorders. For example, substance use/misuse is common among problem gamblers. Use of substances can exacerbate one's gambling as it reduces one's judgement and decision-making abilities. It also increases one's illusions of control. This can lead the individual to continue gambling despite significant losses. Some problem gamblers may continue using substances to cope with the gambling losses and negative consequences. Thus, therapists need to assess the presence of (including a history of) any emotional/ mental health problems, the client's experiences with treatment as well as treatment outcomes in relation to these emotional/psychological problems.

⊙ Physical health – the client's gambling may also be maintained by his/her ongoing physical health problems. Thus, therapists need to assess:

- whether the client is experiencing any health problems;
- whether the client is taking any medication for any health problems;
- whether the client had or is currently receiving any form of treatment for these health problems;
- the medical history of the client;
- the client's experiences with treatment as well as treatment outcomes in relation to physical health problems.

- Legal consequences – financial hardship (via debts and asset losses) may lead to legal consequences such as bankruptcy, loans or criminal acts to gain money. Stress associated with this could encourage one to continue gambling despite significant losses.

- Void/need for stimulation – some problem gamblers may gamble to reach and maintain a subjective state of arousal or excitement. The risk taking becomes more meaningful than wins especially when life is boring and unsatisfying. As the gambling behaviour accelerates, the problem gambler seeks to prolong the experience of arousal by spending more time gambling. Problem gamblers often talk about feeling powerful, excited, satisfied and in control when gambling. Thus, exploring the client's current (and past) interests and hobbies are important.

- Social interaction – an individual's commitment to a gambling institution may be positively reinforced by the social rewards (e.g. social interaction) received from the gambling institution. These rewards may encourage the client to continue gambling despite ongoing losses.

- Personality – many personality factors can play a role in the maintenance of gambling problems including impulsivity and sensation seeking. Comorbid personality disorders that are often associated with pathological gambling include narcissistic personality disorder and antisocial personality disorder.

- Current financial situation – some problem gamblers begin gambling because of the temptation of a big win or to resolve a financial crisis. However, continued gambling often results in further financial loss, which encourages further gambling. Thus, it is important to assess:

  - The client's personal and household income.
  - Whether the client is gambling more than his/her living expenses.
  - Whether the client needs increasing amounts of money to gamble with to enjoy gambling.
  - Whether the client is currently experiencing financial difficulties. If yes, what is the nature of these difficulties?
  - Whether the client is borrowing to finance his/her gambling and/or debts.
  - The extent of the client's debts.
  - To whom does the client owe money?
  - Which individuals are most likely to ask the client to return their money?
  - When does the client have to pay his/her debts by?
  - Is the client considering bankruptcy?

- Family/relationship problems – the client's gambling can be maintained by family/relationship problems in a number of ways. Problem gamblers often lose/damage relationships especially when they borrow money from friends/family members but are unable to pay the money back. This can lead to isolation. Problem gamblers may continue gambling to cope with the stress resulting from these damaged/lost relationships or the resulting isolation. Some problem gamblers continue gambling to escape from ongoing conflicts and tension with friends and family members. Regardless of whether these difficulties preceded the gambling or are a consequence of the gambling, they are likely to interfere with successful treatment (Fanning & McKay, 2000; Hudak, Varghese, & Politzer, 1989). Thus, the therapist needs to evaluate the nature of the client's relationships as well as social interaction with family and friends before and after the gambling problems began.

⊙ Rescuing/enabling behaviours of significant others − the client's gambling could also be maintained by unhelpful behaviours of his/her significant others. Two such behaviours include 'enabling' (e.g. taking up problem gamblers' responsibilities) or 'rescuing' (e.g. paying the problem gamblers' bills). Thus, the therapist need to assess how the client's family and friends react to his/her gambling and whether the client's family and friends are engaging in 'enabling' and 'rescuing' behaviours.

⊙ Occupational problems − problem gambling is associated with reduced job production and increased abstinence from work. This could be related to the preoccupation with gambling and/or finding money to finance their gambling or debts. Among those with employment, embezzlement and forgery are common ways to gain money to continue gambling. The unemployment rates for problem gamblers are double that of the general population. Student problem gamblers' productivity might also suffer (e.g. missed assignment deadlines, reduced exam marks). Continued gambling may be a means of dealing/escaping from these stressors.

3.2.2.5 Prognostic factors

A number of personal factors have been shown to influence treatment outcomes/recovery negatively. These include the presence of severe gambling problems, comorbid problems (e.g. substance misuse, mental health problems), and personality traits (e.g. impulsivity, novelty seeking and neuroticism) (Raylu & Oei, 2007). On the other hand, a number of personal factors have been shown to influence treatment outcomes/ recovery positively. These include personality traits such as persistence, the presence of motivation and readiness to change, and willingness to actively participate in treatment (Raylu & Oei, 2007). Thus, therapists need to assess these variables as well as the client's strengths and weaknesses (e.g. the client's ability to monitor and control levels of arousal, delay gratification, challenge his/her thinking, solve problems, be assertive). They also need to assess positive (e.g. presence of social support) and negative (e.g. presence of familial gambling) aspects about the client's environment that could affect the client's treatment outcomes.

3.2.3 Assess the client's motivation to change and increase motivation through motivational interviewing techniques

The client's readiness to change (e.g. whether the client is ready to change his/her gambling behaviours or is ambivalent about change) is important in determining prognosis. The readiness to change can also determine the extent to which the therapist needs to work on improving the motivation of the client in order to improve the odds of treatment success. Therapists can use Prochaska and DiClemente's Stages of Change Model (Prochaska & DiClemente, 1982; 1986) included in Appendix D to determine which stage of change the client is at (i.e. precontemplative, contemplative, preparation, maintenance or relapse). Some important questions to consider when determining the client's motivation include 'what was the referral source?' and 'was the client coerced into treatment?' It is important that the therapist also uses motivational interviewing techniques (found in Appendix E) to help increase/encourage the client's motivation to change.

3.2.4 Evaluate the client's goals and expectations of treatment

Therapists need to determine the client's treatment goals and expectations. Some questions that would help you achieve this include the following:

- What are your thoughts about receiving treatment for your gambling problems?
- What should treatment be like?
- What do you want out of treatment?
- How will you get what you want out of treatment?
- How would you know that you are making progress?
- What do you need to do before the final goal is possible?
- How long do you think it will take you to reach your goal?
- How confident are you that you can succeed or that you will remain abstinent/in control?

Treatment goals should involve changing things about the client, not others. They should be realistic. Ensure that the goal that the client sets is not a general objective, but rather something that is measurable. For example, a goal 'I want to be able to control my gambling' should be stated as 'I want to be able to gamble only once a week, spending only £5.'

Furthermore, the therapist needs to determine whether the client wants treatment to help him/her abstain from gambling or control his/her gambling behaviours. If the client's gambling is always out of control and the client spends most or all of his/her money on gambling, the client should consider stopping gambling altogether. However, if the client is in control more of the time then controlled gambling may be feasible. For further information on setting controlled gambling goals, please refer to Appendix F.

Often there are disparities in the treatment goals between therapists and clients. Both the therapist and the client need to accept the treatment goals before treatment begins. If the client's goals do not match up with yours, you can use the following options (Miller, 1989).

⊙ Negotiate a period of trial abstinence.

⊙ If you believe that the best goal for the client is abstinence, but your client wants to try controlled gambling, suggest that a period of abstinence would be an advantage before attempting to moderate gambling. Negotiate an agreement to review the treatment goals at the end of this period. If the client insists on a controlled gambling goal, accept the client's chosen goal on a negotiated trial period of controlled gambling. Negotiate an agreement to review the treatment goals at the end of this period. Review the goal at the end of the trial period.

⊙ A gradual tapering of gambling towards abstinence. To achieve this, you will need to set realistic intermediate goals and provide your client with a daily diary for self-monitoring. Negotiate a trial period.

⊙ Try to encourage the client to change his/her goals if you think there is an alternative goal that is best for the client – judging from the client's history of gambling, risk factors, history of treatment or success in the goals previously. This can be achieved via motivational interviewing techniques and educating the client about the disorder and its consequences.

⊙ Decline to help your client toward his/her goal. You might select this option if you feel that it would be unethical for you to support your client's chosen goal. You may want to consider the possibility of all the other options before choosing this one.

3.3 DEVISE A CASE FORMULATION AND TREATMENT PLAN

You can use the information obtained in the interview (especially the five Ps) and questionnaires (if any used) to establish case formulation of the client's problems. Remember, this is only an initial formulation. Over the course of the programme, the formulation will be tested out. The five Ps can be related to one another in many ways. This will differ for each client. See example in Figure 3.1.

A family history of gambling and impulsive personality could pre-dispose someone to gamble after a job loss to cope with the boredom felt as a result of not going to work any longer. Increased gambling would lead to a large debt. The problem gambler continues gambling to try to recoup losses, which would result in even bigger debt. This would exacer-bate not only the extent of the individual's gambling (as the individual

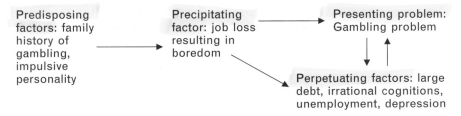

Figure 3.1 Example of how the five Ps interrelate

continues gambling to try to recoup losses) but also lead to depression as a result of feeling hopeless about their situation. Furthermore, irrational thoughts (e.g. I will eventually recoup money lost) maintain gambling despite continuous losses. Thus, for such an individual, it is not only the large debt and irrational cognitions that maintains his/her gambling problems but also ongoing unemployment and depression.

Individualized treatment plans are directly related to the information gathered in the assessment. It should target the factors maintaining the client's gambling problems. Similar to the case formulation, the treatment plan might also change as the therapy progresses.

The initial emphasis of the treatment depends on the client's 'stage of change' (see Appendix D). If the client is in the 'action stage', he/she is ready to begin the programme. If the client is in the contemplative stage, it is important that the education session (Chapter 4) and motivational interviewing techniques are used to increase the client's commitment to change. Several factors are important in planning treatment (highlighted by Adkins, 1988) as they may require urgent attention (i.e. usually dealt with in the initial part of the programme). These include the following:

⊙ Suicide – please refer to Appendix C for information on assessing and managing suicidal clients.

⊙ Housing – housing options would need to be discussed with a client who is homeless. Some housing options include living with a friend, applying for government supported accommodation and other government funded housing initiatives, returning to family with the condition of getting help, halfway houses and emergency housing (e.g. refuges, hostels).

⊙ Vocation – unemployed problem gamblers (especially those that have been unemployed for a long time) may benefit from registering with job seeking agencies, government sponsored work programmes and/or engaging in volunteer work. However, certain jobs place problem gamblers at a high risk of continuing gambling because of the easy access to gambling facilities (e.g. bartenders, casino workers, hotel workers). Workers that are required to handle cash in their work places are also vulnerable as availability of money is often a trigger to gamble (e.g. bank teller, accountant, taxi driver and salesperson). Thus, safeguards may need to be discussed if the client has a high-risk job. Certain employed clients can also take up extra work not only to fill in the time used to gamble but also to pay off debts sooner.

⊙ Finances – if the client is in debt or is having difficulty budgeting/managing finances, he/she might benefit from the elective session in Chapter 14. It is important to address the client's financial difficulties while in treatment. Addressing the client's financial situation will not only reduce the client's stress and negative moods but also enable the client to focus on treatment as he/she is no longer preoccupied with finding ways to improve his/her financial situation. The client might also want to consider taking up a second job to pay off the debts sooner. Referral to financial counselling may also be necessary for some clients and their significant others (Korn & Shaffer, 2004). Some clients will require information on government funded financial assistance. Some charities and churches can also assist problem gamblers (e.g. financial assistance, food vouchers).

⊙ Relationship problems with significant others – if the client's relationships are significantly affected by his/her gambling, the elective sessions in Chapters 13 and 15 might be beneficial for the significant others of problem gamblers as well as the problem gamblers themselves. It is important that significant others and their behaviours support the client's recovery rather than maintain the client's gambling behaviours. For example, significant others need to stop 'rescuing' the gambler from financial crisis as 'rescuing' helps maintain the client's gambling behaviours. It would be useful to engage the family early in the treatment programme. Where marital/family problems are contributing to the gambling, these need to be addressed (either in session or by encouraging the client to receive relationship/family/marriage counselling).

⊙ Legal problems – it is important that therapists are aware of these and the client has enough support and adequate legal advice to cope with such consequences of their gambling problem.

⊙ Physical and mental health – if the client is experiencing major health problems, it is advisable to refer them to their general practitioner. The client's family doctor should also be aware of the gambling problems. Some clients with mental health issues (e.g. depression, anxiety) may benefit from been referred to other health professionals (e.g. a psychiatrist).

⊙ Support – ensure that the client has sufficient support networks in place while completing the programme. If these do not comprise immediate family or friends, it is important that support is received from other means such as helplines and support groups such as Gamblers Anonymous. Gamblers Anonymous is a 12-step peer support recovery programme based on a similar concept to Alcoholics Anonymous. It is based on a medical conceptualization of problem gambling and encourages abstinence rather than controlled gambling.

A sheet such as the one provided in Appendix G can assist you with completing an individualized case formulation and treatment plan. An example of how to complete this form is provided below. A case study has been used to illustrate this example.

Case formulation and treatment plan sheet

Name of client: _David_   Date: _25/03/2009_

DOB: _12/05/1971_   Gender: _Male_

Presenting problems: _problem gambling, low mood, relationship problems, financial problems, unemployment_

Predisposing factors: _parental gambling (father) Big wins in early stages of gambling_

Precipitating factors: _gambling to escape from arguments with wife, switched to playing gambling machines from horse race gambling, desire to win money_

Perpetuating factors: _low mood, erroneous cognitions, financial problems, relationship problems, unemployment_

Prognostic factors: _Positive prognostic factors include: good support network, motivated, good premorbid functioning, late development of problems Negative prognostic factors include: comorbid mood problems, current stressors (i.e. financial, relationship and vocational problems)_

Design how the five Ps are related to one another

Predisposing factors: parental gambling, big wins in early stages of gambling ⟶ *Precipitating factors*: gambling to escape from arguments with wife, switched to playing gambling machines from horse race gambling, desire to win money ⟶ *Presenting problems*: gambling problems, low mood, relationship problems, financial problems, unemployment

Perpetuating factors: erroneous cognitions, low mood, ongoing stressors (i.e. relationship, financial and vocational problems)

Goals of treatment: _Abstinence from gambling learn strategies to cope with low mood and stressors_

Treatment plan

(a) Sessions to be completed: _All core sessions are relevant. Elective sessions: Getting out of debt Teaching significant others strategies to cope/deal with gamblers behaviours_

(b) Any specific intervention/referral needed for suicidal, housing, vocational, financial, relationship, legal, physical/mental health, social support problems:
- Unemployment - encourage client to register with job seeking agencies. Provide information on government sponsored work programmes.
- Relationship problems with wife - provide referrals for relationship counselling.
- Financial problems - provide information on government funded financial assistance.

Case study

David, a 38-year-old salesman self-presented at Gladeview Community Addiction Service stating that he needed to control his gambling because his wife had threatened to leave him. David stated that he currently gambles all his wages on gambling machines. He also presented with very low mood and cried several times during the assessment session.

David first gambled on his 30th birthday when his friends took him to a horse race as a birthday present. He stated that he tripled the amount bet on this first occasion. A week later, he went back to the races on his own. He stated that he was 'curious to find out whether a win could result again'. He continued going to the races at least once a week. 'I was so convinced that I could win because I won large amounts of money at least 3 times within the first month of betting on the horses.'

David's gambling gradually increased after he started playing gambling machines (8 months after he had began betting on horses). He stated that he began gambling on the machines as they were easily accessible and because he 'could gamble small amounts at a time and therefore had more chances of winning'. David reported that a desire to win money and escape from the arguments with his wife also motivated him to continue going to the local club to play the gambling machines.

David stated that it was not long after he began playing gambling machines that he noticed that his bills were piling up and that he had begun borrowing money from his friends. He had to frequently lie to his wife, as he did not want her to discover where the money went. He noticed that he had begun going to the club more frequently in the hope that he could win and pay his debts. The more time he spent gambling, the less he spent at work and with his wife and children. His absence from home often led to arguments with his wife. 'She thought I was having an affair' David reported. He stated that he noticed that he had begun going to the club to gamble whenever he had an argument with his wife or was feeling low about his life situation. Three months after he had begun gambling on the machines David lost his job. He stated that his employer was not satisfied with his sales figures. It was because of this incident that he finally had to tell his wife about the full extent of his gambling and related debts.

David described a happy childhood. He stated he enjoyed school and had a number of close friends. He stated that although his father's gambling habits created some tension between his parents at home, he remembers many happy family occasions. He generally described a good relationship with his parents and elder brother.

When asked about gambling problems, David stated that 'When I gamble, all I think of is winning just that amount of money that will let me draw even again. I don't seem to get the same buzz anymore from gambling but I just can't stop. Everytime I feel stressed, worried or overwhelmed about my life situation, I end up gambling. I feel very bad for hurting my wife and what she and our children are going through, but I just can't seem to stop. I have tried many times. I really want to stop but I feel things are just not going to change.' David stated that although the relationship with his wife is estranged, she is willing to support him through his recovery. His father who has been gamble free for 10 years and a regular Gamblers Anonymous member has also agreed to support him through his recovery.

3.4 PROVIDE TREATMENT RATIONALE AND PLAN

Before the treatment plan is presented to the client, it is important that treatment goals, any fears relating to participating in the programme, the nature of recovery and a treatment rationale is discussed with the client. This will help increase the client's motivation and compliance with the treatment programme. The following format could be used. The information provided here is very comprehensive and therapists are encouraged to discuss only those issues that they feel the client will benefit from.

3.4.1 Normalize fears of giving up gambling or participating in the programme

State that any change is anxiety provoking as change tends to create uncertainty, which frightens many of us. Reassure the client that it is alright to feel anxious throughout the course. However, such anxiety can always be reduced. Encourage the client to seek assistance from family members, friends, helplines (e.g. a problem gambling related helpline) and support groups such as Gamblers Anonymous, whenever anxiety is experienced or when the urge to gamble is strong.

3.4.2 Discuss the nature of recovery from a gambling problem

Many problem gamblers ask whether gambling problems are 'curable'. Thus, there may be a need to discuss the nature of recovery from a gambling problem with the client. Discuss with your client, 'Once we have become used to dealing with stress and meeting our needs through gambling, there is a very high risk of returning to this behaviour/pattern (similar to alcohol or drug dependence). The course of recovery has "ups and downs" and does not normally run smoothly. It can be difficult to stop/control gambling. However, it is possible, as so many other individuals have achieved this successfully.' The client must allow learning to occur from errors or lapses.

3.4.3 Explain treatment rationale and treatment components

Discuss why the programme uses a CBT approach to treat problem gambling. Discuss with your client, 'Although a number of therapies have had varying degrees of success, no single treatment has been shown to be effective for all individuals diagnosed with gambling problems. However, in recent years, evidence is emerging on the efficacy of CBT with gambling problems. CBT has been effective for anxiety and depressive disorders as well as other addictions. It has been tested in a number of controlled studies and has been found to be one to the most effective approaches to the treatment of gambling problems. The benefits of CBT appear to last. Follow-up studies after completion of therapy suggests that most participants maintain their improvements. Although symptoms may occasionally recur, especially during stressful periods, the symptoms can be handled by reimplementing the strategies learned during the course of the treatment and/or returning for a few extra therapy sessions to overcome the relapse quickly.'

Briefly outline the programme. You could say, 'We have already discussed how excessive gambling is maintained despite continuous and/or heavy losses. The treatment programme aims to address these factors.' Review and highlight what may be maintaining the client's gambling problem (you could use the information from the case formulation) and briefly discuss how the treatment programme could target each of these factors. Also, give a brief description of the treatment programme (i.e. the four phases of the treatment programme). You could also briefly discuss the duration of the programme and sessions.

Once the client has decided to commit to completing the programme, you can motivate the client further by encouraging the client to sign a contract (refer to Appendix H for a blank copy). Listed below are several important points to keep in mind when using the contract with the client (Masters et al., 1987; Redd, Porterfield, & Andersen, 1979).

⊙ The contract should be time and frequency limited.

⊙ A very clear and detailed description of the desired behaviour needs to be discussed.

⊙ The client can get a significant other (especially a spouse) to sign the contract. This will not only encourage the client to be open and honest about his/her problems with significant others but also help significant others feel that they are helping and supporting the client through recovery. Self-control techniques are most effective when they are instituted within the client's natural environment (Kanfer, 1977).

⊙ Behavioural contingencies should be stated (e.g. rewards for successfully completing goals (both daily and weekly rewards, as well as costs for not successfully completing goals). These rewards should however, not be gambling related. For example, for each day the client remains gamble free, the client can reward himself/herself with £5 and at the end of the week buy something with the money (e.g. a small dessert or a present). It can also be helpful to provide an additional reward when the individual exceeds the minimal requirements of the contract. For example, if there are no lapses in the first 6 weeks, an additional reward is provided. It is important that the reward is delivered very quickly after the success.

As Kirk (1989) highlighted, it is important to inform the client about the importance of his/her active participation (e.g. collecting information by monitoring, providing feedback on effectiveness of treatment, discussing the treatment progress and completing home exercise tasks) to increase treatment efficacy. The client should be encouraged to buy a folder to collect notes provided/collected during the treatment programme (as the notes would be useful to the client even after the programme has been completed).

3.5 INTRODUCE HOME EXERCISES

Encourage the client to monitor his/her gambling behaviours as a home exercise task. Explain the rationale and advantages of monitoring his/her gambling patterns. You may say something like, 'To get any habit under control, you need to be aware of it. Habits occur without thinking and so you must look closely at your gambling behaviours to get it back under control. One way to do this is by monitoring your gambling patterns.' There are many advantages of monitoring (Barlow & Rapee, 1991). For example it can:

⊙ help the client stay motivated by reminding the client to take an active role in controlling his/her gambling;
⊙ help the client become aware of the many aspects of recovery;
⊙ help the client become aware of the relationship between thoughts, feelings and behaviours;
⊙ help personalize information presented so that the information can relate to the client's unique situation;

⊙ help consolidate learning skills as writing out details in a structured way assists in understanding how each technique works and how it affects one;
⊙ help identify the client's internal and external triggers for gambling so that the client can develop strategies to manage it;
⊙ help the client learn about himself/herself in an objective way;
⊙ help document problems as well as successes with specific changes;
⊙ assist in evaluating progress and thus, keep the client on track.

Go through an example of how to do the monitoring using the Monitoring Gambling Sheet (Appendix I). Below is an example of how to complete the worksheet. Explain how to complete each column carefully. Provide the client with very clear instructions (e.g. 'Complete this every time you gamble and as soon as possible after gambling').

As mentioned in the outline in Chapter 1, at the end of the first session (i.e. assessment), it might be useful to very briefly discuss at least one or two strategies to control gambling (discussed in the next chapter) so that the client can start putting in place some strategies to control his/her gambling. This may improve the client's motivation to continue treatment. Consequently, the first session might need to be covered over two sessions.

Monitoring Gambling Sheet (Example)

Date/ time	Events preceding the gambling situation	Thoughts and feelings before the gambling situation	Gambling situation (a) where (b) with whom (c) available cash	Thoughts and feelings while in the gambling situation	Outcome (a) amount spent (b) amount won/lost	Thoughts and feelings after the gambling situation
Wed 5 pm	Had a fight with wife that morning about my gambling debts.	Feelings: Angry and upset Thoughts: I want to go and gamble to avoid going home the whole day.	(a) local pub (b) Alone (c) £50 cash	Feelings: Excited and lucky Thoughts: last time I won was on a Wednesday. If I go home with winnings, I might avoid an argument with my wife	(a) £50 (b) lost all	Feelings: Guilty and hopeless Thoughts: My wife will hate me even more. My gambling is so out of control.

Session two: Psychoeducation and self-management strategies to stabilize gambling

---

Session content and goals

4.1 Discuss aim and rationale of the session
4.2 Provide psychoeducation
4.3 Discuss self-management strategies to stabilize gambling
4.4 Introduce home exercises

4.1 DISCUSS AIM AND RATIONALE OF THE SESSION

4.1.1 Aim

There are two parts to this session. The main aim of the first part (Part A) is to educate the client about problem gambling and help the client to understand the development and maintenance of his/her own gambling problems. Throughout this, the client can be given feedback on the results of his/her own assessment (i.e. from the information gathered via the interview, standardized questionnaires and monitoring).

The main aim of the second part (Part B) of the session is to teach the client self-management skills to stabilize his/her gambling using both cognitive and behavioural techniques. The second part of the session also discusses strategies to cope with urges to gamble. Some simple strategies to minimize his/her chances of lapsing/relapsing are also discussed.

4.1.2 Rationale for Part A (Psychoeducation)

Many problem gamblers are not fully aware of what pathological gambling consists of and what maintains their gambling problems. Thus, psychoeducation on this instils awareness of not only the client's problems but also why past attempts to control his/her gambling might not have been successful. This gives the client a sense of hope and helps motivate the client to continue treatment. This part of the session was mainly compiled using the findings and content of the Raylu and Oei (2002) review.

4.1.3 Rationale for Part B (Self-management skills to stabilize gambling)

A number of factors play a role in maintaining gambling among problem gamblers despite continuous losses. Before these factors are addressed, the client's gambling behaviours should be stabilized (Sharpe, 1998). This can be achieved via teaching the client self-control strategies to stabilize his/her gambling behaviours.

The self-control literature demonstrates that there are two main strategies of self-control, environmental/stimulus control and behavioural programming (Redd, Porterfield, & Andersen, 1979). Environmental/stimulus control is based on Skinner's (1953) formulations of self-control that emphasize a need to alter relevant situational variables that can have an impact on behaviours. Behavioural programming is based on Kanfer's (1977) model of self-instruction or reinforcing and punishing consequences both through cognitive and behavioural means (Redd, Porterfield, & Andersen, 1979).

The client has an opportunity to control the extent of his/her gambling at a number of different states of a gambling episode: before the client encounters a trigger or an urge to gamble (trigger stage); when the client is experiencing an urge to gamble (urge stage); after a lapse or 'close call' (lapse stage).

- ◉ Trigger stage – there are times when a client can control what happens to him/her and how the individual deals with certain triggers to his/her gambling. For example, if the client knows that going into a betting agency will increase his/her urges to gamble, he/she can control that from occurring by staying away from one. Thus, it is important to teach the client how to cope with triggers. ⇒ *Thus, the client will be taught to identify triggers of gambling and put safeguards in place.*

- ◉ Urge stage – it is difficult for a client to control everything that occurs to him/her as the client only has limited control over some of the events that occur in his/her life. Furthermore, there are times when the client cannot control what occurs at all (e.g. accidentally meeting a person that the client used to gamble with). Thus, in situations such as this, one may not be able to control the trigger but may benefit from learning strategies to control urges to gamble. ⇒ *Thus, the client will be taught both cognitive and behavioural strategies to cope with gambling urges.*

- ◉ Lapse stage – it will take the client time to learn and regularly implement strategies learned throughout this programme. Consequently, lapses or 'close calls' are possible.

Thus, it is important to teach the client strategies that he/she can use to minimize gambling and thus, the negative consequences of gambling if a lapse occurs. ⇒ *Thus, the client will be taught some strategies to cope with lapses/'close calls'.*

4.2 PROVIDE PSYCHOEDUCATION

Educate the client about problem gambling and assist the client to understand the development and maintenance of his/her own gambling problems. Incorporate information collected from the assessment throughout the psychoeducation to personalize the information for the client. Although therapists are encouraged to develop their own style/ format of teaching, a psychoeducation session could have the following format. The information provided here is very comprehensive. What is discussed in this part of the session will vary from client to client depending on his/her level of understanding and insight into his/her problems. This subsection might be more relevant for those clients who are in the precontemplative stage. Therapists are encouraged to discuss only the information that they feel the client will benefit from.

4.2.1 Normalize gambling

Normalize gambling behaviour by discussing the following. Gambling is a common thing that most individuals do. Various studies have shown that 70–90% of adults gamble sometime in their lives (Ladouceur, 1991; Wallisch, 1998). However, there are individual differences in the patterns of gambling. For example there are individual differences in the forms of gambling preferred (e.g. lotto, casino games, gambling machines, sports betting), as well as the nature, frequency, duration and extent of gambling. Gamblers exist on a continuum and we all lie somewhere on the continuum of:

Non-gambler ← ---Social gambler-----Heavy/Regular gambler----Problem gambler-- → Pathological gambler

4.2.2 Discuss problem gambling

Discuss the client's problem gambling behaviours and negative consequences by considering the following. Problem gambling usually occurs when an individual's gambling is out of control and it begins causing the individual problems (i.e. social and personal problems). Problematic gambling behaviours include (American Psychiatric Association, 2000):

- frequently preoccupied with gambling or with obtaining money to gamble;
- frequently gambling for longer than intended;
- irritable when attempting to cut down or stop gambling;
- the need to increase the size or frequency of bets in order to achieve the same degree of excitement;
- restlessness or irritability when gambling is reduced or stopped;
- gambling as a means of escaping problems or negative emotions;
- lying to others in order to conceal the extent of involvement in gambling;
- committing illegal acts to finance gambling or pay debts (e.g. fraud);
- risking or have lost significant relationships because of gambling;
- borrowing money to relieve gambling debts or finance gambling;
- trying to reduce or stop gambling without success;
- risking or have lost significant opportunities because of gambling;
- chasing losses (continued gambling to recoup money lost);
- trying to conceal gambling by manipulation (e.g. hiding casino parking tickets).

Discuss assessment results (e.g. results of any questionnaires administered and information from the interview as well as the data gathered from the client's monitoring). It is important to link this to the current situation of the client and his/her case formulation as this helps increase motivation and personalizes treatment.

4.2.3 Discuss the nature and development of problem gambling

Discuss the nature and development of problem gambling by discussing the following issues:

- It is chronic (lasting) – especially when it becomes pathological. People around the problem gamblers are usually the first to recognize that the individual is having a problem, while the problem gambler continues to deny having a problem.

- It is progressive (i.e. it gradually gets worse).

- It is a chronic disorder that encompasses an unrelenting and recurring failure to resist impulses to gamble and where this 'maladaptive behaviour disrupts, or damages personal, family, or vocational pursuits' (American Psychiatric Association, 1994, p. 615).

- Different forms of gambling have been shown to have the potential of becoming problematic to varying degrees, but research suggest that gaming machines are now the leading form of gambling by problem gamblers treated in several countries (Raylu & Oei, 2002). Its potential to become problematic may be as a result of its easy accessibility, rapid event frequency and short payout intervals (Raylu & Oei, 2002).

⊙ The urge to gamble usually increases with stress.

⊙ As problem gambling develops, it may either increase coexisting anxiety and depressive symptoms or lead to the development of symptoms of anxiety and depression.

⊙ There are three ways in which gambling addiction is similar to other addictions (e.g. substance dependence):

 – Tolerance – problem gamblers often gamble with increasing amounts of money in order to achieve the desired excitement. Chasing losses is common.
 – Loss of control – as gambling increases, less time is spent on other things (e.g. work, family and leisure activities).
 – Withdrawal symptoms – when problem gamblers cannot meet that need to gamble through lack of money or opportunity, negative emotional states (e.g. boredom, irritability, anxiety and depression) may result. These are similar to the withdrawal symptoms that substance addicted individuals experience when drugs or alcohol are given up.

The main difference between addiction to gambling and other substance addictions is that in alcohol and drug addiction, individuals are addicted to the external substance introduced into the body. However, in problem gambling the addiction is related to the internal arousal (rather than an external substance) that problem gamblers experience when gambling.

4.2.4 Discuss reasons people begin gambling

Discuss why the client began gambling initially. Encourage the client to complete Part A of the Motivations Towards Gambling Worksheet (Appendix J) as you discuss the triggers. Possible reasons are discussed in detail in Chapter 2 (i.e. precipitating factors).

4.2.5 Discuss reasons some individuals continue gambling despite losses

Explore factors that may be currently maintaining the gambling problems. Encourage the client to write this list on Part B of the Motivations Towards Gambling Worksheet (Appendix J). Possible factors are discussed in detail in Chapter 2 (i.e. perpetuating factors). A brief discussion on possible predisposing factors can help the client understand the development of his/her problems (a summary of possible predisposing factors can be found in the previous session).

4.3 DISCUSS SELF-MANAGEMENT STRATEGIES TO STABILIZE GAMBLING

Before you discuss self-management strategies to stabilize gambling, explain to the client, 'Some of these strategies to stabilize gambling that we will discuss now just helps stop/control your gambling for a short period of time. This is because there are usually other factors that are maintaining gambling (as we learnt in the last section) such as distorted thinking and negative emotions and these need to be addressed to maintain abstinence/control in the long term. However, the strategies will help stabilize your gambling while you address those factors that are maintaining your gambling problems in subsequent sessions.'

> Since these are a wide number of strategies listed, choose the ones that are more relevant to the client or preferred by the client. You can introduce others in later sessions or if the initial strategies do not work.

4.3.1 Discuss triggers for gambling and safeguards for these triggers

Explain to the client that, 'Gambling does not just happen. There are a range of thoughts, places or actions that can increase urges or thoughts to gamble. These are called "triggers". Triggers can be either external (something outside of the individual) or internal (something internal of the individual).' Some examples of triggers include:

⊙ External
  - having money available;
  - being in a place where gambling is possible such as a club where there are gambling machines;
  - drinking alcohol (or using other drugs);
  - knowing that money will be available shortly (e.g. payday);
  - contact with people, places, times of day and situation commonly associated with gambling (e.g. hanging around with people who gamble);
  - hearing/seeing gambling machines;
  - meeting friends who the client used to gamble with;

- spare time;
- interpersonal conflict with others.
⊙ Internal
  - loneliness;
  - particular emotions (e.g. frustration, boredom, anger, depression, stress);
  - boredom/need for arousal or stimulation;
  - negative/dysfunctional thoughts (e.g. if I continue gambling, I will eventually win all the money I have lost).

Tell the client that, 'Some triggers are hard to recognize. Monitoring your gambling behaviours will help identify some of these triggers. Urges can increase to a level where it is too hard to control. This is why it is important to put safeguards in place. It helps reduce the likelihood of encountering these triggers or putting yourself in high-risk situations that may lead you to have a lapse.'

Use the Identifying Gambling Triggers and Establishing Safeguards Worksheet (Appendix K) to explore which of these triggers apply for the client. Then help the client identify possible safeguards that can be put in place using the three categories of safeguards discussed below. For example, possible safeguards for a common trigger (e.g. the day the client gets paid) include avoiding going past the betting agency, leaving bank cards with a significant other, having a busy day planned, and checking in with a helpline/or friend whenever the urge gets strong. The three categories of safeguards are discussed next.

4.3.1.1 Cash control

The client needs to control the amount of cash available at any given time to reduce the likelihood of gambling. These can be achieved by the following:

⊙ Taking only the necessary amount of cash when leaving the house each day (e.g. enough for lunch, and transport).

⊙ Leaving bank cards and credit cards at home. If there is a danger of going back home and getting cash, the client should consider giving the cash to a trusted individual. If the client is asking his/her partner, a relative or a trusted friend to handle the money, the trusted person should be told about the full extent of gambling problems (e.g. lies told in the past to gain access to the key cards). It might also be necessary to hand over the cards (e.g. credit cards) to the trusted person until the client feels that his/her gambling is stabilized. If the client does not have anyone to have this arrangement with then the client can consult the services of a financial counsellor.

⊙ Arranging wages to be paid directly into the bank rather than receiving cash. It might be beneficial to have another trustworthy person such as a spouse to be a joint account holder (where both signatures are required for any withdrawals or where only the other person can sign to withdraw cash). If this is not possible, the client can arrange a friend or trusted person to collect his/her wages.

- Arranging bills (e.g. electricity, telephone and insurance bills) to be paid using 'direct debit', cheque, or credit card. The client could also ask a significant other to pay the bills on a regular basis. However, the client needs to stay involved in the decision-making process about spending money and paying bills. If the client cannot hand over the cards to someone else, he/she can take a friend to pay the bills.

- Considering disclosure of gambling problems to credit providers to restrict further access to credit.

- Credit cards, store account cards, and other types of accounts with plastic card access are a common source of funds for problem gamblers. If the accounts are in the client's name, he/she needs to return the cards to the card provider and formally request that future credit on the account be denied and the account be closed. Arrangements should be made to repay the outstanding balance. If the account has joint account holders or the client is a secondary cardholder on the other person's account, it is wise to seek advice from the credit provider or an independent financial counsellor about limiting the risk of further extension of credit.

- If the client has pawned or sold items for money, he/she needs to take precautions to secure items of value from impulsive acts (e.g. giving valuables to a trusted friend or family member for safe keeping).

- Regarding the family home, other real estate or other types of investments at risk, it may be appropriate to seek legal advice on safeguarding these.

- Someone other than the problem gambler needs to control bank or other banking type accounts (e.g. building society and credit union). This can generally be achieved by the account being held in another name (usually the spouse).

- Ensuring there are no large sums of cash in the house.

- Keeping all cash flow 'visible' on account statements.

- Using automated teller machines to access limited amounts of cash.

- Avoiding jobs that would require handling cash.

When choosing a significant other to take over financial responsibility for the client's finances, it must be made clear to both the client and the significant other that this is a short-term solution and not intended to be a long-term arrangement. Spouses, in particular, can have difficulty later in treatment allowing the client to resume financial control, as they are often afraid that the client will return to gambling. Regaining financial independence is vital for long-term maintenance of therapeutic gains.

4.3.1.2 Avoidance

The easiest way to avoid urges is to try to avoid triggers and high-risk situations. For example:

⊙ trying not to go near the places where gambling used to occur in the past (e.g. the casino);
⊙ avoiding reading newspapers with horse racing sections;
⊙ avoiding talking to other problem gamblers;
⊙ voluntary self-banning from gambling institutes.

Once again, it is important to note that this is only a short-term solution to help the client stabilize his/her gambling. Later in the programme the client will be encouraged to face triggers and use strategies learnt to control urges/gambling.

4.3.1.3 Alternatives/time control

Hodgins and El-Guebaly (2004) reported that unstructured time or boredom was significantly related to relapse among problem gamblers. Thus, the client needs to arrange alternative things to do for the times when gambling normally occurs to reduce the chances of getting urges or lapsing. If the client has a busy day planned, he/she is less likely to think about gambling. Explain to the client that in order to stop a problematic behaviour, such as gambling, healthy behaviours need to replace gambling behaviours. Engaging in pleasant activities will also assist the client to cope with negative emotional states such as depression. Arranging alternative things to do is especially crucial at high-risk times (e.g. if the client gambles after work, he/she could arrange to meet a friend during this time).

Unlike the above two strategies, this strategy is not a short-term one. It has many long-term advantages including the following:

⊙ Motivates the client to begin doing things that he/she used to do/or wanted to do before gambling became problematic.
⊙ In time, these behaviours/activities can fill the gap left after gambling is stopped/reduced and thus, minimize chances of relapsing.
⊙ Encourages the client to set long-term goals that will improve his/her quality of life.
⊙ Physical/relaxation/recreational exercises can also improve mood and assist with social interactions (Korn & Shaffer, 2004).

Some clients may find it useful to use daily schedules. For example, you could say to a client, 'When you have a whole day planned, you don't give yourself time to go and gamble. Making a daily schedule for a vulnerable day (e.g. payday) before the day actually occurs (e.g. the night before) makes you more confident that you will complete the day without gambling – as in your mind you know what you have thought about the day and have put safeguards in place in order to reduce your chances of gambling.' A number of things should be considered when completing a daily schedule (e.g. include a range of activities, include both 'fun' and 'chore' activities, fill in all the gaps and include rewards for completing the plan). A blank copy of the Daily Schedule is included in Appendix L. The Alternative Activities Worksheet in Appendix M could be used to assist the client to brainstorm a variety of activities to include in his/her daily schedules.

If you have time in session, complete the Alternative Activities Worksheet and practise completing daily schedules (for the rest of the day or the next day) with the client. Alternatively, you could encourage the client to complete these for homework.

4.3.2 Discuss strategies to deal with urges

Discuss the nature of urges with the client.

- Urges are natural reactions following changes in gambling patterns and are often a response to situations (e.g. argument with a spouse), people (e.g. meeting someone that the client used to regularly gamble with) and even moods (e.g. feeling down) that used to be part of the gambling. Urges can also occur in the absence of triggers (Kadden et al., 1995).

- Urges only last a few minutes and rarely last more than an hour. Rather than increasing steadily until they become intense and unbearable, they usually peak and then die down, like a wave (Beck, Wright, Newman, & Liese, 1993). Thus, there is no need to relieve it by gambling. Urges will become less frequent and less intense as the client learns to cope with them. Urges are like stray cats. If the client feeds a stray cat, it will come back more often. Similarly, if the client gives in to the urges by gambling, the urges to gamble will come back more often. If the client does not give in to the gambling urges, the urges are likely to diminish over time.

- Urges are most common early in treatment. The client should expect these urges to occur from time to time and be prepared to cope with them if/when they occur. Several authors have reported both behavioural and cognitive strategies to deal with urges (Beck et al., 1993; Marlatt & Gordon, 1985). Although these strategies were initially introduced for controlling alcohol and drug urges, they can be used with gambling urges. These are discussed below.

4.3.2.1 Behavioural techniques

There are a number of behavioural techniques to cope with urges. These include the following:

⊙ Flashcards – when urges are strong, problem gamblers seem to lose the ability to reason objectively. Generating coping statements regarding why one should not gamble is often difficult for the client. Thus, it is useful to have such statements prepared on a card that the client can carry everywhere. When the client begins experiencing urges, he/she can read the prepared coping statements. Some examples of such statements include:

  - 'Things are good with my wife at the moment. I would like to keep it that way.'
  - 'I have already spent so much and if I continue gambling, there are no guarantees that I will continue winning.'
  - 'I have already made the first step towards seeking help. I don't want to go back.'
  - 'I need to take it one day at a time.'
  - 'Due to my gambling I am in debt.'
  - 'I have saved £__ already by not gambling.'
  - 'I have already paid £___ of my debt by not gambling.'

⊙ Delay decision to gamble for an hour – since urges never last more than an hour, encourage the client to delay the decision to gamble for just one hour.

⊙ Distraction – encourage the client to distract himself/herself when he/she experiences urges. It helps prevent the client from thinking about gambling and stops the client from reinforcing negative attitudes and thinking errors (Kadden et al., 1995). Techniques include:

  - reading a magazine or book;
  - observing what is happening around (e.g. looking in shop windows, watching other people, houses) and thinking about how to change these things;
  - turning on the TV;
  - listening to the radio, CD etc. and singing along to music;
  - going out with a purpose (e.g. library);
  - calling someone to talk to;
  - talking to people around you;
  - visiting a friend;
  - writing a letter or poem;
  - going for a drive, walk, run, swimming etc;
  - doing housework and other chores;
  - reciting a poem or prayer;
  - playing games such as video games, board games or puzzles;
  - watching a movie.

The Alternative Activities Worksheet in Appendix M lists a number of activities that the client can use as distractions when he/she experiences urges.

4.3.2.2 Cognitive/detachment techniques

There are a number of cognitive techniques to cope with urges. These include the following:

- Image replacement – when experiencing an urge, many problem gamblers have a tendency to remember only the positive consequences of gambling (e.g. winning a lot of money) and often forget the negative ones (e.g. losing their whole paypacket). Thus, when experiencing urges, the client may find it helpful to remind himself/herself of the negative consequences of gambling (financial loss). The client can substitute negative images regarding the many negative consequences of gambling. This is called negative image replacement. However, sometimes problem gamblers experience strong negative images about his/her current situation (e.g. losing their family because of their gambling or never being able to pay debts). Such thoughts often lead to feelings of hopelessness, which often leads to a lapse. Thus, at times like this, it is important to think positively (i.e. reminding yourself about the benefits of not gambling) by substituting positive images regarding the many positive consequences of not gambling (positive image replacement).

- Image refocusing/thought stopping – the thought stopping technique involves directing attention away from urges by imagining external events. Bain (1928) first introduced thought stopping. It involves concentrating on unwanted thoughts and after a short period, suddenly stopping and emptying your mind. More specifically, as soon as you start thinking about gambling, call out STOP! STOP! STOP! to yourself as loudly as you can in your head, and simultaneously imagine a stop sign as vividly as possible. Immediately distract yourself by shifting your attention to something else (such as becoming involved in another activity). This technique will require some practice but with enough practice will become a habit.

- Challenging thinking errors – identifying and challenging thinking errors, and replacing them with ones that are more positive. This technique will be discussed in more detail in the next three sessions.

4.3.3 Discuss strategies to deal with lapses/relapses

We cannot assume that the client will not give in to the gambling urges and end up gambling. A single lapse, if not handled well can lead to a full-blown relapse. Thus, it is important to teach the client to cope with a lapse in such a way that it does not lead to a full-blown relapse. The START technique described below can achieve this by guiding the client to get back on track if they encounter a lapse or a 'close call'. The START technique can be used by the client to remove him/her from the gambling environment after a lapse or when strong urges to gamble (but they have not gambled yet) are experienced. The START technique is based on Meichenbaum's (1977) self-instructional training. Meichenbaum introduced a comprehensive model for understanding the role of self-instructions in controlling impulses and behaviours. It assumes that with enough practice, self-instructions to control impulses and behaviours become automatic (Freeman, Pretzer, Fleming, & Simon, 1990). The steps are:

S – stop what I am doing immediately;
T – think of the possible negative consequences of gambling (when a 'close call' is experienced) or continuing gambling (when a lapse is experienced) and all the positive consequences experienced so far by controlling gambling/abstaining from gambling;
A – act by removing myself from the situation;
R – ring someone immediately to talk to (helplines, friends);
T – try the techniques learned in this section to control the urges.

The START technique can be adapted to a contract form (see Appendix N). It includes an agreement between the therapist and client concerning the steps to be taken in the event of a future lapse. It also provides a method of formalizing or reinforcing the client's commitment to change. Rewards and negative consequences for successfully completing the technique and not successfully completing the technique, respectively can be included in the contract.

4.4 INTRODUCE HOME EXERCISES

Discuss the home exercise tasks and any obstacles that can prevent the client from completing the task(s). Ensure that you have given the client the following:

✓ Home exercise sheet (below).
✓ Client Information Handout: Strategies to Stabilize Gambling (below). Ensure that you added the relevant phone numbers (e.g. 24-hour Helpline numbers and support groups such as Gamblers Anonymous numbers) on the handout.
✓ Blank copies of the Daily Schedule (Appendix L).
✓ Either a blank copy of the Alternative Activities Worksheet found in Appendix M (if this was not completed in session) or a completed copy of this sheet (if it was completed in session).
✓ Copies of worksheets completed in session – Motivations Towards Gambling Worksheet (Appendix J), Identifying Triggers and Establishing Safeguards Worksheet (Appendix K) and The START Technique Contract (Appendix N).

Home Exercise Sheet

(1) Try the strategies that you have learnt in this session. A summary of the strategies learnt in this session will be provided to you.

(2) Complete the Alternative Activities Worksheet (if not already completed in session). Choose some of the activities from the Alternative Activities Worksheet to help distract yourself when you are having urges and to begin replacing gambling behaviours with new and healthy behaviours.

(3) Practise making daily action plans daily and implementing it. You could choose some of the activities from the Alternative Activities Worksheet to complete your daily schedules. Try getting into a routine of doing the daily schedules one day in advance. When you have a whole day planned, you don't give yourself time to go and gamble. Making a daily schedule for a vulnerable day (e.g. payday) before the day actually occurs (e.g. the night before) makes you more confident that you will complete the day without gambling – as in your mind you know what you have thought about the day and have put safeguards in place in order to reduce your chances of gambling.

Client Information Handout:
Strategies to Stabilize Gambling

Strategies to deal with triggers
Ensure that you have safeguards in place for your triggers.
⊙ Cash control – control the amount of cash you have access to. Give access to someone else for a while if necessary.
⊙ Alternatives/time control – ensure that you have alternative things (besides gambling) to do and have a full schedule (daily schedule) so you don't have a chance to gamble.
⊙ Avoid triggers of gambling.

Strategies to deal with urges
⊙ Carry flashcards with coping statements.
⊙ DELAY decision to gamble for an hour as urges rarely last more than an hour.
⊙ Use thought stopping and distraction – as soon as you start thinking about gambling call out 'STOP' while imagining vividly a stop sign and immediately distract yourself by shifting attention to something else.
⊙ Image replacement – imagine negative consequences of gambling (negative image replacement) or imagine positive consequences of not gambling (positive image replacement).
(References: Beck et al., 1993; Marlatt & Gordon, 1985).

Strategies to deal with lapses/'close calls'
The START technique (based on Meichenbaum's 1977 self-instructional training) should also be used if your urges have led you to a situation where you are about to gamble (i.e. have a 'close call') or have gambled (i.e. lapsed).

S – stop what I am doing immediately.
T – think of the possible negative consequences of gambling (when a 'close call' is experienced) or continuing gambling (when a lapse is experienced) and all the positive consequences experienced so far by controlling gambling/abstaining from gambling.
A – act by removing myself from the situation.
R – ring someone immediately to talk to (Helpline, family member, friend).
T – try the techniques learnt so far to control the urges.

URGES ARE LIKE STRAY CATS – THE MORE YOU FEED THEM THE MORE LIKELY THEY WILL COME BACK. IF YOU DON'T FEED THEM, THEY ARE LIKELY TO DIMINISH OVER TIME.

Session three: Cognitive-restructuring I – identifying gambling specific thinking errors

---

Session content and goals

5.1 Review home exercises
5.2 Discuss aim and rationale of the cognitive restructuring sessions
5.3 Discuss identifying gambling specific thinking errors
5.4 Practise identifying gambling specific thinking errors
5.5 Introduce home exercises

5.1 REVIEW HOME EXERCISES

Review the client's progress on home exercises and provide as much praise as possible for his/her efforts and accomplishments. Troubleshoot problem areas or reasons for non-compliance. Below are some questions you could ask to initiate discussion on each of the home exercise tasks.

⊙ Trying out the strategies that the client learnt in the last session. Which of the strategies did you try out? Did it work? If so, what were the consequences? If not, what went wrong (you may need to discuss what the client could do the next time to change to a more positive outcome)?

⊙ Completing the Alternative Activities Worksheet. How many items did you manage to come up with? How many of the items did you manage to try over the week? How did it go? How did it make you feel trying them out?

⊙ Making daily schedules. How did you find doing daily schedules? What did you find were the advantages of making daily schedules?

5.2 DISCUSS AIM AND RATIONALE OF THE COGNITIVE RESTRUCTURING SESSIONS

5.2.1 Aim

Introduce the content and goals of the three cognitive restructuring sessions. The main aim of this session is to help the client identify gambling specific thinking errors that encourage the client to continue gambling despite significant losses. Chapter 6 involves teaching the client to challenge these gambling specific thinking errors. Chapter 7 involves teaching the client to identify and challenge other gambling related thinking errors. These include thinking errors regarding perceptions of the client's gambling behaviours, consequences of gambling, ability to stop/control gambling, etc.

5.2.2 Rationale

A number of factors play a role in maintaining gambling problems including inability to cope with stress, insufficient social support, lack of adequate coping skills, poor problem-solving skills, negative emotions and thinking errors (Marlatt, 1988). In subsequent sessions, we will deal with each one separately. We will begin by looking at thinking errors. The cognitive therapy principles described below and in Chapters 6 and 7 are based on the works of a number of authors (e.g. Beck, Rush, Shaw, & Emery, 1979; Ellis & Harper, 1961).

Individuals' thinking (e.g. the way individuals interpret things around them) affect their behaviours and feelings. Such thinking errors (distorted cognitions) are important as it is not necessarily the activating events (e.g. triggers) that cause certain emotional change (e.g. feeling depressed or guilty) or behaviours (e.g. gambling), but rather the automatic thoughts that are triggered. A state of mind characterized by certain dangerous thoughts can often lead one to gamble or to a relapse.

Activating event ⟶ **B**elief/thoughts ⟶ **C**onsequences (behaviours/ emotions/feelings)

⊙ Activating events include both internal (e.g. feelings such as guilt and depression) and external (e.g. going past a casino or betting agency) events.

⊙ Belief/thoughts are what you think determines the consequences (e.g. 'Gambling is the only way I can forget my problems' or 'I feel lucky today').

⊙ Consequences are both the behavioural and emotional consequences that result (e.g. giving into the urges and gambling, or feeling depressed and guilty about having urges to gamble).

If these thinking errors are in operation before gambling (e.g. 'I have to win some money to pay my bills'), they may lead to the client giving into his/her urges to gamble. If these thinking errors are in operation during gambling (e.g. 'I have lost the last three times I have gambled. I am due to win'), they may encourage the client to gamble despite continuous and heavy losses. If these thinking errors are in operation after gambling i.e. after a lapse (e.g. 'I have lost all my pay. My wife will hate me'), they might contribute to the feelings of guilt/hopelessness and encourage continued gambling.

If the client can learn to dismiss such thinking from their minds whenever it appears, or counter it with challenging thoughts to show themselves how distorted the thinking is, it does not need to result in a relapse. This can be achieved by a technique called cognitive restructuring. Several studies have also shown that the cognitive restructuring aspect of CBT can significantly reduce problem gambling symptoms (Ladouceur et al., 1989; 1998; Gaboury & Ladouceur, 1990).

There are three steps to the cognitive restructuring technique. These include:

⦿ identifying thinking errors;
⦿ challenging thinking errors by asking whether it is accurate, helpful and necessary;
⦿ replacing distorted thoughts with more realistic, functional and positive ones.

There are two categories of thinking errors among problem gamblers.

⦿ Gambling specific thinking errors – thinking errors that only problem gamblers have and are specifically related to their gambling skill or chances of winning/losing.

⦿ Other/general thinking errors – general errors in thinking problem gamblers have (similar to individuals who have other psychological problems), about their gambling behaviours, gambling problems, their consequences, ability to stop/control gambling, etc.

This session aims to teach the client how to identify gambling specific thinking errors, while the next session aims to teach the client how to challenge these errors in thinking. The session in Chapter 7 will be dedicated to teaching the client to identify and challenge other/general thinking errors.

5.3 DISCUSS IDENTIFYING GAMBLING SPECIFIC THINKING ERRORS

Toneatto (1999) identified several categories of thinking errors related to the skill of the game and ability to win that can occur before, during or after gambling. Such cognitions encourage problem gamblers to continue gambling despite losses. These can be divided into three broad categories including the following.

5.3.1 Illusion of control of gambling

Illusion of control of gambling involves the belief that one can control gambling outcomes. There are three forms of illusion of control.

⊙ Active illusionary control – believing that you can directly control your gambling outcomes (i.e. whether you win or lose) by gambling in specific places (e.g. where you have won before), carrying special objects (e.g. religious jewellery, or lucky charms), carrying out specific rituals (e.g. making a cross sign or praying before playing) or relying on systems, specific colours or lucky numbers to make gambling decisions.

⊙ Passive illusionary control – believing that you may indirectly have a control in determining whether you win or lose by gambling only when you feel lucky, are having good luck/successes with other areas of your life and by avoiding gamblers that are losing.

⊙ Magnifying your own gambling skills and minimizing other gamblers' skills – overestimating your own ability to win and underestimating others ability to win (e.g. 'This is a sure thing, I will continue with the treatment programme tomorrow').

5.3.2 Predictive control

Predictive control involves the belief that you have the skill of making accurate predictions (e.g. when the machine will payout, which horse will win or predict when you will win or lose) based on the following.

⊙ Salient cues such as omens, unusual events (e.g. the weather), hunches, feelings, instincts, and intuitions.
⊙ Past wins/losses (e.g. gambling the same time you had your past big win; avoiding a particular machine that you lost a lot of money in previously).

5.3.3 Interpretive biases

Interpretative biases involve reframing gambling outcomes in such a way that encourages continued gambling despite continued or heavy losses. There are several types of interpretative biases among problem gamblers. These include the following.

- Internal attributions, external attributions − attributing successes to your own skill or ability and failures to others' influences, bad luck or bad circumstances.

- Gambler's fallacy − reframing a string of losses as an indication that a win is impending (e.g. 'The machine is not paying out at all because the jackpot is just around the corner. If I play long enough, I will ultimately win. I will double my bets so that when I win, I win big').

- Chasing − belief that continued gambling will eventually recoup money lost.

- Reframed losses − reframing continuous losses as a learning experience (e.g. 'A series of losses will provide me with a learning experience that will help me win later').

- Selective memory − recalling wins more easily than losses and thus, expecting to win at games where you have lost previously.

- Hindsight bias − appraising gambling choices based on whether they result in wins or losses. If a win occurs, you decide that your gambling choice was correct and this strengthens your beliefs that you have the skill and ability to predict wins. However, if a loss occurs, you decide that in hindsight you knew this would occur and should have avoided the choice (e.g. 'I knew I should have bet on a red number instead of a black'). This can strengthen your beliefs that you have the skill and ability to predict wins and losses and that you learn from each loss you have at gambling.

Raylu and Oei (2004b) suggested two other cognitions, gambling related expectancies and perceived inability to control/stop gambling that might be relevant for problem gamblers. These are discussed next.

5.3.4 Gambling related expectancies

Gambling related expectancies relate to an individual's perceived expectations about the effects of gambling (e.g. 'Gambling will make me happier/less depressed/less anxious/relaxed/less stressed/powerful/satisfied'). Such expectancies may also be related to rationalizing why the gambler cannot stop gambling (e.g. 'Without gambling I will be very bored' or 'I can't relax without gambling'). Such cognitions also encourage problem gamblers to continue gambling despite continuous losses.

5.3.5 Perceived inability to stop/control gambling

Problem gamblers often try to stop/control gambling several times without success (American Psychiatric Association, 1994). Numerous failed attempts to control/stop gambling can lead to negative thoughts (e.g. 'My gambling is overpowering' or 'I am not strong enough to stop gambling').

Such thoughts can lead a problem gambler to stop trying to stop/control his/her gambling and consequently, confirm their beliefs about being helpless in overcoming their gambling problem.

5.4 PRACTISE IDENTIFYING GAMBLING SPECIFIC THINKING ERRORS

To help the client begin identifying gambling related thinking errors the following methods can be used.

- ⊙ Discuss past gambling sessions. Discuss the incidents (including the feelings, behaviours and especially the thoughts leading up to the events). Explore the thought processes that were occurring before, during and after the gambling episodes in order to elicit the thoughts that led the client to gamble and those that maintain his/her problem gambling behaviours.

- ⊙ Use the downward arrow technique (Burns, 1989) to help identify the distorted cognitions. It involves questioning the client on a chain of events using phrases (e.g. 'What does that mean?', 'What occurred next?', 'What do you mean?', 'What were you thinking?', 'What else would happen?', 'What else do you believe?', 'How would you feel then?').

- ⊙ You can use the Gambling Related Cognitions Scale (Raylu & Oei, 2004b) to help identify what thinking errors the client might have.

- ⊙ Go through each type of thinking error, exploring whether the client can identify with them. Make a list of the thinking errors that the client identifies with.

- ⊙ Use the Irrational Thoughts Record A (Appendix O), the most frequently used sheet to monitor thinking in CBT (Beck et al., 1979).

5.5 INTRODUCE HOME EXERCISES

Ask the client to monitor his/her thinking using the Irrational Thoughts Record A (adapted from Beck et al., 1979). You could introduce the home exercises in the following manner. 'We have just learnt about the types of thinking errors that are common among problem gamblers. You have identified with some of these as well. As mentioned before, some of these thoughts are so automatic that you do not even realize that you are making those thinking errors. The only way to identify these thinking errors is to monitor your thinking patterns. That is, recording your thoughts every time you encounter a trigger, get an urge to gamble or notice a change in your mood. These are the best times to catch these automatic thoughts. You need to be able to identify the thoughts if you are to successfully challenge them.'

Ensure that the client has the following.

✓ Home exercise sheet.
✓ Several copies of the Irrational Thoughts Record A (Appendix O).
✓ Client Information Handout – Identifying Gambling Specific Thinking Errors (below).

Also, encourage the client to continue practising the strategies learnt in the last session and to ring a 24-hour helpline number and/or attend a problem gambling related support group (e.g. Gamblers Anonymous). Tell the client, 'Get into the habit of doing this once a week. Gradually the weekly calls/meetings could be changed into fortnightly ones and then gradually to monthly once you begin feeling more confident about controlling your gambling or abstaining from gambling. This will help to keep you on track after the programme has finished. That is, keeping in touch with someone who can help monitor your gambling on a regular basis after the treatment programme can reduce your chances of lapsing or relapsing.' Provide the client with relevant phone numbers of these organizations.

Home Exercise Sheet

(1) Practise identifying gambling specific thinking errors using the Irrational Thoughts Record A and the Client Information Sheet – Gambling Specific Thinking Errors.

(2) Continue using the strategies learnt in previous sessions.

(3) Ring a 24-hour helpline number and/or attend a problem gambling related support group (e.g. Gamblers Anonymous). Get into the habit of doing this once a week. Gradually the weekly calls/meetings could be changed into fortnightly ones and then gradually to monthly once you begin feeling more confident about controlling your gambling or abstaining from gambling. This will help to keep you on track after the programme has finished. That is, keeping in touch with someone who can help monitor your gambling on a regular basis after the treatment programme can reduce your chances of lapsing or relapsing.

Client Information Handout:
Identifying Gambling Specific Thinking Errors

Toneatto (1999) suggested that a number of gambling specific thinking errors that could play a role in maintaining problem gambling. These include the following.

(1) Illusion of control – belief that one could control gambling outcomes:
  ⊙ active illusionary control – belief that you can directly control your gambling outcomes (i.e. whether you win or lose) by gambling in specific places (e.g. where you have won before), carrying special objects (e.g. religious jewellery or lucky charms), carrying out specific rituals (e.g. making a cross sign or praying before playing) or relying on systems or lucky numbers to make gambling decisions;
  ⊙ passive illusionary control – belief that you may indirectly control winning by gambling only when you feel lucky, are having good luck/ successes with other areas of your life and by avoiding gamblers that are losing;
  ⊙ overestimating own gambling skills or ability to win and underestimating others' gambling skills and ability to win.

(2) Predictive control – belief you have the skill of making accurate predictions (e.g. when you will win or when you will lose/win) based on:
  ⊙ salient cues (using omens or unusual events e.g. the weather);
  ⊙ past wins/losses (e.g. gambling the same time you had your past big win; avoiding a particular machine that you lost a lot of money in).

(3) Interpretive bias – faulty ways of interpreting gambling outcomes:
  ⊙ internal/external attributions – attributing successes to one's own skill/ ability and failures to others' influences, bad circumstances or bad luck;
  ⊙ gambler's fallacy – a series of losses is reframed as indicating that a win is 'very near' (e.g. 'I'm due.');
  ⊙ chasing losses – belief that continued gambling will ultimately recoup money lost;
  ⊙ reframed losses – reframing continuous losses as learning experiences that may eventually help lead to repeated wins;
  ⊙ selective memory – recalling wins more easily than losses and thus, expects to win at games where you have lost previously.

Raylu and Oei (2004b) reported two other gambling specific thinking errors.

(4) Gambling expectancies – faulty expectations of gambling:
  ⊙ 'Gambling will make me happier/less depressed/relaxed/satisfied.'

(5) Perceived inability to stop/control gambling
  ⊙ 'I will never be able to stop gambling' or 'My gambling is overpowering'.

Session four: Cognitive-restructuring II – challenging gambling specific thinking errors

---

Session content and goals

6.1 Review home exercises
6.2 Discuss aim and rationale of the session
6.3 Discuss challenging gambling specific thinking errors
6.4 Practise challenging gambling specific thinking errors
6.5 Generate rational self-statements
6.6 Introduce home exercises

6.1 REVIEW HOME EXERCISES

Review the client's progress on home exercises. Praise his/her efforts and accomplishments. Troubleshoot problem areas or reasons for non-compliance.

6.2 DISCUSS AIM AND RATIONALE OF THE SESSION

6.2.1 Aim

The aim of the session is to teach the client to challenge gambling specific cognitions.

6.2.2 Rationale

The rationale was provided in the previous session. The client should be comfortable with identifying gambling specific cognitions before they move on to this session. If the client has not mastered identifying gambling specific thinking errors, more time should be spent assisting the client to achieve this.

6.3 DISCUSS CHALLENGING GAMBLING SPECIFIC THINKING ERRORS

There are a number of ways you can assist the client to challenge gambling specific thinking errors. These are discussed below.

6.3.1 Psychoeducation

⊙ Educating the client about the nature of gambling, gambling outcomes and the notion of randomness – gambling outcomes are determined by chance, which involves an unpredictable event or accidental occurrence (Ladouceur, 2001). Thus, it is not possible to control or predict a gambling outcome. All gambling specific thinking errors involve the error of believing that there are links between independent chance events rather than understanding that in most forms of gambling all possible outcomes have an equal probability of occurring (Ladouceur, Sylvain, & Boutin, 2000). That is, the outcome of each event/wager is independent to any other event/wager (Sharpe, 1998). For example, just because the last three roulette spin outcomes were black, does not indicate that the chance of obtaining a red in the next spin is higher than obtaining a black. In machine gambling, outcomes are determined by a computer using a randomized system (Sharpe, 1998). Therefore, the likelihood that the machine will pay out following a win is the same as the likelihood it will pay out following a loss (Sharpe, 1998). Thus, the client needs to be educated about the nature of gambling, gambling outcomes and the notion of randomness. Such misconceptions can also be challenged by reminding the client all the times that he/she thought that a possible outcome will occur (e.g. a roulette spin was going to result in a red number) and it did not.

⊙ Educating the client about the level of chance and skill involved in each form of gambling – problem gamblers often have thinking errors related to their skill in gambling or their ability to win (Raylu & Oei, 2004b). Thus, it is important to clarify the level of chance and skill involved in each form of gambling with the client. The client needs to be taught that although different forms of gambling differ in the extent of skill involved, that outcomes of most forms of gambling (e.g. gaming machines) are dependent on only luck and that the outcomes of none of the different forms of gambling are dependent on only skill (Sharpe, 1998).

⊙ Educating the client about the features of gambling machines and gambling environments that foster gambling. The client needs to be aware of the features of gambling machines and gambling environments that encourage gambling despite continuous losses. Gambling institutions are often set up in a way that encourages problem gamblers to continue gambling. This is important for the gambling institutions as the more money individuals gamble the more profits they will make. A number of researchers (e.g. Sharpe, 1998; Griffiths, 1993; Ladouceur, 2001) have outlined the importance of the structural characteristics of gambling machines and gambling environments designed to reinforce beliefs of winning and control and facilitate continued gambling despite continuous losses. These included:

- although the percentage of return on money gambled differs in different places, all gambling machines have a negative return rate (i.e. the machines pay back less money than was staked);

- winnings/pay outs in gambling machines often occur as a small number of credits or free spins, which most problem gamblers end up losing;

- gamblers have to wait only a short time to receive winning payments on a gambling machine;

- the extent to which gamblers are or perceive themselves as taking an active part in the gambling activity while playing on a gambling machine is large (e.g. gamblers have numerous choices in how much credit to use per spin);

- small but frequent wins occur at different intervals;

- structural characteristics exist that temporarily disrupt the gamblers financial value system (e.g. thinking that using 10p coin gambling machines rather than £2 coin gambling machines would allow them to lose little on each gamble);

- environmental properties such as light, colour and sound effects may have the capability of producing psychologically rewarding experiences even when the gambler is losing.

6.3.2 Examining the evidence

Encourage the client to examine the evidence for and against his/her thoughts. For example, for the thought 'I have a better chance of winning on my lucky machine,' a number of questions can be used (such as How many times did you lose when you played on your lucky machine? Have you won using any other machine? How much have you won using your lucky machine? How much have you lost using your lucky machine?). Since problem gamblers have a tendency to remember their wins compared with losses, it is essential that clients are encouraged to remember past losses before challenging their thinking errors (e.g. 'Remember the last time you lost. Did your superstitious beliefs work that time?').

6.3.3 Using behavioural experiments to look at the pattern of wins and losses

For those who continue to maintain some level of belief after a retrospective analysis of their thinking errors, behavioural experiments (e.g. getting a roulette player to predict numbers without actually placing a bet) can be quite useful when set up in an appropriate manner. Keeping a record of predictions will help the client objectively see the inconsistencies between his/her predictions and the actual outcome. It is however, important that the experiment does not involve placing the client in situations that he/she is not yet able to manage without gambling. Thus, it might be advisable for the client to go into the gambling institution with someone, such as a friend, especially if he/she does not feel confident in controlling gambling urges. It is also essential when choosing an appropriate behavioural experiment to try the experiment enough times that the laws of probability will hold true. Therapists should advise their clients not to take any money with them when they try out the behavioural experiments.

6.4 PRACTISE CHALLENGING GAMBLING SPECIFIC THINKING ERRORS

Use the Irrational Thoughts Record B (Appendix P) and the above strategies to challenge gambling specific thinking errors. An example of a completed Irrational Thoughts Record B is below.

6.5 GENERATE RATIONAL SELF-STATEMENTS

The client could write rational thoughts on a card that he/she can carry with him/her. They are especially useful when the urges are strong as this is when it is hard to think rationally. Reading the cards daily can help strength the rational thoughts. Some of these statements could include:

⊙ gambling outcomes are more determined by luck than skill;
⊙ outcomes on gambling machines are determined by a computer using a randomized system so I cannot control or predict gambling outcomes;
⊙ gambling outcomes are not related to previous outcomes or random events so there is no way I can predict gambling outcomes;
⊙ feeling lucky doesn't make it so;
⊙ gaming machines are set in such a way that they pay less than the stake;
⊙ when my urges are strong, I have a tendency to remember only my wins not losses;
⊙ structural factors related to gambling machines and gambling environments encourage continued gambling despite losses.

6.6 INTRODUCE HOME EXERCISES

Use the home exercise sheet to discuss home exercises. Ensure that the client has the following.

✓ Home exercise sheet (below).
✓ Blank copies of the Irrational Thoughts Record B (adapted from Beck et al., 1979) found in Appendix P.
✓ Any completed copies of the Irrational Thoughts Record B (adapted from Beck et al., 1979) including a copy of the example provided below.
✓ Client Information Handout – Challenging Gambling Specific Thinking Errors.

Irrational Thoughts Record B (adapted from Beck et al., 1979) (Example)

Activating experience – events, thoughts, memories, and feelings that trigger negative mood or behaviours (e.g. gambling)	Beliefs – interpretation or thoughts of the experience ⊙ What were you thinking? ⊙ What thinking error are you making?	Consequences – resulting actions and feelings	Challenging irrational thoughts	Consequences – resulting actions and feelings after challenging irrational thoughts
It is payday and I have been feeling vulnerable the whole day. Since I was busy at work I could not go and gamble. As I was leaving work to go home, I met an old friend. My friend invited me to go to the local club where they have gambling machines.	My biggest win was at that club so I may win there again (illusion of control and memory bias). I feel lucky (passive illusionary control). This may help me win back all the money I have lost (chasing).	Anxious Excited about the possibility of winning Disappointment at the circumstance and in myself Gambling urges	I am only focusing on my wins and not the times that I have lost. Despite my big win at that club, I have lost many times in that club. In fact I have lost more money in that club than any other place that I have gambled. Feeling something does not make it so. There are many other times when I have felt lucky but ended up losing significant amounts of money. The machines are fixed anyway. That is how they make money. Outcomes are all random and based on luck so there is no way I can predict whether I will win or lose. Every time I gamble the outcome is not related to previous outcomes so there is no way I can predict whether I will win or lose.	Urges reduced enough for me to go to a safe environment or call someone to talk to about my urges. Feeling less weak in giving in to the urges. Feeling more confident in getting through the rest of the day without gambling.

Challenging: What thinking error am I making? What is the evidence against the thought? What are the disadvantages of thinking this way? What is an alternative way of looking at this? Try behavioural experiments to test your assumptions. For gambling specific thinking errors, also remind yourself of the law of randomness (e.g. 'There are no links between independent chance events so in most forms of gambling all possible outcomes have an equal probability of occurring'), the level of chance and skill involved in each form of gambling (e.g. 'Gambling outcomes are more determined by luck than skill') and structural characteristics of gambling machines and gambling environments that encourage gambling despite losses.

Home Exercise Sheet

(1) Practise identifying and challenging gambling specific thinking errors using the Irrational Thoughts Record B, the Client Information Handout: Challenging Gambling Specific Thinking Errors and the Client Information Handout: Identifying Gambling Specific Thinking Errors (provided in the last session).

(2) Sometimes it is useful to have rational thoughts written down on a card that you can carry. They are especially useful when the urges are strong, as it is hard to thinking rationally when the urges are strong. Make such a card. Statements could include:

- Gambling outcomes are more determined by luck than skill.
- Outcomes on gambling machines are determined by a computer using a randomized system so I cannot control or predict gambling outcomes.
- Gambling outcomes are not related to previous outcomes or random events so there is no way I can predict gambling outcomes.
- Feeling lucky doesn't make it so.
- Gaming machines are set in such a way that they pay less than the stake.
- When my urges are strong, I have a tendency to remember only my wins not my losses.
- Structural factors related to gambling machines and gambling environments encourage continued gambling despite losses.

(3) Continue using the strategies learnt in previous sessions.

(4) Ring a 24-hour helpline number and/or attend a problem gambling related support group (e.g. Gamblers Anonymous). Get into the habit of doing this once a week. Gradually the weekly calls/meetings could be changed into fortnightly ones and then gradually to monthly once you begin feeling more confident about controlling your gambling or abstaining from gambling. This will help to keep you on track after the programme has finished. That is, keeping in touch with someone who can help monitor your gambling on a regular basis after the treatment programme can reduce your chances of lapsing or relapsing.

Client Information Handout:
Challenging Gambling Specific Thinking Errors

(1) Remind yourself of the following.

(a) The nature of gambling, gambling outcomes and notion of randomness – gambling outcomes are determined by chance. Consequently, it is impossible to control or predict a gambling outcome. All gambling specific thinking errors involve the error of believing that there are links between independent chance events. In most forms of gambling all possible outcomes have an equal probability of occurring. That is, the outcome of each event/wager is not dependent on any other event/ wager (e.g. just because the last three roulette spin outcomes were black, does not indicate that the chance of obtaining a red in the next spin is higher than obtaining a black). In machine gambling, outcomes are determined by a computer using a randomized system. Therefore, the likelihood that the machine will pay out following a win is the same as the likelihood it will pay out following a loss. Such misconceptions can be challenged by remembering all the times that you thought that a possible outcome will occur (e.g. the machine was going to pay out or the roulette spin was going to result in a red number) and it did not.

(b) The level of chance and skill involved in each form of gambling – although different forms of gambling differ in the extent of skill involved, outcomes of most forms of gambling (e.g. gaming machines) are dependent on only luck and that the outcomes of none of the different forms of gambling are dependent on only skill. Gambling outcomes are more determined by luck than skill for all types of gambling.

(c) The features of gambling machines and gambling environments that foster gambling – gambling institutions are often set in a way that encourages problem gamblers to continue gambling. This is important for the gambling institutions as the more money individuals gamble, the more profits they will make. There are a number of structural characteristics of gambling machines and gambling environments designed to reinforce beliefs of winning and control to facilitate continued gambling despite continuous losses. Some of these are mentioned below.

- Although the percentage of return on money gambled differs in different places, all gambling machines have a negative return rate (i.e. the machines pay back less money than was staked).
- Winnings/pay outs in gambling machines often occur as small numbers of credits or free spins, which most problem gamblers end up losing.
- Gamblers have to wait only a short time to receive winning payments on a gambling machine.
- The extent to which gamblers are or perceive themselves as taking an active part in the gambling activity while playing on a gambling machine is large (e.g. gamblers have numerous choices in how much credit to use per spin).

⊙ Small but frequent wins occur at different intervals so that they can not be accurately predicted.

⊙ Structural characteristics exist that temporarily disrupt the gamblers financial value system (e.g. thinking that using 10p coin gambling machines rather than £2 coin gambling machines would allow them to lose little on each gamble).

⊙ Environmental properties such as light, colour, and sound effects may have the capability of producing psychologically rewarding experiences even when the gambler is losing.

(2) Examine the evidence against your thoughts.

(3) Use behavioural experiments to look at the pattern of wins and losses (e.g. a horse race gambler could predict which horse would win while watching the race on TV without placing a bet or a roulette player could predict which colour and number the spin would result in without placing a bet). If you are going into a gambling institute to try these experiments, it is advisable to take a friend/family member with you and not to take any money to gamble with. Do not go into a gambling institute if you do not feel confident in controlling your gambling/abstaining from gambling. It is also important when choosing an appropriate behavioural experiment to try the experiment enough times that the laws of probability will hold true.

(4) Remind yourself of your losses and negative consequences of gambling and challenge your irrational thoughts (e.g. remember the last time you lost. Did your predictions work? Did your superstitious beliefs work that time?).

(References: Sharpe, 1998; Griffiths, 1993; Ladouceur, 2001; Ladouceur, Sylvain, & Boutin, 2000).

*Session five: Cognitive-restructuring III –
identifying and challenging other/general
thinking errors*

Session contents and goals

7.1 Review home exercises
7.2 Discuss aim and rationale of the session
7.3 Discuss identifying other/general thinking errors
7.4 Practise identifying other/general thinking errors
7.5 Discuss challenging other/general thinking errors
7.6 Practise challenging other/general thinking errors
7.7 Introduce home exercises

7.1 REVIEW HOME EXERCISES

Review the client's progress on home exercises and provide as much praise as possible for his/her efforts and accomplishments. Troubleshoot problem areas or reasons for non-compliance.

7.2 DISCUSS AIM AND RATIONALE OF THE SESSION

7.2.1 Aim

The aim of the session is to learn to identify and challenge other/general thinking errors that problem gamblers often experience and replace them with more realistic and rational thoughts.

7.2.2 Rationale

Refer to the rationale provided in Session Three (Chapter 5).

7.3 DISCUSS IDENTIFYING OTHER/GENERAL THINKING ERRORS

There are a number of general thinking errors problem gamblers make that are related to their gambling problems, their negative consequences, ability to stop/control gambling, etc. These are similar to the ones displayed by individuals with other psychological/emotional problems. Beck (1963) originally proposed this for depression and later suggested that similar processes underlie other emotional disorders (Beck, 1976). Other authors (such as Burns, 1989) have also discussed these. Similar ones have also been found in problem gamblers (Raylu & Oei, 2004b). If these thinking errors are in operation before gambling, they may lead to the problem gambler giving into his/her urges to gamble. If these thinking errors are in operation during gambling, they may encourage the problem gambler to gamble despite continuous and heavy losses. If these thinking errors are in operation after gambling (e.g. after a lapse), they might contribute to feelings of guilt and hopelessness and encourage the problem gambler to gamble again. These general thinking errors include the following.

7.3.1 All or nothing thinking

This involves making and believing in definite statements or seeing things in black or white categories. If performance falls short of being perfect, the client may begin viewing himself/herself as a total failure. For example:

- 'All lapses are relapses; abstinence once violated can never be regained.'
- 'If I can't be the best, it's pointless in trying at all.'
- 'If I don't succeed in this treatment, I am a total failure.'
- 'If I can't get it completely right, there is no point trying at all.'

7.3.2 Overgeneralization

This involves drawing conclusions based on the occurrence of a single, isolated event. The client may drag up past events, which are similar to today and predict that it will always stay the same. Overgeneralization can lead to a lapse becoming a full-blown relapse as the lapse is taken as a sign of total relapse. For example:

- 'Everything is a mess.'
- 'My future is bleak.'
- 'My situation will never improve.'
- 'Every time I have tried to stop in the past, I didn't succeed. This time won't be any different.'

7.3.3 Mental Filter

This involves picking a single detail and dwelling on it exclusively so that the vision of all reality becomes unclear. For example:

- 'I will never forget the way they treated me the last time I had a lapse.'

7.3.4 Jumping to conclusions

This involves making a negative interpretation even though there are no definite facts that support that conclusion. For example:

- Fortune telling – anticipating that things will turn out a certain way despite a lack of definite facts to support the assertion (e.g. 'My relationship is sure to fail').
- Mind reading – anticipating what others are thinking (e.g. 'My wife will hate me' or 'He is looking at me strangely so I must look stupid or ugly').

7.3.5 Should statements

This includes statements that are used to try to motivate oneself with 'shoulds and shouldn'ts'. When such statements are directed at oneself, the emotional consequence is often guilt. When you direct such statements towards others, the emotional consequence is often anger, frustration or resentment. For example:

- 'I must recoup my losses immediately.'
- 'I must continue gambling to recover my losses.'
- 'I must continue gambling to improve my financial situation.'
- 'I shouldn't have done that. What was I thinking?'

7.3.6 Magnification (catastrophizing) or minimization

This involves exaggerating (magnifying/catastrophizing) or inappropriately reducing (minimizing) the importance of things. For example:

- magnifying/catastrophizing an urge – 'If I get a craving, it will be unbearable.'
- magnify ability to control gambling – 'I will just test myself with £5 and prove that I am in control.'
- minimizing own fault by blaming others – 'It's not my fault if I am nagged into it by my partner who just can't keep off my case.'

7.3.7 Emotional reasoning

This involves assuming that your negative emotions necessarily reflect the way things really are. 'I feel therefore I must be.' For example:

- 'I feel like a loser so I must be one.'
- 'I feel bad about not being able to control my gambling and it means I am a bad person.'
- 'I feel weak when I can't stop my gambling so I must be weak.'

7.3.8 Polarized thinking

This includes focusing entirely on the negatives or entirely on the positives. For example, some problem gamblers tend to focus so much on the fact that they have let others down that they start feeling depressed. Subsequently, this depression can lead to further lapses or a relapse.

- 'I did alright, but why didn't I do this instead.'

7.3.9 Labelling and mislabelling

This is an extreme form of 'overgeneralization'. Instead of describing your error, you attach a negative label to yourself. For example,

- 'I am a loser, I don't deserve any better.'
- 'I'm an idiot.'
- 'I'm weak.'

7.3.10 Personalization

This involves seeing yourself as the cause of some negative external event, which in fact, you are not primarily responsible for. The total responsibility and thus, personal causality for the lapse, makes it more difficult to reassume control.

- 'I keep failing to control my gambling and that is why we are still in this financial mess.'
- 'My wife has come home in a bad mood. It must be something I have done.'

7.4 PRACTISE IDENTIFYING OTHER/GENERAL THINKING ERRORS

Use the adapted Irrational Thoughts Record A in Appendix O to practise identifying other/general thinking errors. An example of this is provided below. You may use the guidelines that are provided in Section 5.4 to help the client identify these thinking errors.

7.5 DISCUSS CHALLENGING OTHER/GENERAL THINKING ERRORS

Hawton, Salkovskis, Kirk, and Clark (1989) highlighted some ways of challenging general thinking errors that are common among problem gamblers. These are summarized below.

7.5.1 Examining the evidence

Examine the evidence. Ask yourself the following.

- What is the evidence for my thinking?
- What is the evidence that if I don't gamble I will . . . ?
- What's the evidence that I will never improve?
- Am I confusing a thought with a fact?

7.5.2 Alternative explanations

Are there any alternative explanations?

- Am I assuming my view of things is the only possibility?
- How would I have looked at this situation before I started gambling excessively?
- How would another person look at the same thing?
- How would I look at it if someone else described it to me?

Irrational Thoughts Record A (adapted from Beck et al., 1979) (Example)

Activating experience – events, thoughts, memories, and feelings that trigger negative mood or behaviours (e.g. gambling)	Beliefs – interpretation or thoughts of the experience ◉ What were you thinking? ◉ What thinking error are you making?	Consequences – resulting actions and feelings
Payday.	The last time I won was on a Thursday (payday). Since today is Thursday, the probability of me winning is high (illusion of control). I feel lucky today (passive illusionary control). I have been losing for a while, so the chance of winning this time is high (gamblers fallacy). Gambling was the only way I can recoup all the money that I have lost (all or nothing, chasing). My wife will think I gambled anyway (jumping to conclusions). I haven't been able to control my urges before so I won't be able to control my urges this time as well (overgeneralization).	Strong urges to gamble which led to a lapse. Felt guilty and angry with myself.

7.5.3 Utility analysis

What is the effect of thinking the way I do?

- Is the way I think now helping me to achieve my goals or is it standing in the way of what I want?
- Am I worrying about the way things ought to be, instead of accepting and dealing with them as they are?
- Would this way of thinking make me feel any better?

7.5.4 Experimental technique

Am I predicting the future instead of experimenting?

- Instead of predicting something, try/test it out in reality.
- Ask people questions to find out if your thoughts and attitudes are realistic.

7.5.5 Standard analysis

What thinking errors am I making?

7.6 PRACTISE CHALLENGING OTHER/GENERAL THINKING ERRORS

Get the client to use the techniques above, including the ones learnt in the previous sessions to practise identifying and challenging other/general thinking errors. Irrational Thoughts Record B (adapted from Beck et al., 1979) included in Appendix P can assist you with this. A completed example is given overleaf. You could also use the Challenge Practice Sheet (on page 97) to help the client practise challenging thinking errors. The Challenge Practice Sheet lists a range of gambling specific and general dysfunctional thoughts. It provides clients with the opportunity to identify the type of thinking error made and to come up with a possible challenge for each dysfunctional thought. A completed example of a practice sheet identifying the type of error made and examples of how to challenge each dysfunctional thought can be seen on page 100.

Irrational Thoughts Record B (adapted from Beck et al., 1979) (Example)

Activating experience – events, thoughts, memories, and feelings that trigger negative mood or behaviours (e.g. gambling)	Beliefs – interpretation or thoughts of the experience ⊙ What were you thinking? ⊙ What thinking error are you making?	Consequences – resulting actions and feelings	Challenging irrational thoughts	Consequences – resulting actions and feelings after challenging irrational thoughts
Came home from work and felt bored and to relieve the boredom I felt like gambling.	Gambling is the only way to relieve my boredom (all or nothing thinking). If I keep at it, I will eventually win (jumping to conclusions, gambler's fallacy). Having a positive attitude will help me win (active illusionary control).	Depressed. Hopeless. Gambling urges.	My therapist has taught me so many ways of relieving boredom. I can try them out. There is no proof that I will eventually win if I continue gambling or if I have a positive attitude. There have been numerous times when I still lost all the money despite having a positive attitude. Outcome of all gaming machines are predetermined so there is no way having a positive attitude can change that.	More hopeful about not gambling. Intensity of urges slightly reduced. Forced myself to go for a run instead of going gambling.

Challenging: What thinking error am I making? What is the evidence against the thought? What are the disadvantages of thinking this way? What is an alternative way of looking at this? Try behavioural experiments to test your assumptions. For gambling specific thinking errors, also remind yourself of the law of randomness (e.g. 'There are no links between independent chance events so in most forms of gambling all possible outcomes have an equal probability of occurring'), the level of chance and skill involved in each form of gambling (e.g. 'Gambling outcomes are more determined by luck than skill') and structural characteristics of the gambling machines and gambling environments that encourage gambling despite losses.

Challenge Practice Sheet

(1) Thought: 'All lapses are relapses; abstinence once violated can never be regained.'

⦿ Type of error: ....

⦿ Challenge: ....

....

....

....

....

(2) Thought: 'I will win today.'

⦿ Type of error: ....

⦿ Challenge: ....

....

....

....

....

(3) Thought: 'Gambling will help pay the bills.'

⦿ Type of error: ....

⦿ Challenge: ....

....

....

....

....

(4) Thought: 'I will never be able to control my urges.'

⦿ Type of error: ....

⦿ Challenge: ....

....

....

....

....

(5) Thought: 'I can't stop thinking about how I gave in to my urges and gambled. I can't believe how weak I am.'

⦿ Type of error: ....

⦿ Challenge: ....

....

....

....

....

(6) Thought: 'I know I will give in to my urge and end up gambling today.'

⦿ Type of error: ....

⦿ Challenge: ....

....

....

....

....

(7) Thought: 'I will just test myself with £5 and prove that I am in control.'

⦿ Type of error: ....

⦿ Challenge: ....

....

....

....

....

(8) Thought: 'It is my fault everything is messed up. I gave in to my urges and gambled after the argument I had with my wife. I did not have enough will-power.'

⦿ Type of error: ....

⦿ Challenge: ....

....

....

....

....

(9) Thought: 'I feel lucky today.'

⦿ Type of error: ....

⦿ Challenge: ....

....

....

....

....

(10) Thought: 'I know my wife will be angry with me again tonight.'

⦿ Type of error: ....

⦿ Challenge: ....

....

....

....

....

(11) Thought: 'After gambling for such a long time, I have developed a system that works on gambling machines.'

  ◉ Type of error: ....
  ◉ Challenge: ....
  ....
  ....
  ....
  ....

(12) Thought: 'If I continue gambling, I will eventually win all the money that I lost.'

  ◉ Type of error: ....
  ◉ Challenge: ....
  ....
  ....
  ....
  ....

(13) Thought: 'I feel weak, so I must be weak.'

  ◉ Type of error: ....
  ◉ Challenge: ....
  ....
  ....
  ....
  ....

(14) Thought: 'I have to pay back the loan by the end of this month.'

  ◉ Type of error: ....
  ◉ Challenge: ....
  ....
  ....
  ....
  ....

Challenge Practice Sheet – Completed (Example)

(1) Thought: 'All lapses are relapses; abstinence once violated can never be regained.'

⊙ Type of error: *All or nothing thinking.*

⊙ Challenge: *Gambling one day is not the same as gambling everyday. If I learn from lapses and deal with them, I can prevent them from becoming relapses.*

(2) Thought: 'I will win today.'

⊙ Type of error: *Jumping to conclusions, predictive control.*

⊙ Challenge: *I may win but there is also a good chance that I will lose. The last time I thought I was going to win, I actually ended up losing a lot of money.*

(3) Thought: 'Gambling will help pay the bills.'

⊙ Type of error: *Gambling related expectancy.*

⊙ Challenge: *I'm thinking like this because I'm stressed. I can end up being worse off by losing all my money. Winning may be a faster way to make money but there is no guarantee I will win. It will take some time to pay off all bills and I have made plans for this which is less risky than gambling.*

(4) Thought: 'I will never be able to control my urges.'

⊙ Type of error: *Overgeneralization.*

⊙ Challenge: *What is so terrible about experiencing an urge? Of course, I can cope with it. Other problem gamblers have managed to cope with it and so can I too. Giving up gambling is hard but I have learnt many strategies that can help me cope with it more effectively. I have managed to control my urges successfully before, so I can this time as well. I have learnt that urges do not get more and more intense unless I gamble, but rather that they eventually die out.*

(5) Thought: 'I can't stop thinking about how I gave in to my urges and gambled. I can't believe how weak I am.'

⊙ Type of error: *Labelling, Mental filter.*

⊙ Challenge: *I am condemning myself as a total person based on a single event. I am a regular human being and have a right to make mistakes. Mistakes always provide us with the opportunity to learn. From each lapse, you learn something about yourself and your problem and it can help you to develop coping skills to control your urges better in future. Thus, I shouldn't beat myself up for one mistake that I obviously learnt from.*

(6) Thought: 'I know I will give in to my urge and end up gambling today.'

⦿ Type of error: *Jumping to conclusion.*

⦿ Challenge: *I am engaging in fortune telling. I don't know that I will give in to my urges as it has not occurred yet. I can try and put safeguards in place. I have learnt a lot of strategies since starting this course that I can use to protect myself. I have already used them with success.*

(7) Thought: 'I will just test myself with £5 and prove that I am in control.'

⦿ Type of error: *Magnifying ability to control gambling.*

⦿ Challenge: *I feel good about my stopping so why do I need to take a risk and prove anything.*

(8) Thought: 'It is my fault everything is messed up. I gave in to my urges and gambled after the argument I had with my wife. I did not have enough will-power.'

⦿ Type of error: *Personalization.*

⦿ Challenge: *I made a mistake. There is no use blaming myself because it will not solve anything. What I learnt from this experience is that when I am starting to get irritable I know that means I am in danger of gambling. Now I can try and think of strategies to handle this better next time.*

(9) Thought: 'I feel lucky today.'

⦿ Type of error: *Illusion of control (passive illusionary control).*

⦿ Challenge: *Feeling lucky doesn't make it so. I felt lucky the last time I went and gambled but I lost all my money. I can't afford to lose anymore money.*

(10) Thought: 'I know my wife will be angry with me again tonight.'

⦿ Type of error: *Jumping to conclusions.*

⦿ Challenge: *I am mind reading. I won't know for sure until I go home. I am just making myself worried thinking in this manner.*

(11) Thought: 'After gambling for such a long time, I have developed a system that works on gambling machines.'

⦿ Type of error: *Illusion of control (active illusionary control)*

⦿ Challenge: *The machines are fixed anyway. That is how they make money. Outcomes are all random and based on luck so there is no way I can control whether I will win or lose. Every time I gamble the outcome is not related to previous outcomes so there is no way I can control whether I will win this time or not. Besides, if I had a system that worked, I wouldn't have the amount of debt I currently have.*

(12) Thought: 'If I continue gambling, I will eventually win all the money that I lost.'

⦿ Type of error: *Interpretative bias (chasing)*

⦿ Challenge: *The last time I lost I thought the same thing. There is no guarantee that I will win. If I lose, I will increase my debt even further.*

(13) Thought: 'I feel weak, so I must be weak.'

⦿ Type of error: *Emotional reasoning*

⦿ Challenge: *How would I see the situation if I was not feeling so bad? I have just lost a lot of money and I am very emotional. I am not thinking clearly. The way you see things is distorted when your emotions take over. Just because I feel a certain way doesn't make it so.*

(14) Thought: 'I have to pay back the loan by the end of this month.'

⦿ Type of error: *should statement*

⦿ Challenge: *This is a should statement. If I continue to think this way, I will give into gambling due to the pressure. I prefer to pay the loan by the end of the month but there is a possibility that I won't be able to. I will need to talk to my financial counsellor about my options.*

7.7 INTRODUCE HOME EXERCISES

Ask the client to practise identifying and challenging irrational cognitions using the skills learnt in the last three sessions. Ensure that the client has:

✓ Home exercise sheet (below).
✓ Client Information Handouts – Identifying General Thinking Errors and Challenging General Thinking Errors.
✓ Several blank copies of the Irrational Thoughts Record B (adapted from Beck et al., 1979) found in Appendix P.
✓ Any completed copies of the Irrational Thoughts Record B (adapted from Beck et al., 1979) including the example provided in this chapter.
✓ Either a completed Challenge Practice Sheet (if it was completed in session) or a blank Challenge Practice Sheet if it was not completed in session.

Home Exercise Sheet

(1) Practise identifying and challenging thinking errors using the Irrational Thoughts Record B, the Client Information Handout: Identifying General Thinking Errors, the Client Information Handout: Challenging General Thinking Errors, the Client Information Handout: Identifying Gambling Specific Thinking Errors (provided in Session Three) and the Client Information Handout: Challenging Gambling Specific Thinking Errors (provided in the last session).

(2) Continue using the strategies learnt in previous sessions.

(3) Ring a 24-hour helpline number and/or attend a problem gambling related support group (e.g. Gamblers Anonymous). Get into the habit of doing this once a week. Gradually the weekly calls/meetings could be changed into fortnightly ones and then gradually to monthly once you begin feeling more confident about controlling your gambling or abstaining from gambling. This will help to keep you on track after the programme has finished. That is, keeping in touch with someone who can help monitor your gambling on a regular basis after the treatment programme can reduce your chances of lapsing or relapsing.

Client Information Handout:
Identifying General Thinking Errors

There are generally ten types of general thinking errors problem gamblers make relating to their problems, consequences, ability to control gambling, etc. similar to the ones displayed by individuals with other psychological/emotional problems (Beck, 1976; Burns, 1989). If these thinking errors are in operation before gambling, they may lead you to give into your urges to gamble. If these errors are in operation during gambling, they may encourage you to gamble despite continuous losses. If they are in operation after gambling (e.g. after a lapse), they might contribute to feelings of guilt and hopelessness and encourage you to gamble despite losses.

(1) All or nothing thinking – seeing things in black or white categories. Making and believing in definite statements. If performance falls short of being perfect, you begin viewing yourself as a total failure.
  ⊙ 'If I do not succeed in this treatment, I am a total failure.'

(2) Overgeneralization – the occurrence of a single, isolated event is over-generalized as a sign of total failure. You drag up past events, which are similar to today and predict that it will always stay the same. Overgeneralization can mediate the escalation from single lapse to total relapse as the lapse is taken as a sign of total relapse.
  ⊙ 'I will never be able to stop gambling.'
  ⊙ 'I relapsed after I stopped 5 years ago, I will never be able to stop gambling.'
  ⊙ 'My future is bleak.'

(3) Mental Filter – picking a single detail and dwelling on it exclusively so that the vision of all reality becomes unclear.
  ⊙ 'I will never forget the way they treated me the last time I had a lapse.'

(4) Jumping to conclusions – making a negative interpretation even though there are no definite facts that support that conclusion.
  ⊙ Fortune telling – anticipating that things will turn out a certain way without definite facts and proof (e.g. 'I will recoup my losses tonight'; 'This relationship is sure to fail'; 'I will never be able to stop gambling').
  ⊙ Mind reading – 'My wife will hate me because I had a lapse.'

(5) Should statements – using statements that contain 'shoulds', 'oughts' and 'musts'. When such statements are directed at oneself, the resulting emotion is often guilt. When you direct should statements towards others, you often feel anger, frustration or resentment.
  ⊙ 'I must recoup my losses immediately.'
  ⊙ 'I must continue gambling to recover my losses.'

(6) Magnification (catastrophizing) or minimization – this involves exaggerating (magnifying/catastrophizing) or inappropriately reducing (minimizing) the importance of things.
- Magnifying/catastrophizing an urge – 'If I get a craving it will be unbearable.'
- Magnify ability to control gambling – 'I will just test myself with £5 and prove that I am in control.'
- Minimizing own fault by blaming others – 'It is not my fault if I am nagged into it by my partner who just cannot keep off my case.'

(7) Emotional reasoning – you assume that your negative emotions necessarily reflect the way things really are. 'I feel therefore I must be.'
- 'I feel like a loser so I must be one.'
- 'I feel bad about not being able to control my gambling and it means I am a bad person.'
- 'I feel weak when I cannot stop my gambling so I must be weak.'

(8) Polarized thinking – focusing entirely on the negatives or entirely on the positives.
- 'The only reason I did not gamble today was that I had too much work.'

(9) Labelling and mislabelling – this is an extreme form of 'overgeneralization'. Instead of describing your error, you attach a negative label to yourself.
- 'I am a loser, I don't deserve any better.'
- 'I'm weak.'

(10) Personalization – you see yourself as the cause of some negative external event which in fact, you are not primarily responsible for. The total responsibility and thus, personal causality for the lapse, makes it more difficult to reassume control.
- 'My wife is in a bad mood it must be something I have done.'

Client Information Handout:
Challenging General Thinking Errors

Strategies for challenging other/general thinking errors.

(1) Examining the evidence:
Examine the evidence. You could ask yourself,
- What is the evidence for my thinking?
- What is the evidence that people who are recovering from a gambling problem do not experience the feelings that I have?
- What is the evidence that there is something wrong with me, that I will never improve?
- Am I confusing a thought with a fact?

(2) Alternative explanations
Are there any alternative explanations out there?
- Am I assuming my view of things is the only possibility?
- How would I have looked at this situation before I started gambling excessively?
- How would another person look at the same thing?
- How would I look at it if someone else described it to me?

(3) Usefulness of my thoughts.
What is the effect of thinking the way I do?
- Is the way I think now helping me to achieve my goals?
- Am I worrying about the way things ought to be, instead of accepting and dealing with them as they are?
- Would this new way making me feel any better?

(4) Experimental technique
Am I predicting the future instead of experimenting?
- Instead of predicting, try/test it out in reality.
- Ask people questions to find out if my thoughts and attitudes are realistic.

(5) Standard analysis
- What thinking errors am I making?

References: Hawtron *et al.*, 1989

CHAPTER 8

Session six: Relaxation and imaginal exposure

Session content and goals

8.1 Review home exercises
8.2 Discuss aim and rationale of the session
8.3 Discuss relaxation techniques
8.4 Discuss imaginal exposure
8.5 Practise relaxation/imaginal exposure
8.6 Introduce home exercises

8.1 REVIEW HOME EXERCISES

Review the client's progress on home exercises. Praise his/her efforts/ accomplishments. Troubleshoot problem areas or reasons for non-compliance.

8.2 DISCUSS AIM AND RATIONALE OF THE SESSION

8.2.1 Aim

The aim of this session is to introduce the client to some relaxation exercises and imaginal exposure techniques.

8.2.2 Rationale

The first part of the session introduces the client to some relaxation exercises. It assumes that the gambling problem is caused or exacerbated by tension or anxiety. Stress plays a major role in the development and maintenance of gambling problems (Raylu & Oei, 2002; Ste-Marie, Gupta,

& Derevensky, 2006). It is common for problem gamblers to lapse or relapse after a stressful encounter.

Relaxation aims to produce a calm body and mind. Relaxation can effectively help:

◉ control the client's gambling by reducing anxiety. McConaghy and his colleagues (1983, 1991) found that a lower level of anxiety at post-treatment was related to better long-term prognosis;

◉ increase the client's sense of perceived control in stressful situations;

◉ relieve anxiety when the client encounters gambling triggers;

◉ prepare the client for the second part of the session, which aims to teach him/her imaginal exposure techniques.

Studies investigating the role of autonomic arousal in problem gambling have found that all forms of gambling are associated with it (Raylu & Oei, 2002). One of the coping skills deficits hypothesized in the development of problem gambling is the inability to control high levels of arousal especially among those that play gaming machines. Thus, it is important to teach problem gamblers ways to control subjective feelings of arousal. By teaching problem gamblers strategies to cope with such arousal it would help them control their urges.

Imaginal exposure is based on the technique of systematic desensitization developed by Wolpe (1958). The technique involves pairing relaxation with imagined scenes depicting situations that the client has indicated as anxiety provoking. Three mechanisms are implicated (Masters et al., 1987).

◉ Counter conditioning – substitution of an emotional response that is appropriate to a given situation for one that is maladaptive.

◉ Extinction – anxiety reduction results when a fear-evoking conditioned stimulus is presented repeatedly without any adverse consequences: this results in an eventual decay of the conditioned response.

◉ Habituation – decrement of a person's response to a stimulus when it is repeatedly presented.

Thus, it could be predicted that when a problem gambler is exposed to an imaginal scene, which is associated with arousal, the resulting arousal would habituate with subsequent presentations. A number of studies (e.g. Blaszczynski, Drobny, & Steel, 2005; Dowling et al., 2007; McConaghy et al., 1983; 1991; Tavares, Zilberman, & El-Guebaly, 2003) show strong support for the use of imaginal exposure in the treatment of problem gambling.

8.3 DISCUSS RELAXATION TECHNIQUES

Before you describe the various relaxation techniques therapists need to remind the client to set up a relaxation environment that is free from distractions/interruptions (e.g. putting phones off the hook, turning off all mobile phones, choosing a quiet time to do the relaxation exercises). The client can do the exercises either lying down or while sitting. It is also advisable to have eyes closed, legs uncrossed and to wear loose clothing while doing the exercises.

Tell the client that there are a number of different types of relaxation exercises. The steps involved in the abdominal breathing exercise are described in Appendix Q. (Some other relaxation techniques are also included.) Provide detailed information and also practise at least one relaxation exercise (the abdominal breathing exercise is highly recommended) and provide brief descriptions for a few others.

Introduce abdominal breathing as a form of relaxation and a way to cope with anxiety/arousal. You can say, 'When you breathe, you typically use one of the following: chest or the abdomen. Chest breathing is associated with anxiety or other emotional distress and is common among those that lead stressful lives. Chest breathing is shallow and often irregular and rapid. When air is inhaled, the chest expands and the shoulders rise to take in the air. If an insufficient amount of air reaches your lungs, your blood is not properly oxygenated, your heart rate and muscle tension increase, and your stress response is turned on. Breathing directly reflects the level of tension you carry in your body. Under tension, your breathing becomes more shallow and rapid, and occurs high in the chest. When relaxed, you breathe more fully, more deeply, and from your abdomen. It is difficult to be tense while breathing from your abdomen. Abdominal breathing is natural breathing for newborn babies and sleeping adults. Inhaled air is drawn deep into the lungs and exhaled (the diaphragm contracts and expands as this occurs). Abdominal breathing takes minutes to learn but needs to be practised often to master it properly.' Abdominal breathing has a number of other benefits that you may want to discuss with the client including improved concentration, improved efficacy of excreting toxins from the body, increased energy levels, improved blood circulation and heart rate, reduced tension and increased relaxation response (Barlow, 1988; Barlow & Rapee, 1991).

Demonstrate how to use abdominal breathing, as described in Appendix Q. If you have time, you could also practise one or more of the other relaxation exercises in the session. Otherwise, just introduce the client to the other exercises and let the client try the exercises out in his/her own time. You might want to check the client's progress in subsequent sessions. If the client prefers to see or practise any of the exercises in Appendix Q you may decide to cover them in an additional session or add it onto the agenda of other sessions. Relaxation exercises can be taped during the session and then played at home.

8.4 DISCUSS IMAGINAL EXPOSURE

Imaginal exposure is beneficial and effective if the imagined situation/scene is related to the client's situation/gambling behaviours. Thus, to create a list of scenes, it will be useful to identify a number of the client's gambling triggers (e.g. going past a gambling venue, having dinner at a club that has gambling machines, meeting a friend that often talks the client into gambling, having an argument with his/her wife).

Each of these scenes/triggers should be divided into four to six sequences. For each trigger, the client needs to include imaginal scenes where he/she is able to resist the urge to gamble (e.g. by using the strategies learnt in this programme so far). For example:

- having an argument with my wife;
- after the argument, feel upset and begin having thoughts of going to the pub;
- walking to the pub;
- entering the pub;
- looking at the gaming machines and thinking how much I have lost on them;
- walking out of the pub feeling proud of myself.

When listing the scenes involved in each scenario, elicit a scene that includes not only the physical location in which the scene occurs, but also the internal changes that are associated with the situation (thoughts, emotions, physical sensations, etc.). Thus, for each scenario/trigger, the scene has to be described as vividly as possible. Pay attention to all five senses when describing the scenes for each trigger.

The list of triggers can be arranged in a hierarchy (e.g. order of most anxiety provoking to least anxiety provoking). In this case imaginal exposure could start with the least anxiety-provoking trigger and when the client has reached a level of anxiety comfortable for him/her for the least anxiety-provoking scenario, the client can begin doing the imaginal exposure using the next scenario in the hierarchy. As the client progresses down the hierarchy, he/she should still be encouraged to occasionally do practices using items higher on the hierarchy. Other outcome variables could also be used to construct the hierarchy of triggers (e.g. triggers in the order of the likelihood that they will lead to lapse, the level of stress related to each trigger, level of confidence in coping with the triggers).

The client should be encouraged to rate his/her anxiety level before, during and after each imaginal exposure practice. He/she should be encouraged to record the strength of urges on a 100-point scale where zero represents that the urges are not strong at all and 100 represents that the urges are very strong. The steps involved include the following.

⊚ Recording the strength of your urge before the imaginal exposure session.

⊚ Lying down on your back, as it is the most relaxing position. Keep your hands and feet uncrossed. Loosen tight clothing. It is also possible to do visualization sitting or even standing, but it is not preferred. Some people find visualization while sitting up dull and unimaginative.

⊚ Closing your eyes gently, not with clenched eyelids. It also helps shut out the real world. Make sure you are in a quiet place.

⊚ Begin by relaxing yourself (use abdominal breathing).

⊚ Try to imagine going through the scenes using your five senses to get a vivid picture of each scene.

⊚ Once the session is over, affirm yourself.

⊚ Don't forget to do a rating of the strength of your urges during and after the session.

The imaginal scene can be taped during the session and then it can be played during the following week as home exercises. An example of a completed Imaginal Exposure Worksheet is provided on page 114.

8.5 PRACTISE RELAXATION/IMAGINAL EXPOSURE

Using the information provided above, make a hierarchy of triggers for each client. Write (and/or make an audiotape) detailed descriptions of the scenes for each scenario/trigger. Using the steps above, begin practising imaginal exposure on the least anxiety-provoking trigger. Use the Imaginal Exposure Worksheet in Appendix R.

8.6 INTRODUCE HOME EXERCISES

Discuss home exercises using the home exercise sheet. Ensure the client has:

✓ Home exercise sheet (page 115).
✓ Notes on the relaxation exercises provided in Appendix Q.
✓ Blank copies of the Imaginal Exposure Worksheet provided in Appendix R.
✓ Client Information Sheet – Steps of Imaginal Exposure (overleaf).

Imaginal Exposure Worksheet (Example)

Date & time	Item	Strength of urge before try (0–100)	Strength of urge after try (0–100)
22/6 9.50am	Scenario 1: Going to the pub after having an argument with my wife	30	20
22/6 10am	Scenario 1: Going to the pub after having an argument with my wife	20	15
22/6 10.15 am	Scenario 1: Going to the pub after having an argument with my wife	15	15
23/6 3pm	Scenario 1: Going to the pub after having an argument with my wife	15	10
23/6 3.10pm	Scenario 1: Going to the pub after having an argument with my wife	10	5

Home Exercise Sheet

(1) Practise identifying and challenging thinking errors both related to your gambling as well as your negative moods using the Irrational Thoughts Record B.

(2) Ring a 24-hour helpline number and/or attend a problem gambling related support group (e.g. Gamblers Anonymous). Get into the habit of doing this once a week. Gradually the weekly calls/meetings could be changed into fortnightly ones and then gradually to monthly ones once you begin feeling more confident about controlling your gambling or abstaining from gambling. This will help to keep you on track after the programme has finished. That is, keeping in touch with someone who can help monitor your gambling on a regular basis after the treatment programme can reduce your chances of lapsing or relapsing.

(3) **EVERYDAY PUT AT LEAST AN HOUR ASIDE** TO DO THE FOLLOWING: (best times are either before you start your day or before you go to sleep). If you prefer to do these twice a day, put half an hour aside in the morning and another half an hour in the evening to:

⦿ practise abdominal breathing exercises and at least one other relaxation technique. When doing abdominal breathing exercises, do at least three sets (one set includes 10 breaths – 10 × inhale, pause and exhale);

⦿ read over all your self-statements you have written on flashcards so far;

⦿ practise imaginal exposure (refer to the Client Information Handout: Steps of Imaginal Exposure).

**Client Information Sheet:
Steps of Imaginal Exposure**

⊙ Record the strength of your urge before the imaginal exposure session.

⊙ Lie down on your back, as it is the most relaxing position. Keep your hands and feet uncrossed. Loosen tight clothing. It is possible to do visualization sitting or even standing, but it is not preferred.

⊙ Close your eyes gently not with clenched eyelids. It also helps shut out the real world.

⊙ Make sure you are in a quiet place.

⊙ Begin by relaxing yourself (you could use abdominal breathing exercises).

⊙ When imagining the scenes, pay attention to all five senses and be as vivid as possible in your imagination of the scenes. This includes physiological reactions, thoughts and feelings.

⊙ If in one of your scenes you are in a gambling environment imagine that you are able to resist the urge to gamble by doing other enjoyable things (e.g. chatting with a friend) and that you leave the gambling environment in a calm state. Imagine using the strategies that you have learnt in this programme so far to help you with this.

⊙ Once the session is over affirm yourself.

⊙ Don't forget to do a rating of the strength of your urges before and after the session.

Session seven: Problem-solving and goal-setting skills training

---

Session content and goals

9.1 Review home exercises
9.2 Discuss the aim and rationale of the session
9.3 Discuss problem solving
9.4 Discuss setting goals
9.5 Practise problem-solving and goal-setting skills
9.6 Introduce home exercises

9.1 REVIEW HOME EXERCISES

Review the client's progress on home exercises and provide as much praise as possible for his/her efforts and accomplishments. Troubleshoot problem areas or reasons for non-compliance. Evaluate the client's progress on the exposure items.

9.2 DISCUSS THE AIM AND RATIONALE OF THE SESSION

9.2.1 Aim

The session aims to teach the client the usefulness of problem solving as well as the steps involved in a problem-solving approach. It also aims to discuss how to set appropriate and achievable goals.

9.2.2 Rationale

Problem gamblers frequently give the impression that they are not able to take account of the long-term consequences of actions and thus, act or react impulsively. Thus, teaching problem gamblers basic problem-solving skills can be vital in helping them consider alternatives before impulsively engaging in gambling behaviours, which they are likely to later regret. Problem gamblers can also use problem-solving techniques to cope with urges to gamble (Korn & Shaffer, 2004). These skills can also be used to cope with negative consequences that arise due to gambling including employment, relationship and financial problems (Korn & Shaffer, 2004).

Problem-solving skills training (usually in conjunction with other techniques) has been used successfully with a range of psychological and behavioural disorders, usually to help maintain treatment gains (D'Zurilla & Nezu, 1982). Empirical treatment studies that have reported good outcomes with problem gamblers (e.g. Doiron & Nicki, 2007; Dowling et al., 2007; Sylvain et al., 1997) usually include problem-solving skills training as one of the treatment components.

For any changes that are to be made, realistic goals need to be set so that the goals are easily attained. Thus, teaching the client goal-setting skills is very important in this programme as the client is encouraged to make many changes (lifestyle changes, behaviour changes, etc.) throughout the treatment programme.

9.3 DISCUSS PROBLEM SOLVING

Problem solving is a process, a skill that the client can learn. It is a 'behavioural process, whether overt or cognitive, which provides a variety of potentially effective responses to the problem situation and increases the likelihood of selecting the most effective response from these various alternatives' (Goldfried & Davison, 1994, p. 187). Although it requires practice and it does not guarantee perfect solutions, it helps an individual to consider all the options available. It helps to control the client's moods by logically focusing on solutions to problems. This is especially helpful when the client feels confused, anxious or depressed. A logical worksheet can be used to solve problems by getting the thoughts, problems and solutions clearly on paper. The steps of problem solving discussed in this section are based on the work of D'Zurilla and Goldfried (1971). There are a number of steps involved in problem solving, which are described in detail below.

Step 1: Identify the problem

The following can help the client to identify the problem.

⊙ Use your feelings as a cue (what is causing the way you feel?).
⊙ Use your behaviour as a cue (what is the situation you are not coping with?).
⊙ Consider the content of your worries.
⊙ Ask yourself 'What is preventing me from achieving my goals?'

Step 2: Define the problem

The following should be considered when defining the problem.

⊙ Be specific and phrase in positive terms (e.g. 'I need to obtain suitable employment' rather than 'I am unemployed').

⊙ Consider one problem at a time.

⊙ If it is a big problem, break it down into sub-problems and take them one at a time. For example, if your gambling behaviour and its consequences have affected your relationships with different people in your life, you might want to deal with the problems you have with each person separately.

Step 3: Brainstorm possible solutions

Brainstorm as many solutions as you can. You do not need to explain your solutions. Do not criticize or judge the possible solutions. You can be creative and imaginative. You can also seek ideas from others (e.g. family members or friends). You can also research for possible ideas/solutions from books or the Internet.

Step 4: Assess each solution by considering the advantages and disadvantages of each option

Evaluate the advantages and disadvantages of each possible solution. Consider both short- and long-term consequences.

Step 5: List the solutions in order of preference and choose a solution

List the solutions in order of preference. Combine solutions as appropriate. It is often useful to choose the solution that can be readily applied and not too difficult to put into practice. This means you can get started right away and are likely to experience some success early, rather than failing with your first attempt.

Step 6: Evaluate the success of the solution

Plan and carry out your solution. If the client is having difficulty planning implementing the solution, the goal-setting skills described in the next section might help the client plan and achieve a goal. Analyse whether the chosen solution was effective. If it was not, you can go back to step five and choose the next preferred solution.

Below is an example of how to use the problem-solving steps to solve a likely problem using the Problem-Solving Worksheet (blank copies can be found in Appendix S).

9.4 DISCUSS SETTING GOALS

There are a number of steps to achieve a goal. These are described below.

Step 1: Define the goal

In order to successfully implement a solution, it is important that the client has a clear goal in mind.

- Be specific and phrase in positive terms (e.g. 'I will visit my family once a week' rather than 'I'll stop avoiding my family').
- State it in behavioural terms (e.g. 'I will go for 30-minute walks four times a week' rather than 'I will improve my health').
- Break large goals into smaller goals so it is attainable.
- Prioritize goals and complete high-priority goals first.

Problem-Solving Worksheet (Example)

Step 1: Identify the problem .... *I owe £5 000 on my credit card.* ....

Step 2: Define the problem (be specific and phrase in positive terms) ....
I need to obtain £5 000 to pay my credit card bill.

Step 3: Brainstorm all possible solutions ....
(1) Borrow the money from my friend Paul.
(2) Organize with the credit card company to pay in instalments.
(3) Borrow the money from mum.
(4) Apply for a personal loan

Step 4: Assess the advantages and disadvantages of each solution

Solution	Advantage	Disadvantage
Borrow the money from my friend Paul	He will definitely have money to spare.	I already owe him £3000. He is likely to say 'no'. It is unlikely I will be able to pay him the money I already owe him within a year.
Organize with the credit card company to pay in instalments	I can pay small amounts that I can afford. I won't be further in debt.	It will take me about 1 year to pay it off.
Borrow the money from mum	She is likely to give it to me without any questions.	I already owe her more than £10,000. It's not fair on mum, as she is no longer working. It is unlikely I will be able to pay her the money I already owe her within a year.
Apply for a personal loan	I am likely to get the loan as the company caters for individuals with a bad credit rating.	I will owe more money than I do now. The interest rate is high. I won't be able to pay it back in the specified time.

Step 5: List the solutions in order of preference and choose a solution ....
Order of preference: (1) Organize with the credit card company to pay in instalments. (2) Borrow the money from mum. (3) Borrow the money from my friend Paul. (4) Apply for a personal loan.

Step 6: Evaluate the success of the solution ....
I managed to organize with the credit card company to pay in instalments. On my current income, I will be able to pay the bill within a year.

Step 2: Reward for completing the goal

How are you going to reward yourself after the goal has been achieved?

Step 3: Plan to achieve the goal

In order to plan the goal the client needs to consider a number of things such as: What needs to be done? Who will be involved? Who will do what? Do you have the cooperation of others in your plan? Do those involved in your plan know what they need to do? Where will the goal be carried out? How are you going to obtain the things needed to complete the goal?

Step 4: Date/time goal to be completed

Decide on a date/time the goal is to be completed.

Step 5: Time spent working on the goal (include a date the goal is to be reviewed)

Decide when, how long and how often you will work on the goal. Decide on a date the goal will be reviewed.

Step 6: Possible obstacles preventing you from reaching the goal and ways to deal with the obstacles

Explore any obstacles that can prevent you from achieving your goal. How are you going to overcome these obstacles? What is the plan if the goal is not attained?

Step 7: Assess the outcome of your goal

When assessing the outcome of your goals consider the following: Did your plan work? If not, why? What went wrong and what went right? What are the alternatives? Acknowledge feelings of disappointment but do not catastrophize when things go wrong. Remind yourself of other successes of your life and that if you can achieve them you can do this too. Label an attempt as partial success rather than total failure. Remind yourself that you only learn from trial and error and that even an attempt at your goal is a sign of success. Adapt, modify and re-plan if necessary. Try again as soon as possible.

Below is an example of how to use the goal-setting skills to accomplish a goal using the Goal-Setting Worksheet (blank copies can be found in Appendix T).

9.5 PRACTISE PROBLEM-SOLVING AND GOAL-SETTING SKILLS

Practise the above problem-solving steps on a real problem the client is experiencing using the Problem-Solving Worksheet. Also, practise the goal-setting skills using the Goal-Setting Worksheet.

9.6 INTRODUCE HOME EXERCISES

Discuss home exercises using the home exercise sheet. Ensure the client has:

✓ Home exercise sheet (overleaf).
✓ Client Information Handout – Problem-Solving and Goal-Setting Skills (on page 126).
✓ Blank copies of the Problem-Solving Worksheet (Appendix S).
✓ Blank copies of the Goal-Setting Worksheet (Appendix T).
✓ Irrational Thoughts Record B and Imaginal Exposure Worksheets (if the client requires more).

Goal-Setting Worksheet (Example)

Step 1: Define the goal (in positive, specific and behavioural terms)
I will find a job as a retail shop assistant.

Step 2: Reward for completing the goal
Buy myself a new dress.

Step 3: Plan to achieve the goal
(1) Do a curriculum vitae (I will need to ask my sister's help to do this).
(2) Join an employment agency. Go and look for any relevant jobs on their noticeboards at least every second day.
(3) Look for jobs in the newspaper and on the Internet on a daily basis.
(4) Apply for any job that seems relevant (I will ask my sister's help if I need help writing application letters).

Step 4: Date/time the goal is to be completed
Midnight, June, 30th.

Step 5: Time spent working on the goal (When, how long and how often will you work on the goal? Date the goal is to be reviewed)
(1) Work on my goal 9-10 am everyday. (2) Continue with the current plan for at least 3 months and if I still haven't found a job at the end of 3 months, I will review my goal.

Step 6: Possible obstacles preventing you from reaching the goal and ways to deal with the obstacles.
Motivation to carry out my plan.
(1) Think positively and encourage myself daily. (2) Imagine/remind myself of the outcome daily (e.g. having a job and thus money to pay off debts). (3) Talk to my sister if I feel that my motivation is low.

Step 7: Assess the outcome of your goal (Did you achieve your goal? If not, why? What are the alternatives? Modify, re-plan and try again as soon as possible)
Yes, I got a full-time job at a large furniture store.

> Remember: Do not catastrophize when things go wrong. Remind yourself of other successes of your life and that if you can achieve them you can do this too. Label an attempt as partial success rather than total failure. Remind yourself that you only learn from trial and error and that even an attempt at your goal is a sign of success.

Home Exercise Sheet

(1) Practise identifying and challenging thinking errors both related to your gambling as well as your negative moods using the Irrational Thoughts Record B.

(2) Ring a 24-hour helpline number and/or attend a problem gambling related support group (e.g. Gamblers Anonymous). Get into the habit of doing this once a week. Gradually the weekly calls/meetings could be changed into fortnightly ones and then gradually to monthly once you begin feeling more confident about controlling your gambling or abstaining from gambling. This will help to keep you on track after the programme has finished. That is, keeping in touch with someone who can help monitor your gambling on a regular basis after the treatment programme can reduce your chances of lapsing or relapsing.

(3) **EVERYDAY PUT AT LEAST AN HOUR ASIDE** TO DO THE FOLLOWING: (best times are either before you start your day or before you go to sleep). If you prefer to do these twice a day, put a half an hour aside in the morning and another half an hour in the evening to:

- practise abdominal breathing exercises and one other relaxation technique. When doing abdominal breathing exercises, do at least three sets (one set includes 10 breaths – 10 × inhale, pause and exhale);
- read over all your self-statements you have written on flashcards so far;
- practise imaginal exposure.

OPTIONAL

- Practise problem-solving skills using the Problem-Solving Worksheet.
- Practise goal-setting skills using the Goal-Setting Worksheet.

Client Information Sheet:
Problem-Solving and Goal-Setting Skills

Steps of problem solving (D'Zurilla & Goldfried, 1971)

(1) *Identify the problem* – use your feelings and behaviours as cues; evaluate content of your worries.
(2) *Define the problem* – consider one problem at a time. Be specific and phrase in positive terms (e.g. 'I need to obtain suitable employment' rather than 'I am unemployed'). If it is a big problem, you may need to break it down into sub-problems and take them one at a time.
(3) *Brainstorm possible solutions.*
(4) *Assess the advantages and disadvantages of each solution.*
(5) *List the solutions in order of preferences and choose a solution.*
(6) *Evaluate the success of the solution.*

Steps of goal setting

(1) *Define the goal* – characteristics of a good goal include:
   ⊙ be specific and phrase in positive terms (e.g. 'I will visit my family once a week' rather than 'I'll stop avoiding my family');
   ⊙ state it in behavioural terms (e.g. 'I will go for 30-minute walks four times a week' rather than 'I will improve my health');
   ⊙ break large goals into smaller goals so it is attainable;
   ⊙ prioritize goals and complete high-priority goals first.
(2) *Reward for completing the goal*
(3) *Plan to achieve the goal* – consider: who will be involved and what will they do? How are you going to obtain the things needed to complete the goal? Where will the goal be carried out? What needs to be done?
(4) *Date/time the goal is to be completed*
(5) *Time spent working on the goal (when, how long and how often will you work on the goal? Date the goal is to be reviewed)*
(6) *Possible obstacles preventing you from reaching the goal and ways to deal with the obstacles*
(7) *Assess the outcome of your goal* – did your plan work? If not, why? What went wrong? What are the alternatives? Modify, re-plan and try again as soon as possible.

Remember: Do not catastrophize when things go wrong. Remind yourself of other successes of your life and that if you can achieve them you can do this too. Label an attempt as partial success rather than total failure. Remind yourself that you only learn from trial and error and that even an attempt at your goal is a sign of success.

Session eight: Management of negative emotions

Session content and goals

10.1 Review home exercises
10.2 Discuss aim and rationale of the session
10.3 Discuss negative emotions that are common among problem gamblers
10.4 Explore the client's negative emotions
10.5 Discuss strategies for dealing with negative emotions
10.6 Introduce home exercises

10.1 REVIEW HOME EXERCISES

Review the client's progress on home exercises and provide praise for his/her efforts and accomplishments. Troubleshoot problem areas or reasons for non-compliance. Evaluate the client's progress on exposure items.

10.2 DISCUSS AIM AND RATIONALE OF THE SESSION

10.2.1 Aim

The aims of this chapter include:

⊙ helping the client understand the role negative emotions may play in the maintenance of gambling problems;
⊙ assisting the client to explore his/her negative emotions;
⊙ helping the client recognize non-productive ways of dealing with negative emotions;
⊙ teaching the client productive strategies of coping with negative emotions.

Remember that this programme assumes that negative emotions (e.g. depression, anger, guilt and anxiety) are not the main issue for the client. As stated at the beginning of this manual if negative emotions are the main issue of concern for the individual, it might be better to deal with them first – and this manual is not designed for that purpose.

10.2.2 Rationale

As discussed in previous chapters, gambling is often used to escape negative emotional states or relieve tension. Numerous studies have found negative emotional states (e.g. depression, guilt, anxiety and anger) and related psychological disorders (e.g. depressive and anxiety disorders) play a role in the development and maintenance of gambling problems (Boughton & Falenchuk, 2007; El-Guebaly et al., 2006; Rush, Bassani, Urbanoski, & Castel, 2008;). Negative emotional states have also been linked to relapse (Hodgins & El-Guebaly, 2004) and treatment drop out (Echeburúa, Fernández-Montalvo, & Báez, 2001) among problem gamblers.

Negative emotions can occur at various stages of gambling (before, during and after gambling). A large number of gamblers gamble to escape from negative emotions. That is, they are unable to cope with these emotions before they become so empowering that they end up gambling. Negative emotions can also occur in problem gamblers after a gambling episode (especially if they have lost a lot of money) or if they have had a lapse. Such emotions after a gambling episode can lead the problem gambler to continue gambling to relieve the negative emotions despite continuous losses. Thus, it is vital that a problem gambler learns how to deal with such negative emotions as they may be playing a role in maintaining his/her gambling problems.

10.3 DISCUSS NEGATIVE EMOTIONS THAT ARE COMMON AMONG PROBLEM GAMBLERS

Emotions are unhelpful when they are ignored, are too intense, interfere with our functioning, are out of control or lead to negative behaviours (i.e. self-harm or hurting others). We need a good balance of emotions because when our emotions are out of control we are unable to do anything productive. On the other hand, when we suppress our emotions and spend too much time doing other activities (such as working) we ignore the signals our emotions are sending us. In order for us to think clearly, effectively handle stressful situations and solve practical problems we need to develop emotional control.

We have already learnt in previous sessions how our thoughts, feelings and behaviours are linked. For some problem gamblers, negative emotions play a role in the initiation of gambling and development of gambling problems. For others, they develop as a consequence of the client's gambling problems. Below are some common examples of negative emotions among problem gamblers.

10.3.1 Anxiety

Many researchers have also associated anxiety with gambling problems (Westphal & Johnson, 2007; Zangeneh, Grunfeld, & Koenig, 2008). Participants that prefer low-skill gambling (e.g. gambling machines) are more likely to experience anxiety and stress (Coman et al., 1997). Miu, Heilman and Houser (2008) found that trait anxiety was related to impaired decision-making. Echeburúa et al. (2001) found that individuals with anxiety and neuroticism were more likely to drop out of treatment or relapse at 1-year follow up.

10.3.2 Guilt

Feelings of guilt are very common among problem gamblers, they may have these feelings relating to letting people in their lives down because of their gambling problems. Guilt may also be related to the problem gambler's manipulative behaviours (e.g. lies they tell their significant others or blaming significant others for their own gambling). Common cognitive distortions related to guilt include:

⊙ magnifying – 'I have my ruined everything';
⊙ labelling – 'I'm such a bad person';
⊙ personalization – 'It is my fault that everything is going bad for my family';
⊙ should statements – 'I should have paid all my debts by now'.

10.3.3 Anger

When a situation falls short of what an individual expects they may believe that their needs (or rights) have not been met and this can result in anger for some people (Johnson, 1990). Anger is caused by both external and internal events (Johnson, 1990). Anger can be disguised as frustration, disappointment, hurt, agitation, sulking, sarcasm, arguing, blaming others, threats and harassment (Johnson, 1990).

Collins, Skinner, and Toneatto (2005) reported that 60% of problem gamblers reported problems with anger compared with about 40% of non-problem gamblers. Numerous studies have also reported high incidents of domestic violence among problem gamblers (Lorenz & Shuttleworth, 1983; Korman et al., 2008; Muelleman, DenOtter, Wadman, Tran, & Anderson, 2002).

10.3.4 Depression

Depression is very common in problem gamblers (Kim, Grant, Eckert, Faris, & Hartman, 2006; Moodie & Finnigan, 2006). Some symptoms of depression include:

⊙ emotional state – sad, tearful, irritable, angry, frustrated, agitation, restlessness, anxious, guilty, fearful, lacking confidence, worthlessness, low self-esteem;

⊙ thought process – poor concentration, slowed thinking, impaired decision-making, forgetfulness, poor memory, pessimism (negative view of self, world and the future), hopeless, suicidal thoughts;

⊙ social functioning – withdrawal, lack of interest or enjoyment, difficulties feeling motivated;

⊙ physical well-being – fatigue, lack of energy, slowed speech and body movements, sleep disturbance, low libido and appetite disturbance.

Participants that prefer skilled gambling (e.g. horse race gambling) are more likely to experience severe depression (Coman et al., 1997). Clarke (2006) reported that impulsivity mediated the path of depression to problem gambling severity.

10.4 EXPLORE THE CLIENT'S NEGATIVE EMOTIONS

Help the client to explore his/her own negative emotions and the ways the client responds to these negative emotions. Ask the client to think of an incident that resulted in a negative emotion (e.g. anger, sadness, guilt, anxiety) recently. Encourage the client to explore his/her thoughts and behaviours by going through the Negative Emotions Worksheet included in Appendix U. This worksheet enables clients to explore their negative emotions by using the following items/questions.

⊙ Describe the negative emotion (what were you feeling?).
⊙ Describe the situation that led to the negative emotion.
⊙ What were you thinking prior to experiencing the negative emotion?
⊙ What were you thinking after experiencing the negative emotion?
⊙ What did you do after experiencing the negative emotion?
⊙ In relation to your thinking and action after experiencing the negative emotion, what was helpful; what was not helpful?
⊙ What would you do differently next time?

10.5 DISCUSS STRATEGIES FOR DEALING WITH NEGATIVE EMOTIONS

Discuss unproductive and productive ways of dealing with negative emotions.

10.5.1 Unproductive ways of dealing with negative emotions

⊙ Emotions accumulate until they become too overwhelming and you direct them towards others. This involves abusing others either verbally (e.g. sarcasm or bullying) or physically (e.g. kicking the cat or furniture).

⊙ Emotions accumulate until they become too overwhelming and you direct them towards yourself (e.g. self-blame).

⊙ Be silent, avoid the problem and withdraw (sulk).

⊙ Deny that negative emotions or the problem that is causing it exist.

⊙ Turn your negative emotions into something else such as overeating, overworking, abusing substances, gambling etc.

10.5.2 Productive ways of dealing with negative emotions

The most productive way of dealing with the negative emotions is to use your negative emotions as a source of energy that can be used effectively/ productively (e.g. used to solve problems) rather than unproductively (e.g. gambling). The following suggestions can help one achieve this.

- Be aware of your negative emotions by monitoring your moods and the situations that influence them. Keep a diary when you have these negative emotions and work through the items of the Negative Emotions Worksheet as this can help increase awareness and understanding of these emotions as well as improve the way you cope with these emotions. Your record should include documenting persons, situations, etc. that precede the negative emotion and thus make you more aware of the triggers, frequency, intensity, circumstances and duration of the negative emotions as well as the positive and negative consequences.

- Change your environment. Sometimes our immediate surroundings can cause negative emotions. Giving yourself a break/time out especially for times of the day that you know are especially stressful is a useful technique. In some situations (e.g. an abusive relationship), it may be beneficial to consider removing yourself from the destructive environment altogether.

- Exercise coping strategies that you have learnt in this programme to control your emotions before they become too overwhelming such as relaxation exercises (including breathing exercises), positive imagery and physical exercises.

- Once emotions seem to be under control, explore causes of emotions (i.e. explore situations, thoughts and feelings that make you feel this way) and use problem-solving techniques to work out a solution. Using a systematic problem-solving approach allows individuals to feel that they have some control over problems in their lives. As the problems are put in a different perspective and usually solved, negative feelings usually begin to fade.

- Use the STAR technique to control your emotions. Similar to the START technique introduced in Chapter 4, it is based on Meichenbaum's (1977) self-instructional training. The steps include the following.

  - **S**TOP – stop what you are doing or thoughts that are producing these negative emotions and take time out. Use breathing exercises if necessary.

  - **T**HINK – think where your negative emotion is coming from and what the main issue is. Try problem solving. Plan on what you can do about it, consider all your options as well as the consequences and try to cope with the emotion in a safe way. Choose the best option.

  - **A**CT – act on your plan. Be task orientated and stick with the issue. It might be beneficial to think of the obstacles that may prevent you from implementing your plan before you act on them.

- REVIEW – review your actions. What worked? What did not work? What needs to change? How can you improve your actions the next time?

⊙ Identify and challenge the negative thinking patterns that are associated with your negative emotion. There are three steps involved: (1) increasing your awareness of these emotions, (2) identifying negative/irrational thoughts associated with them, and (3) challenging these negative/irrational thoughts and replacing them with ones that are more realistic.

Step 1: increase your awareness of these emotions and negative/irrational thoughts associated with them. Some ways you can increase your awareness of your symptoms include the following.

- Paying attention to your mood changes. Every time your mood changes take notice of what is going on and how you are feeling. This may give you important clues to your thinking patterns. You can also use the Irrational Thoughts Record A (Appendix O) to monitor your mood changes and thoughts associated with different moods.

- Discussing your feelings with others (especially those that know you well). Individuals that you often associate with may have important clues about your negative feelings.

- Taking notice of your physical body as this can also provide a clue to your emotions. Notice your posture, your facial expression and movements. Keep a look out for people, places and activities that you once enjoyed but are now avoiding.

Step 2: become aware of your negative thoughts associated with the emotions. You can do this by using a number of techniques, which are described below.

- Ask yourself 'What am I thinking right now?' or 'What is going through my head right now?' whenever your encounter a negative emotion.

- If you have some negative feelings and cannot quite catch the thoughts, re-play the feelings repeatedly until you catch the thoughts. To do this successfully, try to imagine the event as if it were happening right now.

- Write out your thoughts – You can use the Irrational Thoughts Record A (Appendix O) to help you with this.

Step 3: challenge dysfunctional thinking and replace it with thinking that is more rational. When challenging your thoughts try to consider a wide range of possible interpretations, not just the negative ones and question the validity of the thoughts involved. Refer to the different ways of challenging introduced in Session five. For example:

⇒ Thoughts associated with guilt:

- *Thought*: 'I have done something that is very wrong (magnifying).'

- *Challenge*: 'What is the use of thinking such a way? It will not reverse my mistake magically. It will not speed the learning process and reduce the chance that I will make the mistake in future. Other people won't love and respect me more because I am feeling guilty. I may have done something wrong, however, is the behaviour that I am condemning really that terrible? Is it possible that things could have been worse? I did not do it on purpose. I did not intend to hurt anyone. Also, after realizing what I did, I am trying to ensure it does not happen again.'

- *Thought*: 'I am such a bad person (labelling).'

- *Challenge*: 'Why am I labelling myself as a bad person? What is the use of thinking like that? It only diverts energy away from effective problem solving. I need to separate the behaviour from the person. What I did was bad (i.e. my behaviour), not me (person).'

- *Thought*: 'I have to be perfect if I am to control my gambling (all or nothing thinking).'

- *Challenge*: 'Is it realistic to expect myself to be perfect. After all, I am only human and all humans make mistakes. I am learning from each mistake I make.'

- *Thought*: 'I should have been able to take care of my family; I shouldn't have let them down (should statement).'

- *Challenge*: change your 'should statements' to 'I prefer . . .'

- *Thought*: 'I feel guilty so I must be guilty (emotional reasoning).'

- *Challenge*: 'How would I see the situation if I wasn't feeling this way? When emotions are high, it is hard to think clearly.'

⇒ Thoughts related to anger:

- *Thought*: 'My wife should not nag me as that makes me want to gamble more (should statement).'

- *Challenge*: 'People are free to do what they want. I can't control other people's behaviours except mine. I can let them know how I feel but whether they change their behaviours is up to them.'

- *Thought*: 'They are awful for not understanding how hard things are for me (labelling).'

- *Challenge*: 'Just because someone has made you angry doesn't make him/her a bad person. People cope with stress in the best way they can, given their level of awareness and experience. Debating who is right and wrong won't solve anything.'

⇒ Thoughts related to depression:

- *Thought*: 'This is the worst thing that has ever happened to me. I simply won't be able to cope (magnifying).'

- *Challenge*: 'I have coped with other things so I can with this too. I have more strategies now that can help me get through this difficult period.'

- *Thought*: 'They will all hate me for my gambling problem (jumping to conclusions).'

- *Challenge*: 'I don't know whether they hate me as I haven't asked them. They know that I am trying to deal with my gambling problem.'

- *Thought*: 'I always fail at everything I try (overgeneralizing).'
- *Challenge*: 'I have been successful at many things that I have tried. For example . . .'

⊙ Remember your basic human rights (Jakubowski & Lange, 1978, pp. 80–81).

- The right to act in ways that promote your dignity and self-respect as long as others' rights are not violated in the process.
- The right to be treated with respect.
- The right to say 'no' and not feel guilty.
- The right to experience and express your feelings.
- The right to take time and think.
- The right to change your mind.
- The right to ask for what you want.
- The right to do less than you are humanly capable of doing.
- The right to ask for information.
- The right to make mistakes.
- The right to feel good about yourself.

⊙ Use positive affirmation.

- Praise yourself for trying (e.g. 'I am doing the best I can and that's OK').
- Do something nice for yourself or buy yourself something nice occasionally.

⊙ Change your activity level (especially for depressed individuals) – increasing involvement in positive activities and reducing involvement in negative ones can help improve mood.

10.6 INTRODUCE HOME EXERCISES

Use the home exercise sheet to discuss home exercises. Ensure the client has:

✓ Home exercise sheet (overleaf).
✓ Negative Emotions Worksheet (Appendix U).
✓ Client Information Sheet: Strategies to Deal with Negative Emotions (on page 137).
✓ Irrational Thoughts Record A and B and Imaginal Exposure Worksheet (if the client requires more).

Home Exercise Sheet

(1) Practise identifying and challenging thinking errors related to your gambling and your negative moods using the Irrational Thoughts Record B.

(2) Ring a 24-hour helpline number and/or attend a problem gambling related support group (e.g. Gamblers Anonymous). Get into the habit of doing this once a week. Gradually the weekly calls/meetings could be changed into fortnightly ones and then gradually to monthly once you begin feeling more confident about controlling your gambling or abstaining from gambling. This will help to keep you on track after the programme has finished. That is, keeping in touch with someone who can help monitor your gambling on a regular basis after the treatment programme can reduce your chances of lapsing or relapsing.

(3) **EVERYDAY PUT AT LEAST AN HOUR ASIDE** (best times are either before you start your day or before you go to sleep. If you prefer to do these twice a day, put half an hour aside in the morning and half an hour in the evening) to:

- practise abdominal breathing exercises and at least one other relaxation technique.
- read over all your self-statements you have written on flashcards.
- practise exposure items using the Imaginal Exposure Worksheet.

OPTIONAL

Use the Negative Emotions Worksheet, Problem-Solving Worksheet and Goal-Setting Worksheet as required.

Client Information Sheet:
Strategies to Deal with Negative Emotions

- Be aware of your negative emotions by monitoring your moods and the situations that influence them.
- Identify and challenge the negative thinking patterns that are associated with your negative emotion.
- Change your environment if necessary (e.g. time-outs).
- Use coping strategies learnt in this programme to control your emotions such as relaxation exercises, positive imagery and physical exercises.
- Use problem-solving skills to deal with worries and concerns.
- Remember your basic human rights (Jakubowski & Lange, 1978). The right to act in ways that promote your dignity and self-respect as long as others' rights are not violated in the process; the right to be treated with respect; the right to say 'no' and not feel guilty; the right to experience and express your feelings; the right to take time and think; the right to change your mind; the right to ask for what you want; the right to do less than you are humanly capable of doing; the right to feel good about yourself; the right to ask for information; the right to make mistakes.
- Use the STAR technique (based on Meichenbaum's 1977 self-instructional training) to control emotional outbursts.
  - **S**TOP: stop what you are doing or thoughts that are producing these emotions. Take time out. Use your deep breathing if necessary.
  - **T**HINK: think where your negative emotion is coming from and what the main issue is. Try problem solving. Plan on what you can do about it. Consider all your options and consequences and try to cope with the negative emotion in a safe way. Choose the best option.
  - **A**CT: act on your plan. Be task orientated and stick with the issue. It might be beneficial to think of the obstacles that may prevent you from implementing your plan before you act on them.
  - **R**EVIEW: review your actions. What worked? What did not work? How can you improve your action for the next time?
- Use positive affirmations. Praise yourself for trying (e.g. 'I am doing the best I can and that's OK'). Do something nice for yourself or buy yourself something nice occasionally.
- Change your activity level. Increasing involvement in positive activities and reducing involvement in negative ones can help improve mood.

*Session nine: Relapse prevention and
maintenance of therapeutic gains I – balanced
lifestyle*

Session content and goals

11.1 Review home exercises
11.2 Discuss aim and rationale of the session
11.3 Discuss what constitutes a balanced lifestyle while assisting the client to
     assess areas of his/her life that need changing
11.4 Assist the client to change unbalanced areas of his/her life
11.5 Introduce home exercises

11.1 REVIEW HOME EXERCISES

Review the client's progress on home exercises. Praise as much as possible
for his/her efforts and accomplishments. Troubleshoot problem areas or
reasons for non-compliance.

11.2 DISCUSS AIM AND RATIONALE OF THE SESSION

11.2.1 Aim

The aim of this session is to demonstrate to the client the importance of a
balanced lifestyle in minimizing lapses/relapses. It also aims to explore
the client's own lifestyle and help the client to make changes to make his/
her life more balanced.

11.2.2 Rationale

Throughout treatment, the client has been encouraged to make numerous
lifestyle changes (e.g. engagement in alternative and/or pleasant

activities). However, there may still be areas in the client's lifestyle that are not balanced.

A balanced lifestyle is one where different aspects of one's life are reasonably managed. Balanced living is not only healthy but protects against relapse. Although some areas of life may inevitably get temporarily out of balance, due to the demands of work or family, it is important to continuously strive for a balance that works for you and that can accommodate periods of imbalance. If the client only focuses on one aspect of his/her life and that aspect is not going well, the client can easily get upset and depressed. However, if the client has a balanced lifestyle, he/she has other aspects to focus on to keep his/her spirits up. Furthermore, it is important for the client to participate in a range of activities in order to provide a constructive behavioural alternative to gambling and to help counter feelings of boredom and loneliness that many problem gamblers experience when they stop gambling.

11.3 DISCUSS WHAT CONSTITUTES A BALANCED LIFESTYLE WHILE ASSISTING THE CLIENT TO ASSESS AREAS OF HIS/HER LIFE THAT NEED CHANGING

Discuss with the client what a balanced lifestyle consists of, while exploring/assessing the client's lifestyle. Although the client's lifestyle was assessed in the first session it would be beneficial to assess which areas still need changing. Below are some components of a balanced lifestyle. Each subsection below lists questions that therapists can ask the client in order to assess whether that specific component of lifestyle is balanced. It is often useful to ask the client to view his/her lifestyle in a visual manner (i.e. make a pie chart of how much time the client spends on each of the lifestyle areas). This can help the client see what areas of his/her life are not balanced (Beck, 1995).

11.3.1 Personal relationships and social support

We need personal relationships/social contacts as a way of enjoying spending time with people we feel comfortable with and who can be a source of support for us. It is easier to stick to the decision to give up gambling if you tell other people around you of your goal. This is because they can help (for example encourage you to stay gamble free) and support you through your decision. Spending time with family and friends can help fill your time so you spend less time thinking about gambling. It is also helpful to be around people who do not gamble. Thus, it might be beneficial for the client to expand or strengthen personal relationships by re-contacting family and friends who they have been neglecting or have lost due to gambling. Re-contacting lost family and friends also allows us to make amends for things done in the past (e.g. dealing with the guilt feelings that may lead to gambling as a way of escaping the negative feelings). Personal relationships can also be expanded or strengthened by spending time with family and friends, meeting new people by joining organizations/clubs (preferably not gambling ones), participating in community activities and special interest groups and doing voluntary work. Questions that can be used to assess the client's personal relationships and social support include the following.

⊙ Do you have good personal relationships?
⊙ Do you have good social support?
⊙ Are you in regular contact with family members?
⊙ Do you meet up with friends regularly?

11.3.2 Mental/emotional well-being

We all need to be able to effectively express our feelings/opinions, and stand up for ourselves (including our beliefs and values). We also need people we can confide in to express our fears, concerns and joys. Developing the emotional side of our lives can be achieved by expanding our social support network, learning assertiveness skills, learning effective communicative skills, learning strategies to cope with negative emotions, learning techniques to challenge dysfunctional thoughts, etc. Questions that can be used to assess the client's mental/emotional well-being include the following.

⊙ Are you able to express your feelings?
⊙ Are you able to express your opinions?
⊙ Do you feel comfortable standing up for yourself?
⊙ Do you feel comfortable confiding in others?
⊙ Are you able to express your fears, concerns and joys?
⊙ Do you feel you manage stress well?
⊙ Are you able to cope with negative emotions?
⊙ Do you feel you have effective ways of managing stress?

11.3.3 Engagement in intellectual activities

Intellectual activities help us expand our knowledge, increase our opportunities and consequently, build our confidence. Furthermore, if we have a range of things to focus on, we are less likely to gamble. This can be achieved by simple tasks such as reading the paper, magazine or book, completing a course, etc. Questions that can be used to assess the client's engagement in intellectual activities include the following.

⊙ Do you do enough activities to keep your mind stimulated?
⊙ Do you engage in activities that enable you to learn new things?
⊙ Do you engage in activities that help expand your knowledge?

11.3.4 Financial situation

Financial difficulties are very common among problem gamblers (e.g. debts). It is important to get the client's finances back on track. The elective session that deals with getting out of debt (Chapter 14) can be an initial step. Questions that can be used to assess the client's financial situation include the following.

⊙ Are you comfortable with your finances?
⊙ Are you free of debt?
⊙ Are you free of concerns about being in debt?
⊙ Are creditors after you?
⊙ Do you owe people money?

11.3.5 Restoration and recreational activities

We need to participate in activities, not only to rejuvenate us, but also to help fill the time so we do not continue to think about gambling. Such activities may include knitting, drawing, pottery, crossword puzzles, art, painting, cooking or other hobbies. Information on these can be found in libraries, local councils, local community centres, and on the Internet. The importance of relaxation was introduced in Chapter 8 and some useful relaxation exercises were introduced in Appendix Q. It might be useful to review these sections again. Questions that can be used to assess the client's participation in restoration/recreational activities include the following.

⊙ Do you engage in fun activities?
⊙ Do you engage in activities that you enjoy?
⊙ Do you have any hobbies?
⊙ Do you engage in recreational activities?
⊙ Do you engage in positive activities that help you relax?
⊙ Do you have techniques that help you unwind?

11.3.6 Spiritual well-being

Having spiritual well-being does not mean that we have to attend a religious institute (e.g. church or temple). It means periodically examining our beliefs and values to see if they are still working for us. This helps provide meaning and a sense of identity to life. Questions that can be used to assess the client's spiritual well-being include the following.

⊙ Are you comfortable with your beliefs and values?
⊙ Do you think your life has a sense of purpose?
⊙ Do you feel comfortable in yourself?

11.3.7 Physical health

Proper physical health can be obtained in several ways. First, it can be achieved via good nutrition, which involves consuming three healthy meals daily, having sufficient water intake, as well as moderating caffeine and alcohol intake. Regular physical activities such as swimming, walking, jogging or sports help increase energy, motivation and fitness. Sufficient sleep is also important as lack of sleep can lead to negative consequences such as lack of physical energy, irritability, poor concentration, slurred speech, problems with memory and blurred vision. Questions that can be used to assess the client's physical health include the following.

⊙ Do you eat three healthy meals a day?
⊙ Do you limit your caffeine and alcohol intake?
⊙ Are you free of drugs?
⊙ Do you do regular physical activity such as swimming, walking, jogging or other sports?
⊙ Are you in good health?
⊙ Do you get enough sleep?

11.3.8 Work/school situation

Work is an activity that provides us with money and a sense of satisfaction when completed. Work also provides challenges, purpose, skills and experience. If you are finding work itself a stress, you may need to look at either changing your attitude towards it or changing your job. If you are having financial problems because of your gambling, you could take up another part-time job. This will not only help with the finances but also keep you busy so you do not have time to gamble or think about gambling. Questions that can be used to assess the client's work situation include the following.

⊙ Are you satisfied with your work/school?
⊙ Are you satisfied with the amount of work (or schoolwork) you do?

11.4 ASSIST THE CLIENT TO CHANGE UNBALANCED AREAS OF HIS/HER LIFE

Once you have identified areas of the client's lifestyle that appear to be 'unbalanced', discuss and write a plan about how the client can improve the 'unbalanced' areas. Refer to Appendix V for the Balanced Lifestyle Worksheet to assist you with this (below is an example of how to use the form to begin making changes to the 'unbalanced' lifestyle area). Encourage the client to use the goal-setting steps learnt in Chapter 9 when planning to make changes to the unbalanced areas of his/her life.

11.5 INTRODUCE HOME EXERCISES

Use the home exercise sheet to discuss home exercises. Ensure the client has:

✓ Home exercise sheet (below).
✓ Any extra copies of worksheets (e.g. Irrational Thoughts Record B) the client requires.
✓ The Balanced Lifestyle Worksheet that was completed in session.

Balanced Lifestyle Worksheet (Example)

Indicate by ticking whether the following lifestyle areas are balanced or need changing.

Lifestyle areas	Balanced	Needs changing
Personal relationships and social support		✓
Emotional/mental well-being	✓	
Intellectual activities	✓	
Financial status		✓
Recreation/recreational activities	✓	
Spiritual	✓	
Physical health	✓	
Work/school situation		✓

Areas that need balancing

Area 1: _Financial status_

Plan to improve this unbalanced area: _I will talk to my wife about the financial situation tonight after dinner. I will give financial control to my wife for a short time. I will then arrange for us to speak to a financial counsellor to discuss strategies to improve our financial situation._

Area 2: _Work – I am not satisfied with work, as currently with my qualifications I am not able to advance._

Plan to improve this unbalanced area: _look on the Internet at the courses that the local university offers that can further my career in electronics on my day off next Wednesday. If I can't find anything on the Internet, I will arrange to speak to a careers adviser at the university in person the following Wednesday so that I can start a course in 6 months' time._

Area 3: _Personal relationships and support systems._

Plan to improve this unbalanced area:
(1) Talk to my wife about the gambling problems and financial situation.
(2) Agree to see a marriage counsellor, as she has been suggesting it.
(3) Re-contact old school friends and arrange coffee: Ian and Kerry.
(4) Re-contact my former soccer teammate, Brett. Arrange coffee with Brett to recommence our friendship and discuss with Brett the chances of re-joining my old social soccer team.
(5) Start attending the 7 pm Gamblers Anonymous meetings on Mondays and Thursdays (especially as Thursday is payday).

Home Exercise Sheet

(1) Begin making the changes you have planned in your completed Balanced Lifestyle Worksheet.

(2) Continue identifying and challenging thinking errors both related to your gambling as well as your negative moods using the Irrational Thoughts Record A and B.

(3) Ring a 24-hour helpline number and/or attend a problem gambling related support group (e.g. Gamblers Anonymous). Get into the habit of doing this once a week. Gradually the weekly calls/meetings can be changed into fortnightly ones and then gradually to monthly once you begin feeling more confident about controlling your gambling or abstaining from gambling. This will help to keep you on track after the programme has finished. That is, keeping in touch with someone who can help monitor your gambling on a regular basis after the treatment programme can reduce your chances of lapsing or relapsing.

(4) EVERYDAY PUT AT LEAST AN HOUR ASIDE TO DO THE FOLLOWING: (best times are either before you start your day or before you go to sleep). If you prefer to do these twice a day, put half an hour aside in the morning and another half an hour in the evening to:

- practise abdominal breathing exercises and one other relaxation technique. When doing abdominal breathing exercises, do at least three sets (one set includes 10 breaths – 10 × inhale, pause and exhale).
- read over all your self-statements you have written on flashcards so far.
- continue practising exposure items using the Imaginal Exposure Worksheet.

OPTIONAL

Use the Negative Emotions Worksheet, Problem-Solving Worksheet and Goal-Setting Worksheet as required.

12

Session ten: Relapse prevention and maintenance of therapeutic gains II – coping with high-risk situations

---

Session content and goals

12.1 Review home exercises
12.2 Discuss aim and rationale of the session
12.3 Discuss any anxieties the client may have about leaving the programme
12.4 Discuss possible high-risk situations that could lead to a lapse/relapse
12.5 Discuss strategies to avoid a lapse/relapse
12.6 Discuss strategies to deal with lapses

12.1 REVIEW HOME EXERCISES

Review the client's progress on home exercises and provide praise for his/her efforts and accomplishments.

12.2 DISCUSS AIM AND RATIONALE OF THE SESSION

12.2.1 Aim

This session aims to help the client minimize their chances of relapsing and to encourage the client to maintain treatment gains by:

⊙ discussing any anxieties the client may have about leaving the programme;
⊙ discussing possible high-risk situations the client is likely to encounter in future that could result in a lapse/relapse;
⊙ discussing strategies to prevent a lapse/relapse;
⊙ discussing strategies to cope with lapses or 'close calls'.

12.2.2 Rationale

Since this is the last session, the client may feel anxious about leaving the comfort of having therapeutic help as well as his/her ability to successfully carry out the strategies without ongoing therapeutic assistance. Thus, these anxieties need to be addressed.

The client will continue to encounter high-risk situations that could lead to a lapse/relapse. The client needs to be armed with strategies to minimize relapse and maintain treatment gains if or when this occurs.

Lapses or 'close calls' may occur even after the client leaves the programme. Thus, it is important to ensure that the client knows how to deal/cope with a lapse so it does not lead to a full-blown relapse.

12.3 DISCUSS ANY ANXIETIES THE CLIENT MAY HAVE ABOUT LEAVING THE PROGRAMME

Discuss with the client any concerns he/she may have about leaving treatment. Examples of the types of anxieties the client may have include worries that he/she will return to gambling once treatment ceases or concerns that he/she will not be able to cope on their own without input from a therapist if they encounter a major stressor. Thus, it may be important to discuss the following to reduce the client's anxieties.

- Discuss the nature of recovery. The client needs to be reminded that the process of improvement is gradual, and rarely without setbacks as problem gambling is like any other addiction and is thus, difficult to control/stop. That is why there may be difficulties in the future. However, the client has learnt a large number of strategies in the programme that will help him/her cope/deal with these difficulties.

- Highlight the differences between a lapse and a relapse. You can tell the client, 'Be aware of unrealistic expectations (for example I need a guarantee that I will never gamble again). Do not expect to be perfect – two steps forward one step back is not a failure, it is to be expected. Recovery from any medical, psychological or behavioural problems involve lapses or setbacks (and close calls). Lapses/setbacks do not equal failure. Rather, they are signs that signal to you that the recovery process is under way. Lapses are not the same as relapses. A lapse is a short initial episode of gambling following a period of abstinence, whereas a relapse is continuous gambling. Recovery is like learning to ride a bicycle. If you hit a pothole and fall that is not a reason to stop trying. You just need to get back on the bike and keep pedalling, and watch out for potholes so you do not make that mistake again. Time, practise and patience are required when replacing old habits with new ones.'

⊙ Discuss with the client the progress he/she has made so far since the initiation of the treatment programme. This can increase the client's motivation and confidence.

⊙ Review the strategies the client has learnt in the programme, especially the ones the client found successful.

12.4 DISCUSS POSSIBLE HIGH-RISK SITUATIONS THAT COULD LEAD TO A LAPSE/ RELAPSE

A lapse can normally be foreseen and prepared for. There are a number of factors/high-risk situations that can often indicate the possibility of a lapse/relapse occurring. These include the following.

⊙ Feelings – gradual build up of particular feelings (both negative and positive) that increase urges towards gambling such as:

- depression;
- anxiety;
- frustration and anger;
- remorse and guilt (e.g. the client may feel that he/she has let everyone down);
- loneliness;
- boredom;
- resentment – any feelings related to being exploited, dominated or denied (e.g. of not being trusted by significant others);
- happiness;
- overconfidence.

⊙ Thoughts – gradual build up of a particular state of mind (e.g. distorted thinking/ thinking errors) that increase your urges to gamble (e.g. thoughts relating to testing yourself to see how good you are at resisting temptations).

⊙ Behaviours – behaviours that may lead to a lapse/relapse include:

- lifestyle imbalance;
- maladaptive behaviours (e.g. drug and alcohol misuse);
- failure to deal with unexpected high-risk scenarios;
- failure to deal with sights, sounds, smells and moods that remind you of gambling.

⊙ Places – certain places can lead to a lapse/relapse including:

- being in the presence of gambling cues (e.g. watching horse racing on TV);
- gambling venues (e.g. casino, clubs, betting agencies, arcades and pubs).

⊙ Events – certain events can lead to a lapse/relapse including:

- interpersonal conflict;
- traumatic events (e.g. death/illness in the family);

- stressful events – you are more likely to lose control when other areas of your life are under pressure (e.g. financial, family or employment difficulties) as stress makes it difficult for you to follow your action or treatment plan;
- payday – availability of money is often a trigger for gambling;
- social pressure (e.g. spending time with friends who gamble).

12.5 DISCUSS STRATEGIES TO AVOID A LAPSE/ RELAPSE

There are a number of strategies that can help reduce the chances of a lapse/relapse. These include the following suggestions.

⊙ Leading a balanced lifestyle.

⊙ Having reminder cards. Write down your triggers (both internal and external) for gambling on a card and keep it in a place where you can see it often (e.g. in your wallet). You may also want to write down the benefits of not gambling and/or the negative consequences experienced because of gambling on a card. It might be a good idea to have the number of a relevant 24-hour helpline in case you want to talk to someone urgently (e.g. when you are experiencing an urge and have no one with you at that particular time).

⊙ Avoiding high-risk situations. In case you are unable to avoid a particular high-risk situation plan ahead how you are going to cope and prevent a lapse.

⊙ Revising your triggers and safeguards periodically.

⊙ Discussing on a regular basis with someone (helpline, Gamblers Anonymous sponsor, a friend or family member) how you are coping.

⊙ Using the strategies that you have learnt in this programme to deal with your urges such as urge surging, image replacement, thought stopping, imaginal exposure, cognitive restructuring.

⊙ Using daily schedules as they help ensure that you have planned a gamble-free day.

⊙ Reading your notes once a month.

⊙ Challenging negative cognitions as they arise.

⊙ Refusing offers to gamble. If you are easily pressured into gambling by others, it will be useful to prepare a short and assertive response that you can give when you feel pressured to gamble (e.g. 'No, thanks', 'I've decided gambling isn't good for me', 'I am taking a break from gambling' and 'I have stopped gambling as my gambling gets out of control'). You do not have to offer any explanations. Practise this response as this will ensure that you will feel more comfortable saying it when a situation arises where you have to refuse to gamble.

⊙ Monitoring your progress. Lapses do not just happen. There are always warning signs (e.g. negative feelings, thinking errors and particular behaviours). The best way to catch early warning signs is by monitoring your progress. One way to do this is to take a few minutes daily or at least weekly to ask yourself:

- did anything happen today that changed my desire to gamble;
- did I experience strong urges or persistent thoughts of gambling that are still with me;
- did I notice any warning signs of a lapse today?

12.6 DISCUSS STRATEGIES TO DEAL WITH LAPSES

When problem gamblers lapse, they experience a range of feelings (e.g. depression, frustration, anger, anxiety and guilt) and distorted thoughts, which makes them vulnerable to continue gambling. Marlatt and Gordon (1985) reported several strategies/steps that can help individuals get back on the path to recovery once they have lapsed. These include the following suggestions.

⊙ Staying calm. It is natural for the first reaction to be guilt or self-blame. Remind yourself that a lapse is not the same as a relapse. Remind yourself that what is important is that you deal with a lapse properly, so it does not turn into a relapse. Once you learn from a lapse, you can prevent it from happening again in future.

⊙ Reminding yourself of your successes to this point.

⊙ Reminding yourself of your goals and of how important it is not to continue gambling if you are to reach your goals.

⊙ Evaluating the positive and negative consequences of continued gambling.

⊙ Consulting your reminder cards or relapse prevention notes for instructions.

⊙ Making an immediate plan of recovery:

- record your relapse as this will help you determine the factors that led to it (e.g. walking past where you gambled, time of day, who you were with);

- analyse possible triggers, including the 'who', 'when', or 'where' of the situation and negative thoughts relating to your lapse. It is possible that either these triggers were one of your old triggers or they are new ones that did not exist before. Redo your list of triggers and safeguards for the future;

- check your original action plan and see what you are not doing anymore. If needed, revise your action plan. Learn from your mistakes/lapses. Think about ways to use this experience to help you in the future.

⊙ Challenging any negative thoughts that arise. For example:

- *Negative thought*: 'I have tried to give up and it doesn't work.'

Thinking error: magnification/catastrophizing of failures.
Challenge: 'I know I can give up as I have done it before. All I need to do is identify the trigger that set me up for a lapse and put safeguards in place so it does not happen again.'

- *Negative thought*: 'This is just too hard. I really can't stop myself.'
  Thinking error: magnification/catastrophizing of failures.
  Challenge: 'I know deep down that I have the determination to stop and that this may mean an odd lapse but if I get back up and try again then I will feel stronger each time I bounce.'

- *Negative thought*: 'If I can fail this time, I will definitely fail again. Once a gambler, always a gambler.'
  Thinking error: overgeneralization
  Challenge: 'From each lapse/situation, I learn something about myself. Each lapse is a specific and independent event. In the past when I have lapsed I have lost control but since then I have learnt a lot. I have more coping skills handy this time.'

- *Negative thought*: 'All lapses are relapses. Once I have gambled, the control is taken away from me and I am powerless to control my gambling.'
  Thinking error: All or nothing thinking.
  Challenge: 'A lapse does not mean that abstinence is forever lost. All I need to do in order to abstain is not to gamble and thus, regain control.'

- Problem solving – deal with the problems and crises immediately so that these do not build up to the point where you feel tempted to continue gambling. For example, if stress or other problems in life led to your gambling, you need to deal with these problem directly. Use your problem-solving skills to determine the best solution and plan how you are going to begin implementing it.

- Calling someone and ask for help if necessary. Use your support network (e.g. ask family members, friends or your Gamblers Anonymous sponsor for help) or organize to see a psychologist/therapist for a booster session if required.

Provide the client with (1) a plan to remain gamble-free/in control of his/ her gambling; (2) the Client Information Handout – Strategies to Prevent Lapse/Relapse and (3) Client Information Handout – Coping with Lapses (see below). Emphasize that lapses/relapses occur mostly when clients stop practising the strategies that they have learnt. It took years to develop a gambling problem and it is unreasonable to expect several weeks of practice (during the course of the programme) to change these behaviours/ thoughts. Thus, the client needs to continue practising the strategies if he/she is to replace old unhealthy/non-functional behaviours, habits, thoughts and feelings with new ones. In addition, doing something towards your gambling problem everyday helps remind you to put safeguards in place and reduce your chances of lapses/relapses.

My Plan to Remain Gamble Free/In control of my gambling

DO <u>AT LEAST ONE</u> OF THE FOLLOWING <u>EVERYDAY</u>:
(It will only take as little as 10 minutes a day but the benefits will last you a lifetime!)

~~~~~~~~~~~~~

⊙ Read your reminder cards/flashcards.

⊙ Read some part of your notes.

⊙ Practise one of the skills that you have learnt (e.g. challenging thinking errors, abdominal breathing, relaxation exercises, imaginal exposure, problem solving, goal setting).

⊙ Check in with a relevant helpline.

⊙ Attend a Gamblers Anonymous meeting.

⊙ Talk to someone (e.g. a family member, friend, or Gamblers Anonymous sponsor) about your progress.

~~~~~~~~~~~~~

Choose a different option each day

Client Information Handout:
Strategies to Prevent Lapse/Relapse

⦿ Lead a balanced lifestyle.

⦿ Write down your triggers for gambling, benefits of not gambling and/or negative consequences experienced due to gambling on a card and keep it in a place where you can see it often (such as in your wallet). Have the number of a support or helpline handy.

⦿ Avoid high-risk situations. In case you are unable to avoid a particular high-risk situation plan ahead how you are going to cope and prevent a lapse.

⦿ Discuss on a regular basis with someone (helpline, Gamblers Anonymous sponsor, friends or family members) how you are coping.

⦿ Challenge negative thoughts as they arise.

⦿ Prepare (and practise) a short assertive response that you can give when you feel pressured to gamble (e.g. 'No, thanks', 'I've decided gambling isn't good for me', 'I am taking a break from gambling').

⦿ Avoid all triggers of gambling including high-risk situations and revise your triggers and safeguards periodically.

⦿ Monitor your progress. Lapses do not just happen. There are always warning signs (e.g. negative feelings, thinking errors and particular behaviours). The best way to catch early warning signs is by monitoring your progress. Take a few minutes daily or at least weekly to ask yourself: 'Did anything happen today that changed my desire to gamble?', 'Did I experience strong urges/ thoughts of gambling that are still with me?', 'Did I notice any relapse warning signs today?'

⦿ Read your notes once a month.

⦿ Use the strategies that you have learnt to cope with your urges.

⦿ Use daily schedules as they help ensure that you have planned a gamble-free day.

**Client Information Handout:
Coping with Lapses**

⊙ Keep calm – the first reaction often might be guilt or self-blame. This is a normal reaction. Give yourself enough time for it to occur and pass. Look upon the lapse as a single, independent event, something that can be avoided in future. Remind yourself of your successes to this point.

⊙ Consult your reminder cards or notes for instructions.

⊙ Remind yourself of your goals and of how important it is not to gamble if you are to reach your goals.

⊙ Get your motivation back by evaluating the positive and negative consequences of continued gambling (both immediate and delayed ones).

⊙ Challenge any negative thoughts that arise.

⊙ Make an immediate plan of recovery.
  - Record your relapse. This will help you determine the factors that led to your relapse (e.g. walking past a club, time of day, who you were with).
  - Analyse possible triggers, including the 'who', 'when', or 'where' of the situation and anticipatory thoughts. It is possible that either these triggers were one of your old triggers or they are new ones that did not exist before. Redo your triggers list and safeguards for the future.
  - Check your original action plan and see what helpful strategies you are not doing any longer. If needed, revise your action plan. Learn from your mistakes/lapses. Think about ways to use this experience to help you in the future.

⊙ Problem solving – deal with the problems and crises immediately so that these do not build up to the point where you feel tempted to continue gambling. Use your problem-solving skills to determine the best solution and plan how you are going to begin implementing it.

⊙ Call someone and ask for help if necessary. Use your support network (e.g. ask family members, friends or your Gamblers Anonymous sponsor for help) or organize to see a psychologist/therapist for a booster session if required.

Reference: Marlatt & Gordon, 1985.

Elective session: Assertiveness skills training

Session content and goals

13.1 Review home exercises
13.2 Discuss aim and rationale of the session
13.3 Discuss assertiveness
13.4 Discuss ways to be more assertive

13.1 REVIEW HOME EXERCISES

Review the client's progress on home exercises and provide as much praise as possible for his/her efforts and accomplishments. Troubleshoot problem areas or reasons for non-compliance.

13.2 DISCUSS AIM AND RATIONALE OF THE SESSION

13.2.1 Aim

The session aims to help improve the client's interpersonal relationships by teaching the client assertive ways of interacting with others (including effective communication skills).

13.2.2 Rationale

There are many reasons why problem gamblers might benefit from learning assertive ways of interacting with others. They include the following:

⊙ Problem gamblers encounter a range of obstacles in their path to recovery (e.g. meeting a friend who tries to talk the client into going to gamble). An assertive individual is more likely to be able to resist social pressure to gamble. For example, if the client communicates to the other person clearly and assertively about their decision not to gamble they are less likely to be pressured into gambling.

⊙ For some clients, lack of assertiveness or poor communication/social skills may motivate the client to gamble. Thus, such clients would benefit from learning ways to be more direct and appropriate in expressing their thoughts and feelings.

⊙ For some problem gamblers, there may be increased interpersonal conflicts with family and friends due to their gambling behaviours. For such individuals, learning appropriate ways to handle such conflicts will be beneficial. This is important as if such conflicts are not handled properly they will only exacerbate the crisis and possibly lead the problem gambler to have a lapse. Good assertion (and communication) skills are vital for effective conflict resolution.

Therapists need to note that some clients will not require training in the various skills discussed in this session. On the other hand, some clients will require extensive training in these skills and you may need additional sessions to cover all the skills adequately. Furthermore, the significant others of problem gamblers may also benefit from being included in this discussion.

13.3 DISCUSS ASSERTIVENESS

Being assertive means standing up for one's own personal rights and being able to express them without disrespecting other people's rights and needs. There are generally three ways of interacting with others (see Table 13.1).

Discuss the advantages and disadvantages of each approach: for example, the advantages of being passive are that it encourages protection from others, avoids responsibility or conflict, and elicits praise from

Table 13.1 Basic interaction styles

Assertive	Passive	Aggressive
Standing up for personal rights and expressing thoughts, feelings and beliefs in direct, honest and appropriate ways that do not violate others' rights. ⇒ Respect own and others' rights and needs.	Failing to express honest thoughts, feelings & beliefs or expressing them in such a manner that allows others to ignore or violate our rights and needs. ⇒ Respect others' rights and needs but not own.	Standing up for personal rights and expressing thoughts, feelings and beliefs in a way that does not respect the rights and needs of others. ⇒ Respect one's rights and needs but not others'.

others. However, by being passive, one loses independence and power to make decisions as one fails to respect his/her rights and needs.

Alberti and Emmons (1989) highlighted ten key elements of assertive behaviour. These are:

- self-expression;
- being respectful of others' rights;
- being honest;
- being direct and firm;
- benefiting both self and relationships;
- appropriate verbal communication including the content of the message (feelings, rights, facts, opinions, requests and limits);
- appropriate non-verbal communication including the style of the message (eye contact, voice, posture, facial expression, gestures, distance, timing, fluency and listening);
- appropriate for the person and situation;
- socially responsible;
- learnt not inborn.

13.4 DISCUSS WAYS TO BE MORE ASSERTIVE

There are several ways one can be more assertive and these are discussed below. The works of a number of authors were used to compile this session including Alberti and Emmons (2001), Gottman (1976), Hanna (1995), Jakubowski and Lange (1978), Lange and Jakubowski (1976), Tannen (1986), and Smith (1985). You may want to discuss only those strategies from this section that apply to your client. You can give your client the Client Information Handout: Ways to be Assertive at the end of the session.

13.4.1 Problem solving

To effectively deal with a conflict, problem-solving skills that were taught earlier in the programme (Chapter 9) can be used. Remind the client of the steps involved in problem solving and suggest that these steps can be used cooperatively by two or more people to come up with a solution.

13.4.2 Honour your basic human rights (Jakubowski & Lange, 1978, pp. 80–81)

Remind the client of his/her basic human rights.

- The right to act in ways that promote your dignity and self-respect as long as others' rights are not violated in the process.
- The right to be treated with respect.
- The right to say 'no' and not feel guilty.
- The right to experience and express your feelings.
- The right to take time and think.
- The right to change your mind.
- The right to ask for what you want.
- The right to do less than you are humanly capable of doing.
- The right to ask for information.
- The right to make mistakes.
- The right to feel good about yourself.

13.4.3 Deal with negative emotions

The client can use techniques learnt in Chapter 10 to deal with negative emotions that might arise from negative feedback or criticism.

- For example, if someone gets the client to do certain things by making him/her feel guilty the client could explore what is making him/her feel this way by using the Negative Emotions Worksheet (Appendix U). Encourage the client not to say 'sorry' unless he/she is genuinely sorry.

- For example, if someone makes the client angry, the client can use the STAR technique in Chapter 10 to cope with the situation.

13.4.4 Challenge negative thinking

There are a number of thinking errors that can prevent a client from being assertive. Thus, these errors need to be identified and challenged. For example:

- *Thought*: If I assert myself, others will get mad at me (jumping to conclusions).
  Challenge: If I assert myself, the effects may be positive, neutral or negative. However, as assertion involves respecting others' rights and needs as well, the result is more likely to be positive.

- *Thought*: If I assert myself and people do become angry with me, it will be awful (catastrophizing).
  Challenge: Even if others do become angry, I am capable of handling it without falling apart. If I assert myself, when it is appropriate, I do not have to feel responsible for other people's anger, as I am not in control of other people's reactions and actions. I can only control how I react and act.

- *Thought*: By being assertive I may hurt others' feelings (jumping to conclusions).
  Challenge: If I am assertive, other people may or may not feel hurt. If I prefer to be dealt with directly, quite likely, others will too. In addition, if I am being assertive, I am still respecting their rights and needs, so my intention is not to hurt them.

- *Thought*: If my assertion hurts others, I am responsible for their feelings (personalization).
  Challenge: Even if others do feel hurt by my assertive behaviour I can let them know I care for them while also being direct about what I need or want. Most people are not so weak that they will be traumatized by it.

13.4.5 Effective communication

Communication is a two-way process requiring both speakers and listeners. Speaking our mind is usually very easy but clear and effective communication is more difficult to achieve.

13.4.5.1 Explore barriers to effective communication

There are many barriers to effective communication that need to be avoided and these include the following.

- Advising – giving the other person solutions to his/her problems. For example: 'If I were you, I would . . .'.

- Criticizing – making a negative appraisal of the other person. For example: 'You don't do anything right'.

- Diagnosing – scrutinizing why a person is behaving in a particular manner. For example: 'You are just doing this to hurt me'.

- Diverting – pushing away the other person's message via distraction. For example: 'Let's change the subject'.

- Evaluative praise – making a positive judgement of the other person, his/her actions or attitudes, which may make the others feel guilty or feel 'emotionally blackmailed'. For example: 'You have always made the right decision and you will this time as well'.

- Moralizing – telling the other person what he/she should do or not do. For example: 'You should tell him that you will help him out'.

- Name-calling or labelling – putting down or stereotyping others. For example: 'You are a loser'.

- Ordering – commanding the other person to do what you want. For example: 'Make sure you don't mess this up too'.

⊙ Threatening – trying to control the other person's actions by warning them of possible negative consequences if the action is not done. For example: 'If you don't stop nagging, I am going to leave'.

Discuss with the client:

⊙ have you ever used such barriers;
⊙ if you have, what were the results/consequences;
⊙ how do you feel when these occur in an interaction?

13.4.5.2 Rules for effective communication

There are a number of general rules for effective communication. These include:

⊙ using short, clear, simple and positive statements or questions;
⊙ asking one question at a time or making one request at a time;
⊙ being specific;
⊙ avoiding strong emotional statements;
⊙ voice, tone and body language should match words spoken.

More specific advice includes the following.

⊙ Active listening:
  – listen to what the other person is saying. Active listening means that you are concentrating on what the other person is saying;
  – if in doubt, ask what the other person meant;
  – use encouraging statements (e.g. 'Oh', 'I see', 'Go on', 'really') or show that you are paying attention by nodding;
  – ask open-ended questions (e.g. use 'how', 'what', 'where' or 'who') to clarify. However, do not question excessively;
  – paraphrase (acknowledge, and clarify by putting in your own words what you think the other person has said and/or reflect back others' statements or feelings);
  – look at the other person the majority of the time (do not stare) – i.e. make eye contact and look interested in what he/she is saying;
  – minimize distractions (e.g. turn the radio or TV off).

⊙ Praising others:
  – it is important to give praise for even small accomplishments because if you do not praise the small achievements, the big ones may not happen;
  – look at the person and make sure that he/she is listening to you;
  – say exactly what he or she did that pleased you;
  – praise people as soon as they have done something that deserves praise, as this will increase the likelihood that the behaviour will be repeated;
  – avoid backhand compliments (e.g. 'Gosh, you look so much better in a dress').

⊙ Receiving praise:

- look at the person that praised you and say thanks;
- tell them what it is you appreciate;
- tell them how you feel (happy, proud, pleased).

⊙ Asking someone to do something:

- look at the person and make sure he/she is looking at you or listening to you;

- do not nag, demand or make the other person feel guilty in some way;

- say exactly what you would like that person to do (be specific about the behaviour);

- say how you feel about their effort;

- use phrases such as 'I would really appreciate if you would . . .', 'It would make a big difference to me if you could . . .' or 'If you could . . . I would really feel a lot better about . . .';

- remember the tone of voice and body language need to give the same message as the words you use;

- timing is also important;

- do not ask for too much or not give enough information.

⊙ Providing negative feedback:

- look at the person and speak firmly;

- use 'I' statements. Say exactly what the person did to upset you (be specific about the behaviour). Tell the person how that makes you feel (use feeling words). Suggest how the person may prevent this from happening in future and offer an alternative. For example: 'I feel . . . when you . . . because . . . I would like . . .' (I feel = the emotional response, when you = the behavioural response, because = the impact on you, I would like = your preference for the other person's behaviour);

- voice, body language and tone must fit the words spoken.

⊙ Receiving negative criticism:

- if you agree with a negative feedback about your behaviour, it is important that you apologize. Then make the necessary changes you need to your behaviour;

- if the person extends the negative feedback and starts criticizing you, you need to say that you do apologize that you hurt the person's feelings but not accept everything else that he/she said to you.

Remember: non-verbal communication is as important as verbal communication. For example:

⊙ verbal should be congruent with the verbal message;
⊙ speech pattern should be fluent and expressive. Be clear and emphasize keywords;

- voice should be appropriately loud to the situation;
- eye contact should be firm and direct (try not to stare);
- posture should be erect and relaxed;
- body gestures should indicate strength to the verbal message. Try avoiding nervous gestures (e.g. hand wringing or covering the mouth with hand) or threatening gestures (e.g. finger pointing or hands on the hips).

One needs to protect oneself where communication is not working (e.g. when someone is criticizing you, acting irrationally, not listening to you and not responding to your communication). Some techniques include the following.

- Broken record technique – if it becomes clear that the other person is not prepared to listen to you (e.g. refusing inappropriate request from friend), stop giving explanations and answering questions and simply repeat yourself over and over again until the other person gets the message.

- Selective ignoring – refuse to respond to inappropriate conversation or requests until the other person gives up (e.g. someone criticizes you for the mistakes of the past that you know you are trying to rectify and do not wish to discuss with them). You choose to ignore whenever they bring that topic up. It might be a good idea to let them know that you have planned to do this. You could say, 'I hear what you are saying, but I have already discussed this with you and have already told you how I feel about it. I am not prepared to discuss it any further. If this comes up again, I will ignore it. However, you can continue to talk to me about other issues.'

Remind the client that he/she cannot become assertive overnight and it will require practise like most skills and strategies used in this programme.

Client Information Handout:
Ways to be Assertive

⊙ Problem solving.

⊙ Remember your basic human rights (Jakubowski & Lange, 1978, pp. 80–81) including the right to act in ways that promote your dignity and self-respect as long as others' rights are not violated in the process, be treated with respect, say 'no' and not feel guilty, experience and express your feelings, take time and think, change your mind, ask for what you want, do less than you are humanly capable of doing, ask for information, make mistakes, and feel good about yourself.

⊙ Deal with negative emotions – use techniques learnt to deal with negative emotions that might arise from negative feedback or criticism.

⊙ Challenge negative thoughts related to being assertive.

⊙ Effective communication. When communicating:
  - avoid communication barriers (e.g. distractions, judging);
  - be specific;
  - use short, clear, simple and positive statements or questions to express your thoughts or requests;
  - ask one question at a time or make one request at a time;
  - show appreciation for positive behaviours or changes made;
  - show the person you are listening;
  - avoid strong emotional statements;
  - voice, tone and body language should match words spoken;
  - 'I' message formula for expressing negative feedback: 'I feel . . . when you . . . because . . . I would like . . .' (I feel = the emotional response, when you = the behavioural response, because = the impact on you, I would like = your preference for the other person's behaviour).

Remember that you cannot become assertive overnight and it will require practice like most skills and strategies used in this programme.

References: Alberti & Emmons (2001), Gottman (1976), Hanna (1995), Jakubowski & Lange (1978), Lange & Jakubowski (1976), Tannen (1986) and Smith (1985).

Elective session: Getting out of debt

Session content and goals

14.1 Review home exercises
14.2 Discuss aim and rationale of the session
14.3 Discuss steps to getting out of debt

14.1 REVIEW HOME EXERCISES

Review the client's progress on home exercises and provide as much praise as possible for his/her efforts and accomplishments. Troubleshoot problem areas or reasons for non-compliance.

14.2 DISCUSS AIM AND RATIONALE OF THE SESSION

14.2.1 Aim

This session aims to teach the client basic steps in getting out of debt. It also aims to teach the client how to do a budget.

14.2.2 Rationale

Many problem gamblers have problems with debt as a result of borrowing money to gamble with or to pay gambling debts. This session outlines the steps to help the client get out of debt. Obviously, some clients will not be in debt but may benefit from learning how to work out a budget.

This session may not be suitable (i.e. it may be limiting) for clients that have major financial difficulties. Clients with major financial difficulties will need to be referred to a financial counsellor and/or lawyer.

14.3 DISCUSS STEPS TO GETTING OUT OF DEBT

The following are the steps the client can take to begin getting out of debt. The steps have been complied using the information in the NSW Young Lawyers' *Debt Handbook* (2004) and the authors' personal experience working with clients in debt because of their gambling behaviours.

Step One: Make a list of debts

Get the client to make a list of all his/her debts. These should include debts incurred because of fines, loans (from financial institutes, family members, friends, workmates, loan sharks, etc.), pawnbrokers, credit cards, other plastic cards, bounced cheques, unpaid bills (e.g. telephone, electricity, home rent, car registration, insurance policies, rates), tax, rentals (video, stereo, washing machine, dryer, fridge, etc.) and pay TV.

Once the list is made, help the client prioritize the debts. For example, high-priority debts may be the ones where the client is paying high interest rates. Also, paying utility bills might be more important than credit card bills. High-priority debts need to be paid first.

Step Two: Make a list of creditors

Help the client to make a list of his/her creditors. The list needs to include the following information :

- name of creditors (people who the client borrowed money from);
- the total amount owed to each creditor;
- how often the repayments need to be made;
- how much needs to be paid at each repayment point;
- when will payments begin;
- how will payments be made;
- the interest rates involved with each of the debts;
- is it the client's debt or is it a joint debt;
- is there a guarantor associated with the debt;
- is it a secured debt (e.g. Is there a security such as a mortgage associated with the debt)?

Therapists could help the client to write a letter to each of the creditors immediately (e.g. before a debt collector gets involved). The letter needs to explain the client's financial situation, reasons the client is having difficulty paying bills and the client's willingness to negotiate a payment plan that he/she can adhere to. It is a good idea for the client to include as much information as he/she can about his/her financial status in the letter. It is also a good idea for the client to include the following with the letter:

⊙ his/her financial statement;
⊙ a list of assets;
⊙ a list of all sources of income;
⊙ a list of all debts;
⊙ a list of expenses.

Where possible the client needs to provide proof of assets, income, debts and expenses.

Creditors normally contact the sender of the letter after receiving the letter to negotiate a new repayment plan. The client needs to remember that when negotiating with creditors, he/she:

⊙ should not offer all his/her income to one creditor;
⊙ needs to be honest with the creditors;
⊙ needs to ensure that he/she does not offer or commit more than he/she is able to repay;
⊙ needs to ask the creditor to confirm any new agreement in writing;
⊙ needs to keep a record of all correspondence and communication with creditors (e.g. the date of contact, name of the person the client spoke to, the amount agreed upon).

If a creditor is unwilling to change the original repayment plan the client can get a financial counsellor to mediate on his/her behalf.

Step Three – Make a budget

Help the client to start using written budgets; the Budget Worksheet in Appendix W can assist with this. It requires the client to list his/her weekly income and expenses. It is important to ensure that the TOTAL EXPENSES are lower than the TOTAL INCOME so that there are some SAVINGS each week. Initially, when one is trying to pay off the debts, one may not be saving any money but it is important that the TOTAL EXPENSES never exceed the TOTAL INCOME. Furthermore, the client needs to always call creditors before due dates if something has upset his/her repayment plan.

Step Four – Reduce chances of further debt from occurring

The client needs to ensure that his/her debts do not grow any larger. There are a number of ways to keep debt from becoming bigger and these include:

- cutting up credit cards. Use cash and debit cards to pay bills and other expenses. Once credit card debts are paid, close the credit card accounts;
- not taking out any more loans. Consolidation loans often come with high interest rates;
- making lifestyle changes that can reduce expenses (e.g. spending less on clothing, eating home cooked meals rather than takeaway meals, travelling by public transport).

Below are some other points the therapist may need to discuss/emphasize to the client.

- The client may find it helpful to get an additional job so that debts can be paid off sooner. This also keeps the client busy and thus, the client has less time to gamble.

- If the client is having difficulty managing money, he/she could contact an accredited financial counsellor. Financial counsellors are often community-based workers whose services are free of charge. They provide a range of services including giving financial advice, preparing a budget, negotiating with creditors and assisting with the process of bankruptcy.

- It may be beneficial for certain clients to meet with government-related agency personnel to discuss whether the client is eligible for any welfare assistance or temporary financial assistance.

- Some churches or community agencies also provide temporary financial assistance and this might also be worth considering.

- If the client has bankruptcy issues, it may be important for the client to meet with a lawyer.

CHAPTER 15

Elective session: Teaching significant others strategies to cope/deal with the gambler's behaviours

---

Session content and goals

15.1 Discuss aim and rationale of the session
15.2 Assessment of the impact of the client's and his/her significant other's behaviours on each other
15.3 Provide psychoeducation
15.4 Discuss stages in stopping problem behaviours
15.5 Discuss strategies to improve the client's readiness to change and assist him/her through recovery
15.6 Discuss effective strategies to cope with the negative consequences of the client's behaviours
15.7 Discuss self-care strategies with the significant other

15.1 DISCUSS AIM AND RATIONALE OF THE SESSION

15.1.1 Aim

This session caters for the needs of problem gamblers' significant others (including partners, children, parents, work colleagues, friends, siblings, other relatives). The overall goal is to teach the significant other strategies to cope/deal with the client's behaviours so they can assist with achieving and maintaining a change in the client's gambling behaviours. More specifically, the session aims to:

⊙ assist the significant other to understand the client's gambling behaviours;
⊙ assist the significant other to identify ineffective ways of dealing with the client's gambling problems and the resulting consequences;
⊙ teach the significant other strategies to improve the client's readiness to change and assist him/her through recovery;

⊙ teach the significant other strategies to cope with the client's behaviours and negative consequences of his/her gambling;
⊙ discuss self-care strategies (including the importance of self-care) with the significant other.

This session is a guideline to the types of things that might need to be discussed with the significant other but all sections mentioned may not be relevant to all significant others. Therapists need to choose which sections to discuss with the significant other. This will depend on the significant other's current functioning and personal needs, the client's presenting problems as well as the nature of the relationship between the significant other and the gambler. Consequently, the content of this chapter can be covered over one session or over a number of sessions. Furthermore, more than one significant other could be included in the session(s). The therapist also needs to decide whether to include the client in these discussions. It is advisable to include the client when discussing at least some of the sections (such as Section 15.6).

15.1.2 Rationale

Problem gamblers' behaviours can result in enormous negative consequences for their significant others (Hodgins, Shead, & Makarchuk, 2007; Makarchuk, Hodgins, & Peden, 2002). It is common to find that there are serious difficulties in the interpersonal relationships between problem gamblers and their significant others. Interpersonal problems between problem gamblers and their significant others include relationship breakdown, domestic violence, sexual problems and neglecting their family (Lorenz & Yaffee, 1986; 1988; 1989; Muelleman et al., 2002). Problem gambling often results in significant negative financial consequences for significant others (Fanning & McKay, 2000). The problem gamblers' debts can have an enormous impact on significant others' mental well-being and financial situation as well as result in the loss of time from work and other pleasant activities (Ingle, Marotta, McMillan, & Wisdom, 2008). Problem gamblers often lose the ability to carry out their normal family roles and responsibilities (Fanning & McKay, 2000). Loss of trust between problem gamblers and their significant others can produce social (e.g. family members' withdrawal from social contacts to focus on the stress at home), emotional (e.g. depression and anger) and physical changes (e.g. headaches, gastrointestinal problems) in the significant other's well-being. Serious psychosocial maladjustments in the children of problem gamblers such as substance misuse, delinquency, depression, suicide and other behavioural and psychological problems are also common (Lorenz & Yaffee, 1988; Lorenz & Shuttleworth, 1983).

Regardless of whether these difficulties precede the gambling or are a consequence of the gambling, they are likely to interfere with successful treatment outcomes (Raylu & Oei, 2007; Hudak et al., 1989). A number of studies have also found that the significant others of problem gamblers often seek assistance (Hodgins et al., 2001; Potenza, Steinberg, McLaughlin, Wu, Rounsaville, & O'Malley, 2001). Problem gamblers' significant others appear to play an important role in the gamblers' recovery. A number of studies have reported that problem gamblers identify their significant others or concerns about the impact of their gambling on significant others as the main reasons for quitting or reducing gambling behaviours (Hodgins & El-Guebaly, 2000; Hodgins, Makarchuk, El-Guebaly, & Peden, 2002; Makarchuk et al., 2002). A number of studies have shown that engagement of a significant other in treatment can improve outcomes for the problem gambler. For example, Ingle and colleagues (2008) found that having a significant other was associated with treatment success in a group of problem gamblers. Furthermore, their participation in treatment had a positive impact on treatment retention. This supports research that suggests that a good support network and/or involvement of significant others in treatment can improve treatment success (Hudak et al., 1989), reduce severity of relapse (Zion, Tracy, & Abell, 1991) and decrease treatment drop out (Grant, Kim, & Kuskowski, 2004).

Thus, considering the negative consequences of a problem gambler's gambling on his/her significant others and the influence significant others have on the gambler's recovery, it is important to teach significant others strategies to cope with the problem gambler's behaviours and negative consequences of his/her gambling as well as strategies to improve the client's readiness to change and assist him/her through recovery. It would benefit both the problem gambler and his/her significant other if the significant other understands the factors involved in the development and maintenance of the gambling problem and can identify ineffective ways of dealing with the problem gambler's behaviours. Providing such education to the significant other also prevents the significant other from sabotaging the problem gambler's recovery process knowingly or unknowingly (e.g. by rescuing the problem gambler from experiencing the negative consequences of gambling), it helps reinforce therapeutic gains and increases the likelihood that the significant other will support the problem gambler through recovery.

For clients that are experiencing a great deal of marital distress, it is best not to try to deal with all of the complex marital and perhaps sexual dysfunction issues. These clients may benefit from being referred to a specialized relationship/marriage counsellor or psychologist. Similarly, those clients experiencing significant family problems may benefit from specialized family counselling.

15.2 ASSESSMENT OF THE IMPACT OF THE CLIENT'S AND HIS/HER SIGNIFICANT OTHER'S BEHAVIOURS ON EACH OTHER

Provide an opportunity for the client's significant other (and for the client if they present with the significant other) to express his/her feelings, concerns, thoughts, perspectives and expectations in relation to the client's gambling problems and resulting consequences. Explore the nature of conflicts in the relationships and their perceived causes. Identify significant others' ineffective responses to problem gambling. Below is a list of such ineffective responses. The list was compiled from the discussion in Fanning and McKay (2000) and the authors' personal experiences with treating problem gamblers and their significant others.

⊙ Denial – denial is common among problem gamblers' significant others, especially in the early stages of the gambling problem. This can occur in many forms including acting as if the problem does not exist, refusing to talk about it and becoming angry and defensive when the subject comes up with those outside the family. Denial has short-term benefits. It allows significant others to maintain smooth relationships, continue functioning in their daily lives and avoid emotions (e.g. depression, anxiety, anger, guilt or shame). However, in the long term, denial allows significant others to ignore the gambling problem and its consequences (believing that the problem will vanish in time) and prevents them from dealing with the problems directly.

⊙ Minimizing the problem – some significant others respond to the gambler's gambling problems and its consequences by making the problem seem smaller than it is. This is shown in comments such as 'He only gets verbally abusive when he loses a lot of money. It's not something he does all the time' or 'He only gambles a few times a week.' Minimizing the problem leads significant others to believe that the problem is not large or the situation is not too bad even though it may be. They prevent significant others from dealing with problems directly.

⊙ Making excuses – some significant others make excuses for the problem gamblers' behaviours (e.g. He is like this because . . .). Such excuses indicate that the significant other is trying to justify what is happening. However, this stops the significant other from exploring the real reasons for the current problems. It also shifts responsibility for the gambling away from the gambler to the significant other. This often leads to feelings of guilt and powerlessness among significant others.

⊙ 'Enabling' and 'rescuing' behaviours – some significant others engage in actions that may appear appropriate, and/or necessary without recognizing that their behaviours are supporting or reinforcing the problem gambler's behaviours. One such action involves 'enabling'. 'Enabling' behaviours are those that make it easier for the problem gambler to continue gambling (e.g. a wife may take over the husband's responsibilities such as taking the children to soccer practice). 'Enabling' is generally done to keep the family functioning. Another such action involves 'rescuing'. 'Rescuing' behaviours are those that prevent the gambler from experiencing the full negative consequences of his/her gambling behaviours (e.g. bailing the client out of their frequent gambling losses and debts). 'Rescuing' is done to minimize short-term damage to the problem gambler. However, this only results in severe long-term problems for the problem gambler. Sometimes 'enabling' and 'rescuing' behaviours are a result of the fears that the significant others have regarding the negative consequences of the problem gambler's behaviours (e.g. 'If I don't pay his rent, he will be evicted' or 'If I don't wake him up every morning, he will lose his job'). Sometimes 'enabling' and 'rescuing' behaviours occur as a result of thinking in terms of 'shoulds' and 'oughts' (e.g. 'We should always forgive our loved ones' or 'We should always help people we care about').

⊙ Blaming – significant others often blame each other for the problems they are encountering due to the gambler's behaviours. Blaming alleviates the blamer of anxiety from any concerns about failing in his or her responsibilities. Although blaming others may help the blamer to feel better in the short term, there are long-term negative consequences. Those that are blamed often develop negative emotions such as anger, resentment and shame. As a result, they may become defensive or begin denying that a problem exists. It also prevents those concerned from effective communication and problem solving.

⊙ Self-blame – some significant others blame themselves for the problems they are experiencing due to the gambler's behaviours. Focusing on blame means that they become more preoccupied with trying to find out who or what caused the problem rather than how to deal with what has happened.

⊙ Withdrawal and isolation – many significant others withdraw from social contact and isolate themselves from their family and friends (i.e. those that may be able to support them through the difficult time or those that challenge the problem gambler's behaviours) and from the problem gambler. Sometimes as gambling dominates the family's life, a significant other may begin devoting more of his/her life to keeping the family functioning and less for more personal and independent pursuits. Withdrawal and isolation are ineffective ways of dealing with problem gambling as they stop all involved from recognizing and accepting the problem, discussing issues of concern, giving each other support, problem solving and seeking support and information.

15.3 PROVIDE PSYCHOEDUCATION

Use the information and/or format in Chapter 4 to provide the significant other with psychoeducation on problem gambling to increase their awareness and understanding of the problem. This includes a discussion of the nature of gambling problems, the signs that someone has a gambling problem, the consequences of problem gambling on the gambler and his/her significant others, what your treatment involves, the early warning signs of a lapse/relapse (e.g. unexplained absences, mood swings, and financial difficulties), possible triggers for gambling, factors associated with the development and maintenance of problem gambling, as well as problem gamblers' dysfunctional thinking patterns. Also, discuss with the significant other the ineffective responses to problem gambling identified in the last section (e.g. 'enabling' and 'rescuing' behaviours) and the role they play in maintaining gambling problems and difficulties in their relationships. If the significant other is denying, minimizing and/ or making excuses for the gambler's behaviours therapists will need to challenge this so that the significant other is forced to deal with the reality of what is occurring.

15.4 DISCUSS STAGES IN STOPPING PROBLEM BEHAVIOURS

The stages of change model (developed by Prochaska and DiClemente, 1982; 1986) describes the different stages of change involved in stopping problem behaviours. Discuss with the significant other the stages involved. Help the significant other identify what stage the problem gambler is at.

⊙ *Precontemplation*: problem gamblers in the precontemplative stage are not considering altering their gambling behaviours. These individuals could be unaware of the risks or negative consequences of their gambling or do not feel that the risks or negative consequences apply to them. Some gamblers in the precontemplative stage believe they do not have the ability to change their gambling behaviours. For precontemplators, the benefits of continued gambling outweigh the costs or consequences associated with continued gambling.

⊙ *Contemplation*: problem gamblers in the contemplative stage are ambivalent about their gambling. They would like to stop gambling but they still like the benefits of gambling. They are beginning to assess the advantages and disadvantages of changing their gambling behaviours as well as the consequences of not changing. The benefits and consequences of continued gambling are almost even.

⊙ *Preparation*: problem gamblers in the preparation stage are ready to make a decision and plan to change their gambling behaviours. The disadvantages of continued gambling outweigh the advantages. During this stage, the individuals may work on their motivation to change their gambling behaviours (e.g. telling their significant others of their intention and plan to change). Although there may not be any changes in their gambling behaviours, they will have started to plan and prepare for the changes.

- ⦿ *Action*: problem gamblers in the action stage want to make positive changes to their gambling behaviours and make a variety of concerted efforts to change. They may have limited their access to cash or started avoiding certain people, places or situations that trigger gambling. They may also be engaging in alternative activities to gambling (e.g. increased engagement in other pleasant activities such as exercise or new hobbies). For these individuals, the consequences of continued gambling clearly outweigh the benefits of continued gambling.

- ⦿ *Maintenance*: problem gamblers in the maintenance stage are making a sustained effort to keep to the positive changes made to their gambling behaviours by utilizing a number of strategies for preventing gambling (e.g. avoiding certain people, places or situations that trigger gambling, challenging any negative thoughts that can trigger gambling). For these gamblers, the desire and urge to gamble is weak. Their desire and ability to abstain or control their gambling is strong. These individuals are however, still at some risk of relapse during this stage.

- ⦿ *Relapse*: relapse can occur at any time during any of the above stages of change. Changes take time and many problem gamblers may return to gambling excessively. Furthermore, problem gamblers can revert back to any of the earlier stages of change. It is usual for problem gamblers to progress through these stages of change several times before finally successfully stopping or controlling their gambling.

15.5 DISCUSS STRATEGIES TO IMPROVE THE CLIENT'S READINESS TO CHANGE AND ASSIST HIM/HER THROUGH RECOVERY

These stages of changing problem behaviours involve varying degrees of motivation, as well as different patterns of attitudes, intentions and behaviours (Prochaska & DiClemente, 1982; 1986; Prochaska, DiClemente, & Norcross, 1992). Thus, the strategies used should be tailored to match the stage of change the problem gambler is at. Using the information below, help the significant other identify how he/she can assist the problem gambler depending on the stage of change the problem gambler is at. The information below was complied using strategies discussed by Smith and Meyers (2004), Meyers, Smith, and Miller (1998) and the authors' personal experiences working with problem gamblers and their significant others. The strategies mentioned for each stage of change help the gambler move towards the next stage of change. The Client Information Handout: Stages of Change in Stopping Problem Behaviours and Strategies Effective in Changing Behaviours at Each Stage (below) can be given to the significant other at the end of the session.

15.5.1 Precontemplation

◉ Do not lecture the gambler about gambling, as he/she is happy with his/her gambling behaviours and not likely to listen.

◉ Do not argue, threaten or scream at the gambler as it will not work. This is likely to just deteriorate the relationship between the gambler and the significant other and the gambler is less likely to come to the significant other for help when he/she is ready to change.

◉ Do leave the lines of communication open by working at building your relationship and offer to be there when the gambler is ready to change his/her gambling behaviours. The gambler will change his/her gambling behaviours when he/she is ready to do so.

◉ By identifying specific behaviours that you are concerned about explain to the gambler why you are concerned. The significant other can use 'I statements' described in Chapter 13 (Section 13.4.5.2) to discuss their concerns with the problem gambler.

◉ Provide the gambler with information about their gambling problem and treatment. It is important not to be too 'pushy' as this will only make the gambler take less notice. You can just leave the information with them so that they can read the material in their own time.

◉ Set realistic boundaries and be willing to carry out the consequences if boundaries are broken.

◉ Separate the behaviour from the person by reassuring the gambler that you still love, value and accept him/her but you believe his/her gambling behaviours are unacceptable and you do not approve of the gambling.

◉ Avoid 'enabling' and 'rescuing' behaviours.

15.5.2 Contemplation

◉ Use similar strategies to those you would use with someone in the precontemplative stage.
◉ Assist the gambler to evaluate the advantages and disadvantages of gambling.
◉ Suggest the gambler seeks advice from a health professional (e.g. a general practitioner, psychologist).
◉ Continue to provide support and encouragement.

15.5.3 Preparation and action

◉ Continue to provide support and encouragement.
◉ Praise any positive changes in gambling behaviours.
◉ Do not 'nag' about the problem gambler's past.
◉ Do not constantly look over the gambler's shoulders and monitor his/her every move.

⊙ Do not encourage gambling (e.g. go to gambling venues).
⊙ Organize non-gambling activities (e.g. going to the movies, joining a sports club).
⊙ Understand the problem gambler's triggers for gambling and work together to maintain abstinence (e.g. not having any reminders of gambling in the house).
⊙ Organize positive reinforcers for not gambling.

15.5.4 Maintenance

⊙ Use similar strategies to those you would use with someone in the action/preparation stage.
⊙ Understand the problem gambler's early warning signs of lapsing and give feedback to the problem gambler regarding this in a constructive way to prevent relapse.
⊙ Together with the gambler come up with an 'action plan' in case the gambler has a 'close call' or a lapse in order to prevent a relapse from occurring.

15.5.5 Relapse

⊙ If the problem gambler has had a lapse, remind them of the difference between a lapse and relapse. Remind them of the importance of coping with the lapse to prevent it from becoming a full-blown relapse.

⊙ Remind the gambler of all the benefits gained so far from abstaining/controlling his/her gambling behaviours.

⊙ Implement the 'action plan' in order to prevent or minimize the effect of a relapse.

There are a number of important issues that may need to be discussed/ highlighted with the significant other. These include the following.

⊙ Responsibility – significant others need to understand that they cannot force the gambler to change. They can only encourage and motivate the gambler to change by implementing the strategies described above (i.e. precontemplative and contemplative stages). The gambler will change when he/she is ready.

⊙ Trust – trust is often an issue of concern among the significant others of problem gamblers. Lack of trust may have resulted from either the problem gambler's manipulative or secretive behaviours. The gambler and his/her significant other need to know that it will take time to rebuild trust. Furthermore, they need to be aware that trust will be gained gradually.

⊙ Boundaries – it is important to discuss with significant others (especially parents) the importance of setting clear boundaries about what is and is not acceptable behaviour. Significant others need to be clear about the consequences of violating these boundaries and be prepared to follow through with these.

⊙ 'Enabling' and 'rescuing' behaviours – significant others need to be encouraged to avoid 'enabling' (e.g. taking up problem gamblers' responsibilities) or 'rescuing' behaviours (e.g. paying the problem gamblers' bills).

Therapists may also need to challenge some cognitive distortions significant others may have. Epstein and Schlesinger (1991) highlighted five categories of cognitive distortions among significant others (Baucom & Epstein, 1990; Epstein & Baucom, 1989).

⊙ Selective perceptions about what events have occurred during family interactions.
⊙ Biased attributions about the causes of particular family occurrences.
⊙ Inaccurate predictions about probabilities that certain events will occur in the future.
⊙ Unrealistic assumptions about the characteristics of significant others and their relationships.
⊙ Unrealistic expectations regarding characteristics of significant others and their relationships.

15.6 DISCUSS EFFECTIVE STRATEGIES TO COPE WITH THE NEGATIVE CONSEQUENCES OF THE CLIENT'S BEHAVIOURS

As discussed earlier, significant others experience a number of negative consequences as a result of problem gamblers' behaviours. Described below are suggestions of how to assist significant others experiencing various negative consequences.

15.6.1 Health problems

Negative emotions such as depression, anger, guilt and anxiety are common among significant others. Refer to Chapter 10 for strategies to cope with negative emotions. If you think that the significant other has comorbid psychological disorders (eating disorders, substance misuse disorder, etc.) and may require ongoing assistance, he/she can be referred to a psychologist/psychiatrist. Some significant others may experience physical health problems as a result of the ongoing stress. Such significant others should be referred to a general practitioner.

15.6.2 Financial stress/difficulties

If the significant other is experiencing financial stress because of the gambler's behaviours, he/she may need to protect himself/herself financially (e.g. separating or closing joint accounts). The significant other may also benefit from some of the strategies described in the elective session on Getting Out of Debt (Chapter 14) such as the advice on getting out of debt and budgeting. The significant other may also benefit from seeking financial advice (e.g. steps to protect their assets) from an accountant and/or financial counsellor as well as legal advice (e.g. regarding debts on co-signed loans) from a lawyer. In some cases, it would be useful to convince the gambler to give financial control to the significant other for a short period (i.e. until his/her gambling is under control).

15.6.3 Abuse issues

If the significant other is being abused, he/she needs to be encouraged to protect himself/herself physically and emotionally. Furthermore, if the gambler's gambling is affecting his/her children, the significant other (e.g. spouse) needs to take steps to ensure the children are safe from neglect and hurt. Thus, you may need to provide the significant other with relevant referrals (e.g. phone numbers for domestic violence help, refuges, lawyers).

15.6.4 Legal problems

Significant others may need legal advice for a number of reasons (e.g. they have decided to separate from the gambler, they want to get advice on debts on co-signed loans) and should be provided with referrals to appropriate legal agencies.

15.6.5 Relationship problems

Relationship difficulties are common among problem gamblers. Thus, the significant other and gambler may benefit from increasing their commitment and the level of intimacy in the relationship. Several basic strategies can help with this and these are discussed below. Several references were used to produce this section including Baucom and

Epstein (1990), Epstein and Baucom (1989), Epstein and Schlesinger (1991), and Jacobson and Margolin (1979). If the relationship problems are complex or severe the significant other and/or the gambler may need to be referred to a relationship counsellor/psychologist.

◉ Communicate openly with each other.

 - Discuss the gambling problem and its consequences openly so that you are able to produce adequate solutions to dealing with the problem.

 - Do not expect your significant other to know what you are thinking, what you want or how you feel without expressing it.

 - Do not let things build up. If you do not provide constructive feedback at an early stage, the negative impact of saying nothing about something that is annoying you will accumulate. Do not bring them up unless they seem important to you because bringing up every minor issue can make the other person very defensive.

 - Express your positive feelings, not just the negative ones.

 - Compliment, praise or provide positive feedback to your significant other regularly. For example, record a caring behaviour that you have observed your significant other performing on a daily basis and share this with each other at the end of each week.

If the significant other and/or gambler have problems communicating effectively, the strategies discussed in Section 13.4.5 could be useful.

◉ Solve problems together. If the significant other and/or gambler have difficulty problem solving refer to the steps involved in problem solving in Chapter 9 (Section 9.3).
◉ Negotiate fun activities by using quid pro quos (e.g. 'I will do what you want today in exchange for you doing what I want over the weekend').
◉ Carry out some necessary but tedious task that your significant other usually does or complains about without expecting anything in return.
◉ Engage in some positive/leisure activities that you can enjoy together and that do not involve or relate to gambling.

15.7 DISCUSS SELF-CARE STRATEGIES WITH THE SIGNIFICANT OTHER

Discuss with the significant other the importance/benefits of self-care. If you are well:

◉ you are more likely to have the strength to help and support others (for example support the gambler through recovery);
◉ you are more likely to think clearly. Consequently, you are more efficient at solving problems and making logical decisions;

- your emotions are less likely to overwhelm you;
- other areas of your life are less likely to suffer (such as relationships, job, and parenting);
- you are less likely to start taking over the gambler's responsibilities and thus, have clear boundaries;
- you are more likely to be a good role model and show healthy ways to deal with different emotions.

Discuss with the significant other what he/she can do to take care of himself/herself. Listed below are some self-care strategies:

- take care of yourself physically by eating and sleeping sufficiently as well as exercising regularly;
- maintain a positive mind (e.g. by reminding yourself of the positives in your life, reading inspirational quotes/literature and reciting positive affirmations);
- take time out;
- spend time on your relationships as social interactions provide you with a sense of purpose and meaning in life;
- share the responsibility;
- engage in pleasant activities;
- get yourself support (e.g. via support groups for significant others of problems gamblers such as Gam Anon);
- get counselling for yourself (e.g. family counselling, relationships counselling, personal counselling, stress management);
- engage in relaxation exercises. Therapists may want to discuss and/or practise the relaxation exercises in Appendix Q with some significant others.

Client Information Handout:
Stages of Change in Stopping Problem Behaviours and Strategies Effective in Changing Behaviours at Each Stage

Prochaska and DiClemente (1982; 1986) described the different stages of change involved in stopping problem behaviours. These stages involve differing degrees of motivation, as well as different patterns of attitudes, intentions and behaviours. Thus, the strategies used to encourage behaviour change need to match the stage of change the gambler is at.

PRECONTEMPLATION

Problem gamblers in the precontemplative stage are not considering altering their gambling behaviours. These individuals may be unaware of the risks or negative consequences of their gambling (although that is unlikely) or do not feel that the risks or negative consequences apply to them. Some gamblers in the precontemplative stage believe they do not have the ability to change their gambling behaviours. The benefits of gambling outweigh the costs or consequences of continued gambling.

What can you do to help the gambler at the precontemplative stage?

- Do not lecture the gambler about gambling as he/she is happy with his/her gambling behaviours and not likely to listen.
- Do not argue, threaten or scream at the gambler as it will not work.
- Do leave the lines of communication open by working at building your relationship and offer to be there when the gambler is ready to change his/her gambling behaviours. The gambler will change his/her gambling behaviours when he/she is ready to do so.
- By identifying specific behaviours that you are concerned about explain to the individual why you are concerned.
- Provide the gambler with information about their gambling problem and treatment. It is important not to be too 'pushy' as this will only make the gambler take less notice. You could leave the information with the gambler so that the gambler can read the material in his/her own time.
- Set realistic boundaries and be willing to carry out the consequences if boundaries are broken.
- Separate the behaviour from the person by reassuring the gambler that you still love, value and accept him/her but you believe his/her gambling behaviours are unacceptable.
- Avoid 'enabling' and 'rescuing' behaviours.

CONTEMPLATION

Problem gamblers in the contemplative stage are ambivalent about their gambling. They would like to stop gambling but they still like the benefits of gambling. They are beginning to assess the advantages and disadvantages of changing their gambling behaviours as well as the consequences of not changing. The benefits and consequences of gambling are almost even.

What can you do to help the gambler at the contemplative stage?

⊙ Use similar strategies to those you would with someone in the precontemplative stage.
⊙ Help the gambler to evaluate the advantages and disadvantages of continued gambling.
⊙ Suggest to the gambler that they seek advice from a health professional (e.g. a general practitioner, therapist, psychologist).
⊙ Continue to provide support and encouragement.

PREPARATION

Problem gamblers in the preparation stage are ready to make a decision and plan to change their gambling behaviours. The disadvantages of continued gambling outweigh the advantages. During this stage, the individuals may work on their motivation to change their gambling behaviours (e.g. telling their significant others of their intention and plan to change). Although there may not be any changes in their gambling behaviours, they will have started to plan and prepare for the changes.

ACTION

Problem gamblers in the action stage want to make positive changes to their gambling behaviours and make a variety of concerted efforts to change. They may have limited their access to cash or started avoiding certain people, places or situations that triggered gambling. They may also be engaging in alternative activities to gambling (e.g. increased engagement in other pleasant activities such as exercise or new hobbies). The consequences of continued gambling clearly outweigh the benefits.

What can you do to help the gambler at the preparation or action stage?

⊙ Continue to provide support and encouragement.
⊙ Praise any positive changes in gambling behaviours.
⊙ Do not 'nag' about the problem gambler's past.
⊙ Do not constantly monitor the gambler's every move.
⊙ Do not encourage gambling (e.g. go to gambling venues).
⊙ Organize non-gambling activities (e.g. going to the movies).
⊙ Understand the problem gambler's triggers for gambling and work together to help him/her maintain abstinence (e.g. not having any reminders of gambling in the house).
⊙ Organize positive reinforcers for not gambling.

MAINTENANCE

Problem gamblers in the maintenance stage are making a sustained effort to keep the positive changes made by utilizing strategies for preventing gambling (e.g. avoiding certain people, places or situations that trigger gambling, challenging negative thoughts that can trigger gambling). For these gamblers, the desire and ability to abstain or control their gambling is strong. These individuals are however, still at some risk of relapse.

What can you do to help the gambler at the maintenance stage?

⊙ Use similar strategies to those you would with someone in the action/ preparation stage.
⊙ Understand the problem gambler's early warning signs of lapsing and give feedback to the problem gambler regarding this in a constructive way to prevent relapse.
⊙ Together with the gambler come up with an 'action plan' in case the gambler has a 'close call' or a lapse in order to prevent a relapse.

RELAPSE

Relapse can occur at any time during any of the above stages. Changes take time and many gamblers may return to gambling excessively. Furthermore, they can revert back to any of the earlier stages of change. It is usual for problem gamblers to progress through these stages several times before finally successfully quitting or controlling their gambling.

What can you do to help the gambler who has had a lapse or relapsed?

⊙ If a lapse has occurred, remind them of the difference between a lapse and relapse. Remind them of the importance of coping with the lapse to prevent it from becoming a full-blown relapse.
⊙ Remind the gambler of all the benefits gained so far from abstaining/ controlling his/her gambling behaviours.
⊙ Implement the 'action plan' in order to prevent or minimize the effect of a relapse.

The programme requires the client to complete a number of worksheets, or exercises at home so that the client can try the skills/strategies learnt in sessions in real-life situations. Home exercises are a very important part of therapy as they provide the client opportunities to (1) educate himself/herself through readings, (2) increase awareness of his/her own body and functions (e.g. by monitoring feelings, thoughts and behaviours), (3) increase awareness of his/her recovery and progress and (4) practise skills and strategies learnt in session. Home exercises will also reinforce learnt strategies and help increase the client's sense of self-efficacy (Beck, 1995).

Therapists may encounter clients that are either not completing their home exercise tasks, or not completing them properly. It is essential that therapists investigate the reasons behind any non-compliance or poor performances at home exercise tasks. Below are some common problems that therapists may face with home exercise tasks and strategies to overcome these problems and encourage compliance. The works of a number of authors were used to compile this section. These included: Beck, 1995; Kazantzis & Daniel, 2009; Kazantzis, Deane, Ronan, & L'Abate, 2005; Najavits, 2005; Simmons & Griffiths, 2009.

⊙ *Problem*: the client repeatedly forgets to complete the home assignments or does not complete them because of time constraints.

Strategies to overcome the problem: ask the client to identify a specific time that can be set aside to work on the assignment. Discuss with the client a specific place where the handouts/home exercise sheets can be placed so that the client can easily find them when it is time to complete the tasks. It is also important to discuss with the client prior to completing a session any obstacles that you or he/she might think will influence successful completion of the home exercises as well as strategies to overcome these obstacles.

⊙ *Problem*: the client's constant preoccupation with the negative consequences of his/her gambling problems (e.g. financial, accommodation, legal, employment or relationship problems) prevents him/her from completing the home assignments.

Strategies to overcome the problem: it is important to help the client deal with certain factors/stressors in the initial part of the programme as they may require urgent attention. Resolution (or the knowledge of the possibility of resolution) of such factors/stressors will also enable the client to focus more on treatment. Refer to Section 3.3 on devising a case formulation and treatment plan for further information.

⊙ *Problem*: the client has low motivation to complete the home exercise tasks.

Strategies to overcome the problem: encourage the client to set aside a specific time when their motivation tends to be high (e.g. just after a treatment session) to work on the tasks. Encourage the client to spend only small amounts of time on completing the tasks at the beginning of the programme. This time should then be gradually increased as treatment progresses and the client achieves some degree of success and thus, increases his/her motivation and self-efficacy levels. Therapists may also need to use motivational interviewing techniques (refer to Appendix E) to improve the client's motivation towards treatment and completing home exercise tasks.

⊙ *Problem*: the client has negative associations with 'homework' (e.g. clients that did not perform well at school).

Strategies to overcome the problem: avoid using the word 'homework' as there are negative connotations often associated with the term 'homework' (Kadden et al., 1995). Instead, words such as 'practice exercises', 'home exercises' and 'assignments' could be used.

⊙ *Problem*: the client may believe that home exercise tasks are not necessary for treatment success.

Strategies to overcome the problem: explore the client's reasons why he/she believes that the home exercise tasks may not be necessary for treatment success. It is possible that the client is no longer gambling and thus, views homework as unnecessary. It is also possible that the client does not view active participation as necessary for treatment success. The client may not see a clear relationship between completing the home exercise tasks and treatment success. Such erroneous beliefs need to be discussed/ challenged in session. Therapists need to ensure that they always provide careful rationales for each assignment. They need to discuss how specific home exercise tasks will help to put strategies and skills learnt into practice and how they generalize to real life. Home exercises can also be modified to fit the specified details of individual situations of each client more closely.

⊙ *Problem*: the client may find home exercise tasks too difficult to complete.

Strategies to overcome the problem: assignments should not be difficult and should be related to the client's concerns. Ensure that the client not only understands the home exercise tasks but also knows how to do the home exercises before he/she leaves the sessions. Ensure that the client has all the handouts needed to complete the home exercise tasks.

⊙ *Problem*: the client may feel embarrassed that others will see them completing the tasks.

Strategies to overcome the problem: discuss with the client a specific place they can put the handouts/home exercise sheets that would not be accessible to others. Also discuss with them a specific place they can do the exercises that preserves their privacy. If the home exercise requires the client to carry out a task in public (e.g. carrying out a behavioural experiment such as predicting gambling outcomes of roulette spins), the client could always record the outcomes using an audiotape rather than writing them down on a piece of paper.

⊙ *Problem*: the client is avoiding completing the home exercise tasks due to fear.

Strategies to overcome the problem: the client may be avoiding completing the home exercise tasks because of a number of fears. These include the fear of failure, the fear of the negative emotions that will be elicited by tasks and inability to cope with these emotions, the fear that they will not be able to complete them successfully and the fear of change. Therapists need to investigate such fears and any erroneous beliefs need to be discussed/challenged in session.

APPENDIX B *Guidelines for role-plays/behavioural rehearsals*

Behaviour rehearsal (any procedure, where the client practises responses that are to be learned) can be used to acquire new skills via interactions with the therapists (and others) in simulated or *in vivo* situations (Kadden et al., 1995). Forms of practice include overt (practising for real) and covert responses (practising using imagination). The therapeutic environment is a safe place for the client to practise the skills and strategies before trying them out in the real world (Masters et al., 1987).

Goldfried and Davison (1994) outlined four general stages of behaviour rehearsal.

- Preparing the client – discuss the importance and effectiveness of behaviour rehearsal in terms of learning new skills. Reassure the client that it is normal to feel uncomfortable when trying new skills and strategies out initially. Behaviour rehearsal will become easier the more the client does it. Point out that where appropriate, you will demonstrate the skills first.

- Select target situations – therapists can suggest appropriate situations based on their knowledge of the client's recent circumstances. Alternatively, encourage the client to generate and describe personally relevant situations where the new skills and strategies can be practised. To help the client elicit situations, you could ask the client to think of a recent situation where the strategies might have been useful (e.g. refusing when asked to go gambling), or ask the client to think of a probable difficult situation that may arise in the future where the strategies might be useful (e.g. meeting a friend who the client used to go gambling with).

- Rehearsal in session – use modelling, reinforcement and constructive feedback to assist the client to learn new skills. Encouraging the client to practise the strategies/skills in the session a number of times will increase the likelihood that he/she will try them in his/her real life.

- Carrying out learnt skills/strategies *in vivo* – encourage the client to continue practising the skills/strategies in real life (e.g. get the client to practise new strategies/skills learnt in session as a home exercise task).

APPENDIX C *Assessing and managing suicidal clients*

The main goal in managing a suicidal crisis is ensuring the client's survival. Listed below are some steps therapists can take to assess and manage a suicidal client.

Step one

The first step is to identify the client's motivation and risk for suicide. Some useful questions to ask to assess the risk include the following.

- What are the thoughts?
- How long (and how often) have you been having these thoughts?
- When was the last time you had such thoughts?
- What would you do?
- What would you use?
- Do you have access to what you are planning to use (e.g. a gun, pills)?
- What steps if any have you taken (e.g. made plans for possessions, left instructions for people, written/writing a will or a note)?
- Does it involve others?
- Do these thoughts occur at a specific situation/time?
- Do you know why you feel this way?
- Have you attempted before? If so, how long ago and how was it attempted?
- What are your thoughts about staying alive?
- What has stopped you from acting on your thoughts so far?
- What help could make it easier for you to cope with the problems you are currently experiencing?
- What are your thoughts of the effects of suicide on your relatives, family, etc.?

Therapists also need to determine whether the client is able to see/talk about a future.

Likely risk factors for suicide among problem gamblers may be negative life events (e.g. financial losses, relationship failures, legal consequences), lack of social support, depression, genetic/familial predisposition to suicide, isolation, substance misuse, etc.

Step two

If the client appears to be at high risk of attempting suicide, the therapist should try to reduce this risk. Freeman et al. (1990) highlight some ways to achieve this. These include the following.

⊙ Exploring reasons for them not to take their own life and what the client feels would be accomplished by suicide (i.e. explore the advantages and disadvantages of suicide and of continued living). This can be achieved by showing the client that the disadvantages to suicide outweigh the advantages and that there are better alternatives for attaining his or her goals.

⊙ Reinforcing the factors that have stopped the client from acting on his/her thoughts so far.

⊙ Reminding the client of the effect the suicide will have on his/her family and friends.

⊙ Helping the client brainstorm options that will make it easier for him/her to cope with his/her current problems.

⊙ Challenging the client's thinking errors (e.g. 'Things are hopeless') that have led him/her to want to commit suicide. For example: 'What is the evidence that the situation is hopeless?', 'Will this hopeless situation last forever?', 'What is the evidence that things will never change?' and 'Are there other options?' When a client can see the errors in their thinking, he/she will realize that the situation may be difficult but not hopeless.

⊙ Dealing with the negative emotions (after the immediate crisis is dealt with) if the suicidal impulses are a product of negative emotions (e.g. anger at oneself or others).

Step three

Depending on how committed the client still is about attempting suicide, different approaches will need to be taken. If the client cannot make a commitment to refrain from a suicidal attempt, he/she may require hospitalization. Once the client has made a believable commitment to refrain from a suicide attempt, steps can be taken to minimize the risks of a suicide attempt. Treatment Protocol Project (1997) presents a management plan for individuals who may be contemplating suicide to assist these individuals to get through this period safely. Their suggestions for this management plan included the following.

⊙ Devising a suicide contract to delay the client's suicidal impulses. A suicide contract is an agreement (preferably written) between the client and the therapist in which the client agrees to a particular plan of action other than suicide if he/she experience suicidal thoughts (Callahan, 1996). It is vital that a good therapeutic relationship between the client and therapist exist before such contracts are used (Jacobs, Brewer & Klein-Benheim, 1999). This contract lays out:

- the client's promise not to attempt suicide for an arranged period of time;

- alternative things the client can do if he/she has suicidal thoughts;

- the frequency and timing of therapeutic visits, problems tackled, who else will be involved and what to do in emergencies;

- numbers to call when the client feels vulnerable. If the client is not currently at risk, ensure that he/she has 24-hour access to suitable clinical care (e.g. numbers of relevant helplines, crisis/extended hours mental health team, general practitioner, friends and family members). Also, provide explicit contingency plans if one of more of the contacts are not available.

⊙ Ensuring the client does not have the means of suicide (e.g. guns, pills, chemicals, car keys, knives, rope or other weapons).

⊙ Reassuring the client that most problems can be solved and that he/she will be taught how to achieve this. Highlight to the client that he/she has already made a step towards improving his/her situation by seeking help for his/her gambling.

⊙ Including significant others in the treatment programme.

⊙ Discussing high-risk situations where crisis may develop that could result in suicidal ideations as well as ways to cope with these high-risk situations.

⊙ Challenging thinking errors that may be maintaining suicidal ideations (e.g. 'Nothing is ever going to change').

⊙ Keeping in regular contact with members of a multidisciplinary team if the client is associated with one.

> Ongoing monitoring of suicide throughout the programme is very important especially for at-risk clients.

Prochaska and DiClemente (1982; 1986) described the different stages of change involved in stopping problem behaviours. It is important to note that behaviour change is not a linear process but rather a circular process where a client can move back or forward to any stage (Korn & Shaffer, 2004). These stages involve differing degrees of motivation, as well as different patterns of attitudes, intentions and behaviours (Prochaska & DiClemente, 1982; 1986; Prochaska, DiClemente, & Norcross, 1992). Therapists are required to respond differently depending on the stage the client is at. This is discussed below. Several references were used to compile this information including Bell and Rollnick (1996), Miller (1989) and Miller and Rollnick (1991). For more specific notes on motivational interviewing techniques, see Appendix E.

Precontemplation stage

Individuals at this stage do not believe that they have a problem, as they are not aware of the connection between their gambling behaviours and problems in their lives (Korn & Shaffer, 2004). These clients are not usually seen in the treatment setting. However, some problem gamblers are coerced or pressured into seeking help from significant others or legal systems. Thus, if these individuals do present for treatment they may not be concerned about gambling behaviours or their negative consequences. Problem gamblers that are at the precontemplative stage often minimize their problems (e.g. 'I can stop if I want to. I just choose not to'), deny the effects of their gambling (e.g. 'My wife is overreacting'), appear defensive ('I am hardly an addict') and/or defend their gambling ('I win more than I lose').

Therapist action: it is likely that the client is not ready to change, unaware that a problem exists, has low self-esteem or does not want to acknowledge that he/she has a problem. Thus, it is best not to give direct advice. Build rapport by understanding the client and his/her concerns. Introduce ambivalence by discussing the negatives and positives of gambling and offer information. The focus should be on raising some doubt (and thus, increase awareness) in the client and to increase the perception of risks associated with continued gambling by educating the client via providing information and feedback (Bell & Rollnick, 1996). Encourage the client to examine his/her gambling behaviours and resulting negative consequences via self-monitoring. Tell the client that if he/she decides to give up gambling how he/she can go about doing so.

Contemplative stage

Individuals begin to think about the possibility of having a gambling problem but are ambivalent whether they should continue gambling or stop/reduce it and do not take any action to make changes.

Therapist action: explore the client's concerns. If you are met with resistance, move to the previous stage. Explore the pros and cons of continued gambling as well as the pros and cons of stopping or reducing gambling. Highlight negative consequences compared with the positive ones. Highlight reasons to change and the risks involved in not changing and strengthen self-efficacy. It is best not to confront the client as this can push him/her towards defending the benefits of continued gambling or even denial (Rollnick, Kinnersley, & Stott, 1993).

Preparation/Determination stage

Individuals believe that they have a problem that needs addressing and begin to consider change options (i.e. prepares herself/himself to make a change).

Therapist action: help the client explore the therapeutic options, to determine the best course of action and to strengthen his/her commitment for change (Miller & Rollnick, 1991). This is a very important stage, as reasons for attempting change and the strength of the initial resolution will affect the likelihood of relapse (Allsop & Saunders, 1991). Increase client's sense of self-efficacy or belief in his/her ability to make the change (Bell & Rollnick, 1996).

Action stage

Individuals begin to make specific behavioural changes. New coping skills are taught to replace old dysfunctional ones (e.g. gambling behaviours).

Therapist action: help the client to take steps towards change by going through the programme. It is important that the client is allowed to choose his/her own action plan and perceives that change is desirable (Bell & Rollnick, 1996). Acknowledge that it is normal to feel ambivalent from time to time. Rewards to reinforce successes are very important.

Maintenance stage

Individuals have made certain changes and now they are making efforts to maintain these changes. This is a very important stage as it is this stage that determines whether the results of the action stage are maintained over time and that lapses/relapses do not occur (Marlatt, 1988).

Therapist action: teach the client skills/strategies to maintain changes he/she has made. Encourage practice of the new skills and behaviours as in order to learn new behaviours they need to be rehearsed (Korn & Shaffer, 2004).

Relapse

Individuals begin gambling again.

Therapist action: help the client to recover from the lapse as quickly as possible by learning from it.

APPENDIX E *Notes on motivational interviewing*

Motivational interviewing is a therapeutic technique that can be used to help problem gamblers that are ambivalent about their gambling behaviours. For example, there is a conflict between their gambling behaviours (e.g. 'It's the only enjoyable thing in my life' or 'I have to win the money I have lost before I quit') and their need to stop gambling (e.g. 'I can't afford to continue gambling' or 'I will lose my job if I continue to gamble'). It aims is to explore and amplify this conflict by eliciting problem gamblers concerns and reasons to change their dysfunctional behaviours using non-directive counselling skills such as open-ended questions, affirmation, summarization and reflection. At the same time, it helps motivate problem gamblers to change their current dysfunctional behaviours by creating cognitive dissonance between current behaviours and personal goals and encourage expression of arguments for change (Rollnick, Heather, & Bell, 1992).

Miller and Rollnick (1991) outlined some principles used in motivational interviewing. These include the following.

⊙ Empathy – reflect the client's concerns about his/her behaviours and normalize ambivalence. This does not necessarily mean identification with the client but rather understanding and acceptance of his/her problems and concerns.

⊙ Develop discrepancy between consequences of gambling and the client's personal goals by highlighting negative consequences of gambling.

⊙ Avoid arguing to reduce defensiveness from the client.

⊙ Reduce resistance from the client through reflection, reframing, inviting new perspectives and exploring rather than confronting.

⊙ Support the client's sense of their ability to change as the perception of his/her abilities to accomplish a plan and achieve certain goals will affect the probability that change is attempted (Bell & Rollnick, 1996).

Eliciting self-motivational statements

In motivational interviewing it is important not to present to the client the arguments for change as it can push both the therapist and the client into the confrontational–denial spiral (Miller & Rollnick, 1991). Thus, it is important to facilitate the client's expression of the following self-motivational statements using non-directive counselling skills (Miller & Rollnick, 1991). There are three categories of self-motivational statements. Described below are questions therapists could use to elicit these self-motivational statements.

⊙ Problem recognition (cognitive) – agreeing that there is a problem (e.g. eliciting statements such as 'This is serious, I didn't realize how much I have been gambling'). This can be achieved by asking:

- 'What difficulties have you had in relation to your gambling?'
- 'In what ways has gambling harmed you or others?'
- 'What makes you think that this is a problem?'

⊙ Expression of concern about perceived problem (emotional) – this is often displayed through non-verbals (e.g. 'I'm worried about this' or 'I feel pretty hopeless'). This can be achieved by asking:

- 'What is it about your gambling that you or others see as reasons for concern?'
- 'What worries you about your gambling?'
- 'What can you imagine happening in the long run without change?'
- 'How do you feel about your gambling?'
- 'How does it concern you?'

⊙ Displaying an intention, commitment or decision to change (behavioural) – this may be displayed by eliciting statements (e.g. 'I think it's time for me to stop' or 'I have to do something to change'). This can be achieved by asking:

- 'What are the reasons you see for making change?'
- 'What makes you think you may need to change?'
- 'What are the advantages of changing?'

Once the client shows some optimism for change (i.e. the client indicates hopefulness or optimism about his or her ability to change), the following needs to be assessed: 'What makes you think you could change?' and 'What encourages you that you can change if you wanted to?'

Motivational interviewing techniques that can be used with problem gamblers

The following strategies can be used to increase problem gamblers' motivation to change their gambling behaviours. The work of Miller & Rollnick (1991) and Rollnick et al. (1992) were used to compile this list.

⊙ Give clear advice (e.g. negative consequences of gambling and positive consequences of not gambling) to change the desirability of gambling and attitudes towards gambling and thus advocating the client to stop gambling. Provide practical steps to achieve the goal.

⊙ Provide the client with alternatives to choose from.

⊙ Remove practical obstacles to stopping gambling (e.g. highlighting how this programme has helped treat other problem gamblers).

⊙ Provide the client with objective feedback on his/her gambling behaviours and comorbid problems (e.g. financial problems, relationship difficulties).

⊙ Help the client to set realistic, attainable and specific goals for change.

⊙ Actively assist the client (e.g. by facilitating a referral to a relationships counsellor for a gambler who is experiencing marital problems).

⊙ Build rapport and understand the client's reluctance to change despite negative consequences by empathetic inquiry (objectively explore how the client views his/her gambling in his/her life) and acknowledge that you can see how important his/her gambling is to him/her. This can also be achieved by explore a typical day or session of gambling.

⊙ Raise doubts and increase perceptions of risks and problems. This can be achieved by introducing negative consequences by:

  – asking 'How does your enjoyment of gambling affect your health/relationships/etc?';
  – discussing 'The advantages and disadvantages of gambling';
  – asking 'Where would you like to see yourself in five years' time?' . . . 'What needs to happen for you to achieve your goals in five years' time?';
  – asking 'What were things like for you when you weren't gambling?'

⊙ Offer information about the negative consequences. However, timing is important. For example, when the client appears curious ask if he/she would like some information. Another good time to offer such information is after you ask what he/she thinks of his/her situation and how might it relate to his/her gambling. Be casual and refer to people in general. Also, try to externalize the problem (e.g. 'Experts think . . .')

⊙ Explore concerns – explore each concern and thus, allow the client to contemplate his/her position while assisting him/her through the decision-making process (Bell & Rollnick, 1996). However, it is important to note that this assumes that the client has a problem. If the client is in the precontemplation stage he/she is likely to resist or feel confused.

⊙ Get the client to calculate how much money and/or time has been spent on gambling. For example, to calculate the amount he/she spends per year on gambling multiply the amount he/she spends per week by 52 (52 weeks in a year).

APPENDIX F *Notes on controlled gambling*

Clients that have chosen their treatment goal as 'control gambling' rather than 'abstinence' need to decide on the *maximum amount to be spent on gambling per week*. The client needs to decide how much he/she can afford to lose each week. If the client's spending appears greater than his/her income the client will need to consider changing the treatment goal to 'abstinence'. It is important to discuss with the client that if some or all of the money is not used in a particular week it should not be carried over to the next week. Once the client has decided how much money he/she can afford to spend/lose per week, the client needs to work out:

⊙ Days of the week the client plans to gamble – if the client misses a gambling day, he/she cannot make it up by gambling another day;

⊙ Total amount spent on each of the planned gambling days – the amount spent on each of the planned gambling days cannot add up to more than the maximum amount to be spent on gambling per week.

For example:

⊙ maximum amount to be spent on gambling per week: £50;
⊙ days of the week the client plans to gamble: Saturday and Sunday;
⊙ total amount spent on each of the planned gambling days: Saturday £25, Sunday £25.

Please highlight the following 'control gambling' rules to the client.

⊙ The limits set (e.g. amount of money and time to be spent on gambling) should be revised regularly (e.g. fortnightly or monthly).

⊙ Any winnings cannot be counted. The client needs to have a plan for the winnings (e.g. put it in an account where he/she can only deposit the money and not withdraw it easily). Any amount that is not gambled can also go into this account.

⊙ The client should only take with him/her the exact amount of money that he/she is supposed to gamble.

⊙ If the client does not end up gambling on a planned day, he/she cannot make it up by gambling on a non-gambling day or use that money in addition on the next gambling day. This money goes into the account immediately.

Encourage the client to write down these limits and rules on a card and put the card in a place that he/she sees frequently (e.g. on the fridge or in their wallet).

APPENDIX G *Case formulation and treatment plan sheet*

Name of client: .... Date: ....

DOB: .... Gender: ....

Presenting problems: ....
....
....

Predisposing factors: ....
....
....

Precipitating factors: ....
....
....

Perpetuating factors: ....
....
....

Prognostic factors: ....
....
....
....

Design how the five Ps are related to one another

Goals of treatment: ....
....
....
....

Treatment plan

(a) Sessions to be completed: ....
....
....
....
....
....

(b) Any specific intervention/referral needed for suicidal, housing, vocational, financial, relationship, legal, physical/mental health, social support problems: ....
....
....
....
....
....
....
....
....
....
....
....
....
....
....
....
....
....

APPENDIX H *Contract for completion of the treatment programme*

I, ... *(client's name)* promise myself to complete this 12-week programme (from date .... to ....) in order to stop or control my gambling *(choose one)* and stay gamble free or only do controlled gambling *(choose one)* during this time.

Daily reward for successfully completing goal ....
....
....
....
....

Weekly reward ....
....
....
....
....

Costs for not successfully completing goal ....
....
....
....
....

Client: ....   Date: ....

Therapist: ....   Date: ....

Witness: ....   Date: ....

APPENDIX 1 *Monitoring gambling sheet*

Date/time	Events preceding the gambling situation	Thoughts and feelings before the gambling situation	Gambling situation (a) where (b) with whom (c) available cash	Thoughts and feelings while in the gambling situation	Outcome (a) amount spent (b) amount won/lost	Thoughts and feelings after the gambling situation

APPENDIX J *Motivations towards gambling worksheet*

PART A: why did I start gambling?

....
....
....
....
....
....
....
....
....
....
....
....

PART B: what makes me continue gambling?

....
....
....
....
....
....
....
....
....
....
....
....

APPENDIX K *Identifying gambling triggers and establishing safeguards worksheet*

Trigger: ....

Possible safeguards: ....

....

....

....

....

....

Trigger: ....

Possible safeguards: ....

....

....

....

....

....

Trigger: ....

Possible safeguards: ....

....

....

....

....

....

Trigger: ....

....

Possible safeguards: ....

....

....

....

....

....

Trigger: ....

....

Possible safeguards: ....

....

....

....

....

....

Trigger: ....

....

Possible safeguards: ....

....

....

....

....

Date ....

Time	Activity

Things to consider when you are completing a daily schedule –
include a range of activities, include both 'fun' and 'chore' activities, fill in all the
gaps, include rewards for completing the schedule.

APPENDIX M *Alternative activities worksheet*

Tick the activities that you are willing to try. Think of things you used to enjoy in the past but do not do anymore. Think of things you always wanted to do. Do not wait until you feel like it. Make the decision to do something whether or not you feel like it. Action comes before motivation and not visa versa. You are more likely to do an activity if you plan ahead.

ACTIVITY	
Exercise	
Surfing	
Swimming	
Bike riding	
Walking/walking the dog	
Running	
Playing sports/join a sports club (soccer, tennis, skiing, rugby, bowling, netball)	
Self-defence classes or karate	
Yoga/Pilates/meditation/tai chi	
Join the gym	
Chores	
Gardening	
Complete housework	
Complete a task you've been meaning to do	
Clean your garage	
Redecorate your room/home	
Organize your files	
Engage in pleasant activities	
Rent a movie or go to the movies	
Go to a live show (concerts, comedy shows, plays, sports event)	
Read a magazine, book or newspaper	
Cook a meal/try a new recipe	
Take a relaxing bath	
Go for a drive	

Take a train ride	
Go shopping or window shopping	
Go to the zoo	
Write a letter to a friend or relative	
Phone a friend or relative	
Go to a garage sale	
Plan a day trip	
Go to the beach	
Go to a cafe/restaurant	
Do a relaxation exercise	
Play computer games	
Surf the net	
Take photographs	
Go fishing	
Go on a picnic	
Have a barbecue	
Learn to dance or dance	
Write a diary	
Work on your car/motorcycle/bicycle	
Organize a weekend away	
Volunteer for a charity	
Spend time with your children	
Play with your pets	
Learn to sing or sing	
Play pool	
Visit people (friends and relatives)	
Go to the park	
Write a story	
Learn a musical instrument	
Go to the museum	
Go to the art gallery	
Play a board game	
Go to the markets	
Go to the library	

Listen to music	
Go camping	
Write a poem/song	
Start a collection (e.g. coin, stamps)	
Do a puzzle or crossword	
Do model building	
Pamper yourself	
Get a facial	
Get a haircut/new hair style	
Get a massage	
Enrol in a short course	
Community college class or other further education (e.g. to learn a new skill or language, update computer skills, update work skills)	
Art and Craft	
Pottery making	
Painting/drawing/sketching	
Making presents for family and friends	
Knitting, crocheting, cross stitching, quilting, sewing, needlepoint	
Jewellery making	
Scrap-booking	
Candle making	
Woodworking	
Join a club/group (e.g. church, youth club)	

APPENDIX N *The START technique contract*

I .... (client's name) agree that if I have a slip or strong urges during the course of the programme, I will use the START technique.

S – Stop what I am doing immediately.

T – Think of the possible negative consequences of gambling (when a 'close call' is experienced) or continuing gambling (when a lapse is experienced) and all the positive consequences experienced so far by controlling gambling/ abstaining from gambling.

A – Act by removing myself from the situation.

R – Ring someone immediately to talk to (helplines, friends).

T – Try the techniques learnt in this section to control the urges.

Every time I am successful at completing this technique I will: ....

....

....

....

....

....

....

....

Every time I am unsuccessful at completing this technique I will: ....

....

....

....

....

....

....

....

Client's signature & date

Therapist's signature & date

Significant other's signature & date

⊙ *The START technique is based on Meichenbaum's (1977) self-instructional training.*

APPENDIX O *Irrational thoughts record A (adapted from Beck et al., 1979)*

Activating experience – events, thoughts, memories and feelings that trigger negative mood or behaviours (e.g. gambling)	Beliefs – interpretation or thoughts of the experience ⊙ What were you thinking? ⊙ What thinking error are you making?	Consequences – resulting actions and feelings

APPENDIX P *Irrational thoughts record B (adapted from Beck et al., 1979)*

Activating experience – events, thoughts, memories, and feelings that trigger negative mood or behaviours (e.g. gambling)	Beliefs – interpretation or thoughts of the experience ⦿ What were you thinking? ⦿ What thinking error are you making?	Consequences – resulting actions and feelings	Challenging irrational thoughts	Consequences – resulting actions and feelings after challenging irrational thoughts

Challenging: What thinking error am I making? What is the evidence against the thought? What is an alternative way of looking at this? Try behavioural experiments to test your assumptions. For gambling specific thinking errors, also remind yourself of the law of randomness (e.g. 'There are no links between independent chance events so in most forms of gambling all possible outcomes have an equal probability of occurring'), the level of chance and skill involved in each form of gambling (e.g. 'Gambling outcomes are more determined by luck than skill') and structural characteristics of the gambling machines and gambling environments that encourage gambling despite losses.

APPENDIX Q *Relaxation techniques*

Abdominal breathing exercise

Breathing directly reflects the level of tension you carry in your body. When under tension your breathing becomes more shallow and rapid and occurs high in the chest. When relaxed you breathe more fully, more deeply and from your abdomen. It is difficult to be tense and breathe from your abdomen at the same time.

⦿ Become aware of your breathing by placing one hand on your upper chest and one hand on your tummy. If your chest is rising and falling as you breathe, this means that you are using your chest to breathe.

⦿ Practise breathing through your tummy rather than the chest. When you are doing this, your tummy should rise and fall as you breathe out and in and your chest should only move slightly.

⦿ Inhale slowly and fully through your nose into the 'bottom' of your lungs. That is, send the air as low down as you can. Do slow full breathing NOT deep breathing as this can cause hyperventilation. That is, breathe a normal amount of air rather than forcing a large amount of air in and out of you.

⦿ Try to get a steady rhythm going, take the same depth of breath each time (e.g. don't gulp in a big breath or let breath out all at once). Make sure you exhale fully. As you exhale it is a good idea to allow your whole body to let go (it helps visualizing your arms and legs going loose and limp like a rag doll).

⦿ Do ten slow full abdominal breaths. *Pause* briefly after you inhale and before you exhale. If you feel lightheaded, stop for 30 seconds and try again. It is not uncommon for people to feel lightheaded initially especially if they are not used to breathing this way. At first you may feel you are not getting enough air in, but with regular practise this slower rate will soon feel comfortable.

⦿ When practising do at least 30 breaths (three × 10 inhales, pause, exhale).

Progressive muscle relaxation (Jacobsen, 1968)

Progressive muscle relaxation (PMR) is a muscular relaxation exercise which involves daily practise of tensing and relaxing each muscle group in your body until you become an expert in ridding your body of tension. The goal of PMR is to reduce muscle tension in your body. To be able to do this you will need to recognize and feel excessive tension by producing it deliberately and to recognize the release of the tension. This technique targets 16 muscle groups throughout your body. Initially it may take 30 minutes to complete, but with practice, you will be able to reduce this time.

Make sure you are wearing loose, comfortable clothing. Sit on a comfortable chair. Try to clear your mind of all worries or disturbing thoughts. If these worries or thoughts drift back into your mind while you are relaxing let them float gently out of your mind without reacting to them. Let your mind be clear and calm. When tensing each muscle group, squeeze the muscles immediately (i.e. not slowly or gradually). Also, try to keep all other muscles relaxed when you are tensing a particular muscle group. Try to practise this technique once per day. For each of the muscle groups in your body, tense the muscles for 7–10 seconds and then relax for 10–15 seconds. The steps include:

⊙ tense the muscles of your right hand and lower arm by making a tight fist and then relax;

⊙ tense the muscles of your right biceps by pushing your right elbow down against the arm of the chair and then relax;

⊙ tense the muscles of your left hand and lower arm by making a tight fist and then relax;

⊙ tense the muscles of your left biceps by pushing your left elbow down against the arm of your chair and then relax;

⊙ tense the muscles of your forehead by lifting your eyebrows as high as you can and then relax;

⊙ tense the muscles in your upper face, cheeks and nose by squinting your eyes and wrinkling your nose and then relax;

⊙ tense the muscles in your lower face and jaw by biting your teeth together and pulling back the corners of your mouth and then relax;

⊙ tense the muscles in your neck by pulling your chin downward toward your chest and at the same time prevent it from touching your chest and then relax;

⊙ tense the muscles in your chest, shoulders and upper back by taking a deep breath, holding it and, at the same time pulling the shoulder blades together and then relax;

⊙ tense the muscles in your abdomen by making your stomach as hard as possible and then relax;

⊙ tense the muscles in your right thigh by pushing down with the top muscles and up with the muscles underneath and then relax;

⊙ tense the muscles in your right calf by pointing your toes upward towards your head and then relax;

- tense the muscles in your right foot by pointing the toe, turning the foot inwards and, at the same time, curling your toes and then relax;

- tense the muscles in your left thigh by pushing down with the top muscles and up with the muscles underneath and then relax;

- tense the muscles in your left calf by pointing your toes upward towards your head and then relax;

- tense the muscles in your left foot by pointing the toe, turning the foot inwards and, at the same time, curling your toes and then relax.

Relaxation by imagery

Begin by focusing on your breathing. Spend a few minutes breathing slowly and smoothly.

- As you breathe, slowly count backwards from five, sinking deeper and deeper into a state of relaxation. Say to yourself, 'I feel deeply relaxed'.

- Next imagine a pleasant place that you can return to whenever you need relaxation or anxiety relief. For example, a warm, quiet beach. Close your eyes to help you concentrate.

- Experience the place with all your senses – sight, touch, smell, hearing and taste. Remain there for about 5 minutes or longer, depending on the time you need for anxiety or stress relief.

- Let your imagination run free.

- Slowly let the image you have chose fade from the centre of your attention as you focus again on your breathing. Maintain a relaxed feeling. When you feel ready, count slowly to five and open your eyes.

Autogenic training

Autogenic training teaches the body and mind to respond quickly and effectively to your verbal commands to relax and help return to a balanced state (Davis, Eshelman & McKay, 1982). This is important, as arousal appears to play a role in the maintenance of gambling problems. Johannes Schultz (1932) first introduced it. It incorporated the hypnotic work of the nineteenth century physiologist Oskar Vogt and Yoga techniques. The exercises are targeted at reversing the fight or flight states that occur when one is stressed (Davis et al., 1982).

First, make yourself comfortable and close your eyes. Then slowly and thoughtfully repeat the following sentences to yourself.

⦿ My feet feel warm, heavy and relaxed. My ankles feel warm, heavy and relaxed. My knees feel warm, heavy and relaxed. My hips feel warm, heavy and relaxed. My feet, ankles, knees and hips all feel warm, heavy and relaxed.

⦿ My stomach and the centre of my body feel warm, heavy and relaxed.

⦿ My hands feel warm, heavy and relaxed. My arms feel warm, heavy and relaxed. My shoulders feel warm, heavy and relaxed. My hands, arms and shoulders all feel warm, heavy and relaxed.

⦿ My neck feels warm heavy and relaxed. My jaw feels warm, heavy and relaxed. My face feels warm, heavy and relaxed. My forehead feels warm, heavy, and relaxed. My neck, jaw, face, and forehead all feel warm, heavy and relaxed.

⦿ My whole body feels warm, heavy and relaxed. My whole body feels warm, heavy and relaxed (repeat these last two sentences several times).

⦿ Remain relaxed for 2–5 minutes. When you feel ready, slowly open your eyes and remain relaxed for another 2–5 minutes before you start an activity. If you are in a warm environment use the words 'cool' and 'light' instead of 'warm' and 'heavy'.

APPENDIX R *Imaginal exposure worksheet*

Date and time	Item	Strength of urge before try (0–100)	Strength of urge after try (0–100)

Step 1: Identify the problem

....
....
....

Step 2: Define the problem (be specific and phrase in positive terms) ....

....
....
....
....
....
....

Step 3: Brainstorm all possible solutions ....

....
....
....
....
....
....
....
....
....
....
....
....
....
....

Step 4: Assess the advantages and disadvantages of each solution

Solution	Advantage	Disadvantage

Step 5: List the solutions in order of preference and choose a solution ....

....

....

....

Step 6: Evaluate the success of the solution ....

....

....

....

....

....

APPENDIX T *Goal-setting worksheet*

Step 1: Define the goal (in positive, specific and behavioural terms) ....

....

....

Step 2: Reward for completing the goal ....

....

....

Step 3: Plan to achieve the goal ....

....

....

....

....

....

....

....

....

....

....

....

....

....

....

....

....

Step 4: Date/time goal to be completed ....

....

....

Step 5: Time spent working on the goal (When, how long and how often will you work on the goal? Date the goal is to be reviewed) ....

....

....

Step 6: Possible obstacles preventing you from reaching that goal and ways to deal with the obstacles ....

....

....

....

....

....

....

....

Step 7: Assess the outcome of your goal (Did you achieve your goal? If not, why? What are the alternatives? Modify, re-plan and try again as soon as possible) ....

....

....

....

....

....

....

....

....

....

....

Remember: Do not catastrophize when things go wrong. Remind yourself of other successes in your life and that if you can achieve them you can do this too. Label an attempt as partial success rather than total failure. Remind yourself that you only learn from trial and error and that even an attempt at your goal is a sign of success.

Describe the negative emotion (What were you feeling?) ....

....

....

....

....

....

....

Describe the situation that led to the negative emotion ....

....

....

....

....

....

....

....

What were you thinking prior to experiencing the negative emotion? ....

....

....

....

....

....

....

....

....

What were you thinking after experiencing the negative emotion? ....

....

....

....

....

....

....

What did you do after experiencing the negative emotion? ....

....

....

....

....

....

....

In relation to your thinking and action after experiencing the negative emotion, what was helpful; what was not helpful? ....

....

....

....

....

....

....

What would you do differently next time? ....

....

....

....

....

APPENDIX V *Balanced lifestyle worksheet*

Indicate by ticking whether the following lifestyle areas are balanced or need changing.

Lifestyle areas	Balanced	Needs changing
Personal relationships and social support		
Emotional/mental well-being		
Intellectual activities		
Financial status		
Recreation/recreational activities		
Spiritual		
Physical health		
Work/school situation		

Areas that need balancing

Area 1: ....
....

Plan to improve this unbalanced area: ....
....
....
....
....
....
....
....
....
....
....
....
....
....

Area 2: ....

....

Plan to improve this unbalanced area: ....

....

....

....

....

....

....

Area 3: ....

....

Plan to improve this unbalanced area: ....

....

....

....

....

....

....

Area 4: ....

....

Plan to improve this unbalanced area: ....

....

....

....

....

....

....

Fill in the amount you receive on these per week

Net pay	£	....
Pension/benefit	£	....
Family payment	£	....
Additional payment	£	....
Board/rent received	£	....
Child support/maintenance	£	....
Other	£	....
TOTAL INCOME		£ ....

Fill in the amount you spend on these per week

Rent or mortgage	£	....
Rates	£	....
Insurance (car)	£	....
Insurance (medical)	£	....
Insurance (house)	£	....
Insurance (other)	£	....
Electricity	£	....
Gas	£	....
Telephone/mobile	£	....
Transport/petrol	£	....
Food and groceries	£	....
Clothes	£	....
Car registration	£	....
School fees	£	....
Child care	£	....
Cigarettes	£	....
Entertainment	£	....
Hire purchase/repayments	£	....
Any other regular payments	£	....
Current bills (e.g. credit card)	£	....
Other expenses	£	....
TOTAL EXPENSES		£ ....

TOTAL SAVINGS (TOTAL INCOME MINUS TOTAL EXPENSES)   £ ....

References

Adkins, B. J. (1988). Discharge planning with pathological gamblers: An ongoing process. *Journal of Gambling Behavior, 4*, 208–218.

Alberti, R. E., & Emmons, M. L. (1989). *Your perfect right: A guide to assertive living*. California: Impact Publishers.

Alberti, R. E., & Emmons, M. L. (2001). *Your perfect right: Assertiveness and equality in your life and relationships* (8th ed.). California: Impact Publishers.

Allcock, C. C. (1986). Pathological gambling. *Australian & New Zealand Journal of Psychiatry, 20*, 259–265.

Allsop, S., & Saunders, B. (1991). Reinforcing robust resolutions: Motivation in relapse prevention with severely dependent problem drinkers. In W. R. Miller, & S. Rollnick (Eds.), *Motivational interviewing: Preparing people to change addictive behavior*. New York: Guildford Press.

American Psychiatric Association (1994). *Diagnostic and statistical manual of mental disorders* (4th ed.). Washington, DC: American Psychiatric Press.

American Psychiatric Association (2000). *Diagnostic and statistical manual of mental disorders* (4th ed., Text Revision). Washington, DC: American Psychiatric Press.

Amor, P. J., & Echeburúa, E. (2002). Psychological treatment in pathological gambling: A case study. *Análisis y Modificacion de Conducta, 28*, 71–107.

Anderson, G., & Brown, R. I. F. (1984). Real and laboratory gambling, sensation-seeking and arousal: Towards a Pavlovian component in general theories of gambling and gambling addictions. *British Journal of Psychology, 75*, 401–411.

Anjoul, F., Milton, S. & Roberts, R. (2000). *An Empirical Investigation of DSM-IV Criteria for Pathological Gambling*. Paper presented at the International Conference on Gaming and Risk Taking, Las Vegas, USA.

Arribas, M. P., & Martinez, J. J. (1991). Tratamiento individual de jugadores patologicos: Descripcion de casos. *Analisis y Modificacion de Conducta, 17*, 255–269.

Bagby, R. M., Vachon, D. D., Bulmash, E., & Quilty, L. C. (2008). Personality disorders and pathological gambling: A review and re-examination of prevalence rates. *Journal of Personality Disorders, 22*, 191–207.

Bagby, R. M., Vachon, D. D., Bulmash, E. L., Toneatto, T., Quilty, L. C., & Costa, P. T. (2007). Pathological gambling and the five-factor model of personality. *Personality & Individual Differences, 43*, 873–880.

Bain, J. A. (1928). *Thought control in everyday life*. New York: Funk & Wagnalls.

Bannister, G. (1977). Cognitive and behavior therapy in a case of compulsive gambling. *Cognitive Therapy & Research, 1*, 223–227.

Barker, J. C., & Miller, M. (1968). Aversion therapy for compulsive gambling. *Journal of Nervous & Mental Disease, 146*, 285–302.

Barlow, D. H. (1988). *Anxiety and its disorders: The nature and treatment of anxiety and panic*. New York: Guilford Press.

Barlow, D. H., & Rapee, R. M. (1991). *Mastering stress: A lifestyle approach*. Dallas, Texas: American Health Publishing Co.

Baron, E., & Dickerson, M. (1999). Alcohol consumption and self-control of gambling behavior. *Journal of Gambling Studies, 15*, 3–15.

Baucom, D. H., & Epstein, N. (1990). *Cognitive-Behavioral Marital Therapy*. New York: Brunner/Mazel.

Beck, A. T. (1963). Thinking and depression: I. Idiosyncratic content and cognitive distortions. *Archives of General Psychiatry, 9*, 324–333.

Beck, A. T. (1976). *Cognitive therapy and the emotional disorders*. New York: International Universities Press.

Beck, A. T., Rush, A. J., Shaw, B. F., & Emery, G. (1979). *Cognitive therapy of depression*. New York: Guilford.

Beck, A. T., Wright, F. D., Newman, C. F., & Liese, B. S. (1993). *Cognitive therapy of substance abuse*. New York: Guilford Press.

Beck, J. S. (1995). *Cognitive therapy: Basics and beyond*. New York: Guilford Press.

Bell, A., & Rollnick, S. (1996). Motivational interviewing in practice: A structured approach. In F. Rotgers, D. S. Keller, & J. Morgenstern (Eds.), *Treating substance abuse: Theory and technique*. New York: Guildford Press.

Bergh, C., Eklund, T., Soedersten, P., & Nordin, C. (1997). Altered dopamine function in pathological gambling. *Psychological Medicine, 27*, 473–475.

Bergler, E. (1957). *The psychology of gambling*. New York: International Universities Press.

Black, D. W. (2004). An open-label trial of Bupropion in the treatment of pathologic gambling. *Journal of Clinical Psychopharmacology, 24*, 108–110.

Black, D. W., Monahan, P. O., Temkit, M., & Shaw, M. C. (2006). A family study of pathological gambling. *Psychiatry Research, 141*, 295–303.

Black, D. W., & Moyer, T. (1998). Clinical features and psychiatric comorbidity of subjects with pathological gambling behavior. *Psychiatric Services, 49*, 1434–1439.

Black, D. W., Moyer, T., & Schlosser, S. (2003). Quality of life and family history in pathological gambling, *Journal of Nervous & Mental Disease, 191*, 124–126.

Black, D. W., Shaw, M. C., & Allen, J. (2008). Extended release Carbamazepine in the treatment of pathological gambling: An open-label study. *Progress in Neuro-Psychopharmacology & Biological Psychiatry, 32*, 1191–1194.

Black, D. W., Shaw, M. C., Forbush, K. T., & Allen, J. (2007). An open-label trial of Escitalopram in the treatment of pathological gambling. *Clinical Neuropharmacology, 30*, 206–212.

Blanco, C., Ibáñez, A., Saiz-Ruiz, J., Blanco-Jerez, C., & Nunes, E. V. (2000). Epidemiology, pathophysiology and treatment of pathological gambling. *CNS Drugs, 13*, 397–407.

Blanco, C., Orensanz-Munoz, L., Blanco-Jerez, C., & Saiz-Ruiz, J. (1996). Pathological gambling and platelet MAO activity: A psychobiological study. *American Journal of Psychiatry, 153*, 119–121.

Blanco, C., Petkova, E., Ibáñez, A., & Saiz-Ruiz, J. (2002). A pilot placebo-controlled study of Fluvoxamine for pathological gambling. *Annals of Clinical Psychiatry, 14*, 9–15.

Blaszczynski, A. P., Drobny, J., & Steel, Z. (2005). Home-based imaginal desensitisation in pathological gambling: Short-term outcomes. *Behaviour Change, 22*, 13–21.

Blaszczynski, A. P., & Farrell, E. (1998). A case series of 44 completed gambling-related suicides. *Journal of Gambling Studies, 14*, 93–109.

Blaszczynski, A. P., Ladouceur, R., & Nower, L. (2007). Self-exclusion: A proposed gateway to treatment model. *International Gambling Studies, 7*, 59–71.

Blaszczynski, A. P., & Nower, L. (2002). A pathways model of problem and pathological gambling. *Addiction, 97*, 487–499.

Blaszczynski, A. P., & Silove, D. (1995). Cognitive and behavioral therapies for pathological gambling. *Journal of Gambling Studies, 11*, 195–220.

Blaszczynski, A. P., & Steel, Z. (1998). Personality disorders among pathological gamblers. *Journal of Gambling Studies, 14*, 51–71.

Blaszczynski, A. P., Winters, S. W., & McConaghy, N. (1986). Plasma endorphin levels in pathological gambling. *Journal of Gambling Behavior, 2*, 3–14.

Bolen, D. W., & Boyd, W. H. (1968). Gambling and the gambler: A review and preliminary findings. *Archives of General Psychiatry, 18*, 617–630.

Boughton, R., & Falenchuk, O. (2007). Vulnerability and comorbidity factors of female problem gambling. *Journal of Gambling Studies, 23*, 323–334.

Brewer, J. A., Grant, J. E., & Potenza, M. N. (2008). The treatment of pathologic gambling. *Addictive Disorders & their Treatment, 7*, 1–13.

Brown, R. I. F. (1986). Arousal and sensation-seeking components in the general explanation of gambling and gambling addictions. *International Journal of the Addictions, 21*, 1001–1016.

Bujold, A., Ladouceur, R., Sylvain, C., & Boisvert, J. M. (1994). Treatment of pathological gambling: An experimental study. *Journal of Behavior Therapy & Experimental Psychiatry, 25*, 275–282.

Burns, D. D. (1989). *The feeling good handbook: Using the new mood therapy in everyday life.* New York: William Morrow & Co.

Callahan, J. (1996). Documentation of client dangerousness in a managed care environment. *Health Social Work, 21*, 202–207.

Campbell, F., & Lester, D. (1999). The impact of gambling opportunities on compulsive gambling. *Journal of Social Psychology, 139*, 126–127.

Carlton, P. L., & Manowitz, P. (1994). Factors determining the severity of pathological gambling in males. *Journal of Gambling Studies, 10*, 147–157.

Cavedini, P., Riboldi, G., Keller, R., D'Annucci, A., & Bellodi, L. (2002). Frontal lobe dysfunction in pathological gambling patients. *Biological Psychiatry, 51*, 334–341.

Clarke, D. (2004). Impulsiveness, locus of control, motivation and problem gambling. *Journal of Gambling Studies, 20*, 319–345.

Clarke, D. (2006). Impulsivity as a mediator in the relationship between depression and problem gambling. *Personality & Individual Differences, 40*, 5–15.

Collins, J., Skinner, W., & Toneatto, T. (2005). *Beyond assessment: The impact of comorbidity of pathological gambling, psychiatric disorders and substance use disorders on treatment course and outcome.* http://www.gamblingresearch.org/download.sz/025%20Final%20 Report%20-%20posted%20version%2030May05.pdf?docid=6649.

Coman, G. J., Burrows, G. D., & Evans, B. J. (1997). Stress and anxiety as factors in the onset of problem gambling: Implications for treatment. *Stress Medicine, 13*, 235–244.

Comings, D. E., Rosenthal, R. J., Lesieur, H. R., Rugle, L. J., Muhleman, D., Chiu, C., Dietz, G., & Gade, R. (1996). A study of the dopamine D2 receptor gene in pathological gambling. *Pharmacogenetics, 6*, 223–234.

Cotler, S. B. (1971). The use of different behavioural techniques in treating a case of compulsive gambling. *Behavior Therapy, 2*, 579–584.

Coventry, K. R., & Brown, R. I. F. (1993). Sensation-seeking, gambling and gambling addictions. *Addiction, 88*, 541–554.

Coventry, K. R., & Constable, B. (1999). Physiological arousal and sensation-seeking in female fruit machine gamblers. *Addiction, 94*, 425–430.

Crisp, B. R., Thomas, S. A., Jackson, A. C., Thomason, N., Smith, S., Borrell, J., Ho, W., & Holt, T. A. (2000). Sex differences in the treatment needs and outcomes of problem gamblers. *Research on Social Work Practice, 10*, 229–242.

Custer, R. L. (1982). An overview of compulsive gambling. In P. A. Carone, S. F. Yoles, S. N. Kiefer, & L. Krinsky (Eds.), *Addictive disorders update: Alcoholism, drug abuse, gambling.* New York: Human Sciences Press.

da Silva Lobo, D. S., Vallada, H. P., Knight, J., Martins, S. S., Tavares, H., Gentil, V., & Kennedy, J. L. (2007). Dopamine genes and pathological gambling in discordant sib-pairs. *Journal of Gambling Studies, 23*, 421–433.

Dannon, P. N., Lowengrub, K., Gonopolski, Y., Musin, E., & Kotler, M. (2005a). Topiramate versus Fluvoxamine in the treatment of pathological gambling: A randomized, blind-rater comparison study. *Clinical Neuropharmacology, 28*, 6–10.

Dannon, P. N., Lowengrub, K., Musin, E., Gonopolski, Y., & Kotler, M. (2005b). Sustained-release Bupropion versus Naltrexone in the treatment of pathological gambling: A preliminary blind-rater study. *Journal of Clinical Psychopharmacology, 25*, 593–596.

Dannon, P. N., Lowengrub, K., Shalgi, B., Sasson, M., Tuson, L., Saphir, Y., & Moshe, K. (2006). Dual psychiatric diagnosis and substance abuse in pathological gamblers: A preliminary gender comparison study. *Journal of Addictive Diseases, 25*, 49–54.

Davis, M., Eshelman, E. R., & McKay, M. (1982). *The relaxation & stress reduction workbook* (2nd ed.). Oakland, CA: New Harbinger Publications.

DeCaria, C. M., Hollander, E., Nora, R., Stein, D., Simeon, D., & Cohen, I. (1997). *Gambling: biological/genetic, treatment, government, and gambling concerns: neurobiology of pathological gambling.* Presented at the American Psychiatric Association Annual Meeting, San Diego, CA.

Dell'Osso, B., Allen, A., & Hollander, E. (2005). Comorbidity issues in the pharmacological treatment of pathological gambling: A critical review. *Clinical Practice & Epidemiology in Mental Health, 10*, 1–21.

Dickerson, M. G. (1984). *Compulsive Gamblers.* London: Longman.

Dickerson, M. G. (1993). Internal and external determinants of persistent gambling: Problems in generalising from one form of gambling to another. *Journal of Gambling Studies, 9*, 225–245.

Dickerson, M. G., & Weeks, D. (1979). Controlled gambling as a therapeutic technique for compulsive gamblers. *Journal of Behavior Therapy & Experimental Psychiatry, 10*, 139–141.

Dickson, L., Derevensky, J. L., & Gupta, R. (2008). Youth gambling problems: Examining risk and protective factors. *International Gambling Studies, 8*, 25–47.

Dickson-Gillespie, L., Rugle, L. J., Rosenthal, R. J., & Fong, T. (2008). Preventing the incidence and harm of gambling problems. *Journal of Primary Prevention, 29*, 37–55.

Diener, E., Emmons, R. A., Larsen, R. J., & Griffin, S. (1985). The satisfaction with life scale. *Journal of Personality Assessment, 49*, 71–75.

Doiron, J. P., & Nicki, R. M. (2007). Prevention of pathological gambling: A randomized controlled trial. *Cognitive Behaviour Therapy, 36*, 74–84.

Donald W., B., Stephan, A., Coryell, W. H., Argo, T., Forbush, K. T., Shaw, M. C., Perry, P., & Allen, J. (2007). Bupropion in the treatment of pathological gambling: A randomized, double-blind, placebo-controlled, flexible-dose study. *Journal of Clinical Psychopharmacology, 27*, 143–150.

Dowling, N., Smith, D., & Thomas, T. (2007). A comparison of individual and group cognitive-behavioural treatment for female pathological gambling. *Behaviour Research & Therapy, 45,* 2192–2202.

D'Zurilla, T. J., & Goldfried, M. R. (1971). Problem solving and behavior modification, *Journal of Abnormal Psychology, 78,* 107–126.

D'Zurilla, T. J., & Nezu, A. (1982). Social problem solving in adults. In P. C. Kendall (Ed.), *Advances in cognitive-behavioral research and therapy* (Vol. 1). New York: Academic Press.

Echeburúa, E. (2005). Challenges in the treatment for pathological gambling. *Adicciones, 17,* 11–16.

Echeburúa, E., Báez, C., & Fernández-Montalvo, J. (1996). Comparative effectiveness of three therapeutic modalities in the psychological treatment of pathological gambling: Long-term outcome. *Behavioural & Cognitive Psychotherapy, 24,* 51–72.

Echeburúa, E., & Fernández-Montalvo, J. (2002). Psychological treatment of slot machine pathological gambling: A case study. *Clinical Case Studies, 1,* 240–253.

Echeburúa, E., Fernández-Montalvo, J., & Báez, C. (1999). Relapse prevention in the treatment of pathological gambling: Comparative effectiveness of therapeutic modalities. *Análisis y Modificación De Conducta, 25,* 375–403.

Echeburúa, E., Fernández-Montalvo, J., & Báez, C. (2000). Relapse prevention in the treatment of slot-machine pathological gambling: Long-term outcome. *Behavior Therapy, 31,* 351–364.

Echeburúa, E., Fernández-Montalvo, J., & Báez, C. (2001). Predictors of therapeutic failure in slot-machine pathological gamblers following behavioural treatment. *Behavioural & Cognitive Psychotherapy, 29,* 379–383.

Eisen, S. A., Lin, N., Lyons, M. J., Scherrer, J., Griffith, K., True, W. R., Goldberg, J., & Tsuang, M. T. (1998). Familial influences on gambling behavior: An analysis of 3,359 twin pairs. *Addiction, 93,* 1375–1384.

Eisen, S. A., Slutske, W. S., Lyons M. J., Lassman, J., Xian, H., Toomey, R., Chantarujikapong, S., & Tsuang, M. T. (2001). The genetics of pathological gambling. *Seminars in Clinical Neuropsychiatry, 6,* 195–204.

El-Guebaly, N., Patten, S. B., Currie, S. R., Williams, J. V. A., Beck, C. A., Maxwell, C. J., & Wang, J. L. (2006). Epidemiological associations between gambling behavior, substance use and mood and anxiety disorders. *Journal of Gambling Studies, 22,* 275–287.

Ellis, A., & Harper, R. A. (1961). *A guide to rational living.* Hollywood, CA: Wilshire Books.

Epstein, N., & Baucom, D. H. (1989). Cognitive-behavioral marital therapy. In A. Freeman, K. M. Simon, L. Beutler, & H. Arkovitz (Eds.), *Comprehensive handbook of cognitive therapy.* New York: Plenum.

Epstein, N., & Schlesinger, S. E. (1991). Marital and family problems. In W. Dryden, & R. Rentoul. *Adult clinical problems: A cognitive-behavioural approach.* New York: Routledge.

Fanning, P., & McKay, M. (2000). *Family guide to emotional wellness: Proven self help techniques and exercises for dealing with common problems and building crucial life skills.* Oakland, CA: New Harbinger Publishings Inc.

Fernández-Montalvo, J., & Echeburúa, E. (2004). Pathological gambling and personality disorders: An exploratory study with the IPDE. *Journal of Personality Disorders, 18,* 500–505.

Fong, T., Kalechstein, A. D., Bernhard, B., Rosenthal, R. J., & Rugle, L. J. (2008). A double-blind, placebo-controlled trial of Olanzapine for the treatment of video poker pathological gamblers. *Pharmacology, Biochemistry & Behavior, 89,* 298–303.

Freeman, A., Pretzer, J., Fleming, B., & Simon, K. M. (1990). *Clinical applications of cognitive therapy*. New York: Plenum Press.

Friedland, N., Keinan, G., & Regev, Y. (1992). Controlling the uncontrollable: Effects of stress on illusory perceptions of controllability. *Journal of Personality & Social Psychology*, *63*, 923–931.

Frisch, M. B. (1994). *Quality of life inventory: manual and treatment guide*. Minneapolis, MN: Pearson Assessments.

Gaboury, A., & Ladouceur, R. (1989). Erroneous perceptions and gambling. *Journal of Social Behavior & Personality*, *4*, 411–420.

Gaboury, A., & Ladouceur, R. (1990). Correction of irrational thinking during American roulette. *Canadian Journal of Behavioural Science*, *22*, 417–423.

Galdston, I. (1960). The gambler and his love. *American Journal of Psychiatry*, *117*, 553–555.

Goldfried, M. R., & Davison, G. C. (1994). *Clinical behavior therapy*. New York: John Wiley & Sons.

Goldstein, L., Manowitz, P., Nora, R., Swartzburg, M., & Carlton, P. L. (1985). Differential EEG activation and pathological gambling. *Biological Psychiatry*, *20*, 1232–1234.

Gooding, P., & Tarrier, N. (2009). A systematic review and meta-analysis of cognitive-behavioural interventions to reduce problem gambling: Hedging our bets? *Behaviour Research & Therapy*, *47*, 592–607.

Goorney, A. B. (1968). Treatment of a compulsive horse race gambler by aversion therapy. *British Journal of Psychiatry*, *114*, 329–333.

Gottman, J. (1976). *A couples guide to communication*. Champaign, IL: Research Press.

Grant, J. E., & Kim, S. W. (2001). Demographic and clinical features of 131 adult pathological gamblers. *Journal of Clinical Psychiatry*, *62*, 957–962.

Grant, J. E., Kim, S. W., & Kuskowski, M. (2004). Retrospective review of treatment retention in pathological gambling. *Comprehensive Psychiatry*, *45*, 83–87.

Grant, J. E., Kim, S. W., & Potenza, M. N. (2008). Psychopharmacological management of pathological gambling. In M. Zangeneh, A. Blaszczynski, & N. E. Turner (Eds.), *In the pursuit of winning: Problem gambling theory, research and treatment* (pp. 199–210). New York: Springer Science and Business Media.

Grant, J. E., Kim, S. W., Potenza, M. N., Blanco, C., Ibáñez, A., Stevens, L., Hektner, J. M., & Zaninelli, R. (2003). Paroxetine treatment of pathological gambling: A multi-centre randomized controlled trial. *International Clinical Psychopharmacology*, *18*, 243–249.

Grant J. E., & Potenza, M. N. (2006). Escitalopram treatment of pathological gambling with co-occurring anxiety: an open-label pilot study with double-blind discontinuation. *International Clinical Psychopharmacology*, *21*, 203–209.

Grant, J. E., & Potenza, M. N. (2007). Treatments for pathological gambling and other impulse control disorders. In P. E. Nathan, & J. M. Gorman (Eds.), *A guide to treatments that work* (3rd ed., pp. 561–577). New York: Oxford University Press.

Grant, J. E., Potenza, M. N., Hollander, E., Cunningham-Williams, R., Nurminen, T., Smits, G., & Kallio, A. (2006). Multicenter investigation of the opioid antagonist Nalmefene in the treatment of pathological gambling. *American Journal of Psychiatry*, *163*, 303–312.

Grant, J. E., Schreiber, L., Odlaug, B. L., & Kim, S. W. (2010). Pathologic gambling and bankruptcy. *Comprehensive Psychiatry*, *51*, 115–120.

Greenberg, H. R. (1980). Psychology of gambling. In H. Kaplan, A. Freedman, & B. Sadock (Eds.), *Comprehensive textbook of Psychiatry* (pp. 3274–3283). Baltimore, MA: Williams and Wilkins.

Greenson, R. (1948). On gambling. *Yearbook of Psychoanalysis, 4,* 110–123.

Griffiths, M. D. (1991). Psychobiology of the near miss in fruit machine gambling. *The Journal of Psychology, 125,* 347–357.

Griffiths, M. D. (1993). Fruit machine gambling: The importance of structural characteristics. *Journal of Gambling Studies, 9,* 101–120.

Hanna, S. B. (1995). *Person to person: Positive relationships don't just happen.* Englewood Cliffs, NJ: Prentice-Hall.

Hardoon, K. K., Gupta, R., & Derevensky, J. L. (2004). Psychosocial variables associated with adolescent gambling. *Psychology of Addictive Behaviors, 18,* 170–179.

Harris, H. (1964). Gambling addiction in an adolescent male. *Psychoanalytic Quarterly, 34,* 513–525.

Hawton, K., Salkovskis, P. M., Kirk, J., & Clark, D. M. (1989). *Cognitive behaviour therapy for psychiatric problems.* Oxford: Oxford University Press.

Henry, S. L. (1996). Pathological gambling: Etiologic considerations and treatment efficacy of eye movement desensitization/reprocessing. *Journal of Gambling Studies, 12,* 395–405.

Hodgins, D. C., Currie, S. R., & El-Guebaly, N. (2001). Motivational enhancement and self-help treatments for problem gambling. *Journal of Consulting & Clinical Psychology, 69,* 50–57.

Hodgins, D. C., Currie, S. R., El-Guebaly, N., & Peden, N. (2004). Brief motivational treatment for problem gambling: A 24-month follow-up. *Psychology of Addictive Behaviors, 18,* 293–296.

Hodgins, D. C., & El-Guebaly, N. (2000). Natural and treatment-assisted recovery from gambling problems: A comparison of resolved and active gamblers. *Addiction, 95,* 777–789.

Hodgins, D. C., & El-Guebaly, N. (2004). Retrospective and prospective reports of precipitants to relapse in pathological gambling. *Journal of Consulting & Clinical Psychology, 72,* 72–80.

Hodgins, D. C., Makarchuk, K., El-Guebaly, N., & Peden, N. (2002). Why problem gamblers quit gambling: A comparison of methods and samples. *Addiction Research & Theory, 10,* 203–218.

Hodgins, D. C., Mansley, C., & Thygesen, K. (2006). Risk factors for suicide ideation and attempts among pathological gamblers. *The American Journal on Addictions, 15,* 303–310.

Hodgins, D. C., Shead, N. W., & Makarchuk, K. (2007). Relationship satisfaction and psychological distress among concerned significant others of pathological gamblers. *Journal of Nervous & Mental Disease, 195,* 65–71.

Hollander, E., Buchalter, A. J., & DeCaria, C. M. (2000). Pathological gambling. *Psychiatric Clinics of North America, 23,* 629–642.

Hollander, E., DeCaria, C. M., Finkell, J. N., Begaz, T., Wong, C. M., & Cartwright, C. (2000). A randomized double-blind Fluvoxamine placebo crossover trial in pathologic gambling. *Biological Psychiatry, 47,* 813–817.

Hollander, E., Pallanti, S., Allen, A., Sood, E., & Rossi, N. B. (2005). Does sustained-release lithium reduce impulsive gambling and affective instability versus placebo in pathological gamblers with bipolar spectrum disorders? *American Journal of Psychiatry, 162,* 137–145.

Hudak, C. J., Varghese, R., & Politzer, R. M. (1989). Family, marital, and occupational satisfaction for recovering pathological gamblers. *Journal of Gambling Behavior, 5,* 201–210.

Iancu, I., Lowengrub, K., Dembinsky, Y., Kotler, M., & Dannon, P. N. (2008). Pathological gambling: An update on neuropathophysiology and pharmacotherapy. *CNS Drugs, 22,* 123–138.

Ibáñez, A., Perez de Castro, I., Fernandez-Piqueras, J., Blanco, C., & Saiz-Ruiz, J. (2000). Pathological gambling and DNA polymorphic markers at MAO-A and MAO-B genes. *Molecular Psychiatry, 5,* 105–109.

Ingle, P. J., Marotta, J., McMillan, G., & Wisdom, J. P. (2008). Significant others and gambling treatment outcomes. *Journal of Gambling Studies, 24,* 381–392.

Jackson, P. R., & Oei, T. P. S. (1978). Social skills training and cognitive restructuring with alcoholics. *Drug & Alcohol Dependence, 3,* 369–374.

Jacques, C., Ladouceur, R., & Ferland, F. (2000). Impact of availability on gambling. A longitudinal study. *Canadian Journal of Psychiatry, 45,* 810–815.

Jacobs, D. G., Brewer, M., & Klein-Benheim, M. (1999). Suicide assessment: An overview and recommended protocol. In D. G. Douglas (Ed.), *The Harvard Medical School Guide to suicide assessment and intervention.* San Francisco, CA: Jossey-Bass Publishers.

Jacobsen, E. (1968). *Progressive relaxation.* Chicago, IL: University of Chicago Press.

Jacobson, N. S., & Margolin, G. (1979). *Marital therapy: Strategies based on social learning and behavior exchange principles.* New York: Brunner/Mazel.

Jakubowski, P., & Lange, A. J. (1978). *The assertive option: Your rights and responsibilities.* Champaign, IL: Research Press Co.

Johnson, E. H. (1990). *The deadly emotions: The role of anger, hostility, and aggression in health and emotional well-being.* New York: Praeger.

Jiménez-Murcia, S., Álvarez-Moya, E. M., Granero, R., Aymamí, M. N., Gómez-Peña, M., Jaurrieta, N., Sans, B., Rodriguez-Marti, J., & Vallejo, J. (2007). Cognitive-behavioral group treatment for pathological gambling: Analysis of effectiveness and predictors of therapy outcome. *Psychotherapy Research, 17,* 544–552.

Kadden, R., Carroll, K., Donovan, D. M., Cooney, N. Monti, P., Abrams, D., Litt, M., & Hester, R. (1995). *Cognitive behavioral coping skills therapy manual: A clinical research guide for therapists treating individuals with alcohol abuse and dependence.* Rockville, MA: National Institute on Alcohol Abuse and Alcoholism: Project Match.

Kalechstein, A. D., Fong, T., Rosenthal, R. J., Davis, A., Vanyo, H., & Newton, T. F. (2007). Pathological gamblers demonstrate frontal lobe impairment consistent with that of methamphetamine-dependent individuals. *Journal of Neuropsychiatry & Clinical Neurosciences, 19,* 298–303.

Kalischuk, R. G., Nowatzki, N., Cardwell, K., Klein, K., & Solowoniuk, J. (2006). Problem gambling and its impact on families: A literature review. *International Gambling Studies, 6,* 31–60.

Kanfer, F. H. (1977). Self-regulation and self-control. In H. Zeier (Ed.), *The psychology of the 20th century* (Vol. 4). Zurich: Kindler Verlag.

Kausch, O., Rugle, L. J., & Rowland, D. Y. (2006). Lifetime histories of trauma among pathological gamblers. *The American Journal on Addictions, 15,* 35–43.

Kazantzis, N., & Daniel, J. (2009). Homework assignments in cognitive behavior therapy. In G. Simos (Ed.), *Cognitive behaviour therapy: A guide for the practising clinician, vol 2.* (pp. 165–186). New York: Routledge.

Kazantzis, N., Deane, F. P., Ronan, K. R., & L'Abate, L. (2005). *Using homework assignments in cognitive behavior therapy.* New York: Routledge.

Kim, S. W., & Grant, J. E. (2001). An open Naltrexone treatment study in pathological gambling disorder. *International Clinical Psychopharmacology*, *16*, 285–289.

Kim, S. W., Grant, J. E., Adson, D. E., & Shin, Y. C. (2001). Double-blind Naltrexone and placebo comparison study in the treatment of pathological gambling. *Biological Psychiatry*, *49*, 914–921.

Kim, S. W., Grant, J. E., Adson, D. E., Shin, Y. C., & Zaninelli, R. (2002). A double-blind placebo-controlled study of the efficacy and safety of Paroxetine in the treatment of pathological gambling. *Journal of Clinical Psychiatry*, *63*, 501–507.

Kim, S. W., Grant, J. E., Eckert, E. D., Faris, P. L., & Hartman, B. K. (2006). Pathological gambling and mood disorders: Clinical associations and treatment implications. *Journal of Affective Disorders*, *92*, 109–116.

Kirk, J. (1989). Cognitive-behavioural assessment. In K. Hawton, P. M. Salkovskis, J. Kirk, & D. Clark. (1989). *Cognitive behaviour therapy for psychiatric problems*. Oxford: Oxford University Press.

Korman, L. M., Collins, J., Dutton, D., Dhayananthan, B., Littman-Sharp, N., & Skinner, W. (2008). Problem gambling and intimate partner violence. *Journal of Gambling Studies*, *24*, 13–23.

Korn, D. A., & Shaffer, H. J. (2004). *Massachusetts Department of Public Health's Practice Guidelines for Treating Gambling-Related Problems. An Evidence-Based Treatment Guide for Clinicians*. Toronto: Massachusetts Council on Compulsive Gambling.

Kraft, T. (1970). A short note on forty patients treated by systematic desensitization. *Behavior Research & Therapy*, *8*, 219–220.

Kyngdon, A., & Dickerson, M. (1999). An experimental study of the effect of prior alcohol consumption on a simulated gambling activity. *Addiction*, *94*, 697–707.

Ladouceur, R. (1991). Prevalence estimates of pathological gamblers in Quebec, Canada. *Canadian Journal of Psychiatry*, *36*, 732–734.

Ladouceur, R. (2001). *Diagnostic and treatment of pathological gamblers: A cognitive approach*. Workshop presentation at National Association for Gambling Studies Conference. Sydney, Australia.

Ladouceur, R., Boisvert, J. M., Pepin, M., Loranger, M., & Sylvain, C (1994). Social costs of pathological gambling. *Journal of Gambling Studies*, *10*, 399–409.

Ladouceur, R., Jacques, C., Ferland, F., & Giroux, I. (1999). Prevalence of problem gambling: a replication study 7 years later. *Canadian Journal of Psychiatry*, *44*, 802–804.

Ladouceur, R., Jacques, C., Giroux, I., Ferland, F., & Leblond, J. (2000). Analysis of a casino's self-exclusion program. *Journal of Gambling Studies*, *16*, 453–460.

Ladouceur, R., Sévigny, S., Blaszczynski, A. P., O'Connor, K., & Lavoie, M. E. (2003). Video lottery: Winning expectancies and arousal. *Addiction*, *98*, 733–738.

Ladouceur, R., & Sylvain, C. (1999). Treatment of pathological gambling: A controlled study. *Anuario de Psicologica*, *30*, 127–135.

Ladouceur, R., Sylvain, C., & Boutin, C. (2000). Pathological gambling. In M. Hersen, & M. Biaggio (Eds.), *Effective Brief Therapies: A Clinician's Guide* (pp. 303–318). New York: Academic Press.

Ladouceur, R., Sylvain, C., Boutin, C., Lachance, S., Doucet, C., & Leblond, J. (2003). Group therapy for pathological gamblers: A cognitive approach. *Behaviour Research & Therapy*, *41*, 587–596.

Ladouceur, R., Sylvain, C., Boutin, C., Lachance, S., Doucet, C., Leblond, J., & Jacques, C. (2001). Cognitive treatment of pathological gambling. *Journal of Nervous & Mental Disease*, *189*, 774–780.

Ladouceur, R., Sylvain, C., Duval, C., & Gaboury, A. (1989). Correction of irrational verbalizations among video poker players. *International Journal of Psychology, 24*, 43–56.

Ladouceur, R., Sylvain, C., & Gosselin, P. (2007). Self-exclusion program: A longitudinal evaluation study. *Journal of Gambling Studies, 23*, 85–94.

Ladouceur, R., Sylvain, C., Letarte, H., Giroux, I., & Jacques, C. (1998). Cognitive treatment of pathological gamblers. *Behaviour Research & Therapy, 36*, 1111–1119.

Langenbucher, J., Bavly, L., Labouvie, E., Sanjuan, P. M., & Martin, C. S. (2001). Clinical features of pathological gambling in an addictions treatment cohort. *Psychology of Addictive Behavior, 15*, 77–79.

Lange, A. J., & Jakubowski, P (1976). *Responsible assertive behavior: Cognitive/behavioral procedures for trainers.* Champaign, IL: Research Press Co.

Langer, E. (1975). The illusion of control. *Journal of Personality & Social Psychology, 32*, 311–328.

Leary, K., & Dickerson, M. (1985). Levels of arousal in high- and low-frequency gamblers. *Behaviour Research & Therapy, 23*, 635–640.

Leblond, J., Ladouceur, R., & Blaszczynski, A. P. (2003). Which pathological gamblers will complete treatment? *British Journal of Clinical Psychology, 42*, 205–209.

Ledgerwood, D. M., & Petry, N. M. (2006). Psychological experience of gambling and subtypes of pathological gamblers. *Psychiatry Research, 144*, 17–27.

Ledgerwood, D. M., Steinberg, M. A., Wu, R., & Potenza, M. N. (2005). Self-reported gambling-related suicidality among gambling helpline callers. *Psychology of Addictive Behaviors, 19*, 175–183.

Lesieur, H. R., & Blume, S. B. (1987). The South Oaks Gambling Screen (SOGS): A new instrument for the identification of pathological gamblers. *American Journal of Psychiatry, 144*, 1184–1188.

Lesieur, H. R., & Blume, S. B. (1991). Evaluation of patients treated for pathological gambling in a combined alcohol, substance abuse and pathological gambling treatment unit using the Addiction Severity Index. *British Journal of Addiction, 86*, 1017–1028.

Lindner, R. (1950). The psychodynamics of gambling. *Annals of American Academy of Political & Social Sciences, 269*, 93–107.

Loo, J. M. Y., Raylu, N., & Oei, T. P. S. (2008). Gambling among the Chinese: A comprehensive review. *Clinical Psychology Review, 28*, 1152–1166.

Lorenz, V. C., & Yaffee, R. A. (1986). Pathological gambling: Psychosomatic, emotional, and marital difficulties as reported by the gambler. *Journal of Gambling Behavior, 2*, 40–49.

Lorenz, V. C., & Yaffee, R. A. (1988). Pathological gambling: Psychosomatic, emotional and marital difficulties as reported by the spouse. *Journal of Gambling Behavior, 4*, 13–26.

Lorenz, V. C., & Yaffee, R. A. (1989). Pathological gamblers and their spouses: Problems in interaction. *Journal of Gambling Behavior, 5*, 113–126.

Lorenz, V. C., & Shuttleworth, D. E. (1983). The impact of pathological gambling on the spouse of the gambler. *Journal of Community Psychology, 11*, 67–76.

Lovibond, S. H., & Lovibond, P. F. (1995). The structure of negative emotional states: Comparison of the Depression Anxiety Stress Scales (DASS) with the Beck Depression and Anxiety Inventories. *Behaviour, Research & Therapy, 33*, 335–343.

Loxton, N. J., Nguyen, D., Casey, L., & Dawe, S. (2008). Reward drive, rash impulsivity and punishment sensitivity in problem gamblers. *Personality & Individual Differences, 45*, 167–173.

Maccallum, F., & Blaszczynski, A. P. (2002). Pathological gambling and comorbid substance use. *Australian & New Zealand Journal of Psychiatry, 36,* 411–415.

Maccallum, F., & Blaszczynski, A. P. (2003). Pathological gambling and suicidality: An analysis of severity and lethality. *Suicide & Life-Threatening Behavior, 33,* 88–98.

Maccallum, F., Blaszczynski, A. P., Ladouceur, R., & Nower, L. (2007). Functional and dysfunctional impulsivity in pathological gambling. *Personality & Individual Differences, 43,* 1829–1838.

Makarchuk, K., Hodgins, D. C., & Peden, N. (2002). Development of a brief intervention for concerned significant others of problem gamblers. *Addictive Disorders & their Treatment, 1,* 126–134.

Manowitz, P., Amorosa, L. F., Goldstein, H. S., & Carlton, P. L. (1993). Uric acid level increases in humans engaged in gambling: A preliminary report. *Biological Psychology, 36,* 223–229.

Marazziti, D., Dell'Osso, M. C., Conversano, C., Consoli, G., Vivarelli, L., Mungai, F., Nasso, E. D., & Golia, F. (2008a). Executive function abnormalities in pathological gamblers. *Clinical Practice & Epidemiology in Mental Health, 4,* 7.

Marazziti, D., Golia, F., Picchetti, M., Pioli, E., Mannari, P., Lenzi, F., Conversano, C., Carmassi, C., Dell'Osso, M. C., Consoli, G., Baroni, S., Giannaccini, G., Zanda, G., & Dell'Osso, L. (2008b). Decreased density of the platelet serotonin transporter in pathological gamblers. *Neuropsychobiology, 57,* 38–43.

Marlatt, G. A. (1988). Matching clients to treatment: Treatment models and stages of change. In D. M. Donovan, & G. A Marlatt (Eds.), *Assessment of addictive behaviors.* New York: The Guilford Press.

Marlatt, G. A., & Donovan, D. M. (2005). *Relapse prevention: Maintenance strategies in the treatment of addictive behaviours* (2nd ed.). New York: The Guilford Press.

Marlatt, G. A., & Gordon, J. R. (1985). *Relapse prevention: Maintenance strategies in the treatment of addictive behaviors.* New York: Guilford Press.

Masters, J. C., Burish, T. G., Hollon, S. D., & Rimm, D. C. (1987). *Behavior therapy: Techniques and empirical findings* (3rd ed.). Orlando, FL: Harcourt Brace Jovanovich.

McConaghy, N., Armstrong, M. S., Blaszczynski, A. P., & Allcock, C. C. (1983). Controlled comparison of aversive therapy and imaginal desensitization in compulsive gambling. *British Journal of Psychiatry, 142,* 366–372.

McConaghy, N., Armstrong, M. S., Blaszczynski, A. P., & Allcock, C. C. (1988). Behavior completion versus stimulus control in compulsive gambling: Implications for behavioural assessment. *Behavior Modification, 12,* 371–384.

McConaghy, N., Blaszczynski, A. P., & Frankova, A. (1991). Comparison of imaginal desensitisation with other behavioural treatments of pathological gambling: A two- to nine-year follow-up. *British Journal of Psychiatry, 159,* 390–393.

Meichenbaum, D. (1977). *Cognitive behavior modification: An integrative approach.* New York: Plenum Press.

Meyers, R. J., Smith, J. E., & Miller, E. J. (1998). Working through the concerned significant other. In W. R. Miller, & N. Heather (Eds.), *Treating addictive behaviors* (2nd ed., pp. 149–161). New York: Plenum Press.

Miller, W. R. (1989). Matching individuals with interventions. In R. K. Hester, & W. R. Miller (Eds.), *Handbook of alcoholism treatment approaches: Effective alternatives* (pp. 261–271). Elmsford, NY: Pergamon Press.

Miller, W. R., & Rollnick, S. (1991). *Motivational interviewing: Preparing people to change addictive behaviours.* New York: Guilford.

Milton, S., Crino, R., Hunt, C., & Prosser, E. (2002). The effect of compliance-improving interventions on the cognitive-behavioural treatment of pathological gambling. *Journal of Gambling Studies, 18,* 207–229.

Miu, A. C., Heilman, R. M., & Houser, D. (2008). Anxiety impairs decision-making: Psychophysiological evidence from an Iowa gambling task. *Biological Psychology, 77,* 353–358.

Molde, H., Ingjaldsson, J., Kvale, G., Pallesen, S., Stoylen, I. J., Prescott, P., & Johnsen, B. H. (2004). Pathological gambling – assessment, prevalence, aetiology and treatment. *Tidsskrift for Norsk Psykologforening, 41,* 703–722.

Moodie, C., & Finnigan, F. (2006). Association of pathological gambling with depression in Scotland. *Psychological Reports, 99,* 407–417.

Moran, E. (1970). Varieties of pathological gambling. *British Journal of Psychiatry, 116,* 593–597.

Moskowitz, J. A. (1980). Lithium and lady luck: Use of lithium carbonate in compulsive gambling. *New York State Journal of Medicine, 80,* 785–788.

Muelleman, R. L., DenOtter, T., Wadman, M. C., Tran, T. P., & Anderson, J. (2002). Problem gambling in the partner of the emergency department patient as a risk factor for intimate partner violence. *Journal of Emergency Medicine, 23,* 307–312.

Myrseth, H., Pallesen, S., Molde, H., Johnsen, B. H., & Lorvik, I. M. (2009). Personality factors as predictors of pathological gambling. *Personality & Individual Differences, 47,* 933–937.

Najavits, L. M. (2005). Substance abuse. In N. Kazantzis, F. P. Deane, K. R. Ronan & L L'Abate. *Using homework assignments in cognitive behavior therapy* (pp. 263–282). New York: Routledge.

Newman, S. C., & Thompson, A. H. (2007). The association between pathological gambling and attempted suicide: Findings from a national survey in Canada. *The Canadian Journal of Psychiatry, 52,* 605–612.

NSW Young Lawyers (2004). *The Debt Handbook.* Retrieved May 23, 2009 from http://www.lawsociety.com.au/idc/groups/public/documents/internetyounglawyers/027208.pdf.

Oei, T. P. S., & Gordon, L. M. (2008). Psychosocial factors related to gambling abstinence and relapse in members of gamblers anonymous. *Journal of Gambling Studies, 24,* 91–105.

Oei, T. P. S., & Jackson, P. R. (1980). Long-term effects of group and individual social skills training with alcoholics. *Addictive Behaviors, 5,* 129–136.

Oei, T. P. S., & Jackson, P. R. (1982). Social skills and cognitive behavioral approaches to the treatment of problem drinking. *Journal of Studies on Alcohol, 43,* 532–547.

Oei, T. P. S., & Jackson, P. R. (1984). Some effective therapeutic factors in group cognitive-behavioral therapy with problem drinkers. *Journal of Studies on Alcohol, 45,* 119–123.

Oei, T. P. S., Lin, C. D., & Raylu, N. (2007a). Validation of the Chinese version of the Gambling Related Cognitions Scale (GRCS-C), *Journal of Gambling Studies, 23,* 309–322.

Oei, T. P. S., Lin, C. D., & Raylu, N. (2007b). Validation of the Chinese version of the Gambling Urges Scale (GUS-C). *International Gambling Studies, 7,* 101–111.

Oei, T. P. S., Lin, C. D., & Raylu, N. (2008). The relationship between gambling cognitions, psychological states, and gambling: A cross-cultural study of Chinese and Caucasians in Australia. *Journal of Cross-Cultural Psychology, 39,* 147–161.

Oei, T. P. S. & Raylu, N. (2003). Parental influences on offspring gambling cognitions and behaviour: Preliminary findings. *Journal of the National Association for Gambling Studies, 15*, 8–15.

Oei, T. P. S., & Raylu, N. (2004). Familial influence on offspring gambling: A possible mechanism for transmission of gambling behaviour in families. *Psychological Medicine, 34*, 1279–1288.

Oei, T. P. S., & Raylu, N. (2007). *Gambling and problem gambling among the Chinese.* Brisbane: Behaviour Research and Therapy Centre.

Oei, T. P. S., & Raylu, N. (2009). Factors associated with the severity of gambling problems in a community gambling treatment agency. *International Journal of Mental Health & Addiction, 7*, 124–137.

Oei, T. P. S., & Raylu, N. (2010). Gambling behaviors and motivations: A cross-cultural study of Chinese and Caucasians in Australia. *International Journal of Social Psychiatry, 56*, 23–34.

Oei, T. P. S., Raylu, N., & Casey (in press). Group versus individual cognitive behavioral treatment for problem gambling: A randomized controlled trial. *Behavioural and Cognitive Psychotherapy.*

Oei, T. P. S., Raylu, N., & Grace, R. (2008). *Self help program for problem gamblers.* Brisbane: Behaviour Research and Therapy Centre.

O'Neil, M., Whetton, S., Dolman, B., Herbert, M., Giannopolous, V., O'Neil, D., & Wordley, J. (2003). *Part A – Evaluation of self-exclusion programs in Victoria and Part B – Summary of self-exclusion programs in Australian States and Territories.* Melbourne: Gambling Research Panel.

Pallanti, S., Quercioli, L., Sood, E., & Hollander, E. (2002). Lithium and Valproate treatment of pathological gambling: A randomized single-blind study. *Journal of Clinical Psychiatry, 63*, 559–564.

Pallanti, S., Rossi, N. B., Sood, E., & Hollander, E. (2002). Nefazodone treatment of pathological gambling: A prospective open-label controlled trial. *Journal of Clinical Psychiatry, 63*, 1034–1039.

Pallesen, S., Mitsem, M., Kvale, G., Johnsen, B. H., & Molde, H. (2005). Outcome of psychological treatments of pathological gambling: A review and meta-analysis. *Addiction, 100*, 1412–1422.

Pallesen, S., Molde, H., Arnestad, H. M., Laberg, J. C., Skutle, A., Iversen, E., Stoylen, I. J., Kvale, G., & Holsten, F. (2007). Outcome of pharmacological treatments of pathological gambling: A review and meta-analysis. *Journal of Clinical Psychopharmacology, 27*, 357–364.

Perez de Castro, I., Ibáñez, A., Saiz-Ruiz, J., & Fernandez-Piqueras, J. (1999). Genetic contribution to pathological gambling: Association between a functional DNA polymorphism at the serotonin transporter gene (5-HTT) and affected males. *Pharmacogenetics, 9*, 397–400.

Perez de Castro, I., Ibáñez, A., Torres, P., Saiz-Ruiz, J., & Fernandez-Piqueras, J. (1997). Genetic association study between pathological gambling and a functional DNA polymorphism at the D4 receptor. *Pharmacogenetics, 7*, 345–348.

Petry, N. M. (2002). Psychosocial treatments for pathological gambling: Current status and future directions. *Psychiatric Annals, 32*, 192–196.

Petry, N. M. (2003). Patterns and correlates of Gamblers Anonymous attendance in pathological gamblers seeking professional treatment. *Addictive Behaviors, 28*, 1049–1062.

Petry, N. M., Ammerman, Y., Bohl, J., Doersch, A., Gay, H., Kadden, R., Molina, C., &

Steinberg, K. (2006). Cognitive-behavioral therapy for pathological gamblers. *Journal of Consulting & Clinical Psychology*, *74*, 555–567.

Petry, N. M., Stinson F. S., & Grant, B. F. (2005). Comorbidity of DSM-IV pathological gambling and other psychiatric disorders: results from the National Epidemiologic Survey on Alcohol and Related Conditions. *Journal of Clinical Psychiatry*, *66*, 564–574.

Potenza, M. N., Steinberg, M. A., McLaughlin, S. D., Wu, R., Rounsaville, B. J., & O'Malley, S. S. (2001). Gender-related differences in the characteristics of problem gamblers using a gambling helpline. *American Journal of Psychiatry*, *158*, 1500–1505.

Powell, J., Hardoon, K. K., Derevensky, J. L., & Gupta, R. (1999). Gambling and risk-taking behavior among university students. *Substance Use & Misuse*, *34*, 1167–1184.

Prochaska, J. O., & DiClemente, C. C. (1982). Transtheoretical, therapy: Toward a more integrative model of change. *Psychotherapy: Theory, Research, & Practice*, *19*, 276–288.

Prochaska, J. O., & DiClemente, C. C. (1986). Toward a comprehensive model of change. In W. R. Miller, & N. Heather (Eds.), *Treating addictive behaviors: Processes of change*. New York: Plenum Press.

Prochaska, J. O., DiClemente, C. C., & Norcross, J. C. (1992). In search of how people change: Applications to addictive behaviors. *American Psychologist*, *47*, 1102–1114.

Productivity Commission Report (1999). *Australia's Gambling Industries: Final Report*. Canberra: Government Press.

Rankin, H. (1982). Control rather than abstinence as a goal in the treatment of excessive gambling. *Behaviour Research & Therapy*, *20*, 185–187.

Ravindran, A.V., Telner, J., Bhatla, R., Cameron, C., Horn, E., Horner, D., Cebulski, L., & Davis, S. (2006). Pathological gambling: treatment correlates. *European Neuropsychopharmacology*, *16*, S506.

Rawson, R. A., & Obert, J. L. (2002). Relapse prevention groups in outpatient substance abuse treatment. In D. W. Brook, & H. I. Spitz (Eds.), *The group therapy of substance abuse* (pp. 121–138). New York: Haworth Press.

Raylu, N., & Oei, T. P. S. (2002). Pathological gambling: A comprehensive review. *Clinical Psychology Review*, *22*, 1009–1061.

Raylu, N., & Oei, T. P. S. (2004a). Role of culture in gambling and problem gambling. *Clinical Psychology Review*, *23*, 1087–1114.

Raylu, N. & Oei, T. P. S. (2004b). The Gambling Related Cognitions Scale (GRCS): Development, confirmatory factor validation and psychometric properties. *Addiction*, *99*, 757–769.

Raylu, N. & Oei, T. P. S. (2004c). The Gambling Urge Scale (GUS): Development, confirmatory factor validation and psychometric properties. *Psychology of Addictive Behaviors*, *18*, 100–105.

Raylu, N., & Oei, T. P. S. (2007). Factors that predict treatment outcomes in a community treatment agency for problem gamblers. *International Journal of Mental Health & Addiction*, *5*, 165–176.

Raylu, N., & Oei, T. P. S. (2009). Testing the validity of a cognitive behavioral model for gambling behavior. (Manuscript submitted for publication).

Raylu, N., Oei, T. P. S., & Loo, J. M. Y. (2008). The current status and future direction of self-help treatments for problem gamblers. *Clinical Psychology Review*, *28*, 1372–1385.

Redd, W. H., Porterfield, A. L., & Andersen, B. L. (1979). *Behavior Modification: Behavioral approaches to human problems*. New York: Random House.

Reuter, J., Raedler, T., Rose, M., Hand, I., Gläscher, J., & Büchel, C. (2005). Pathological gambling is linked to reduced activation of the mesolimbic reward system. *Nature Neuroscience, 8,* 147–148.

Roca, M., Torralva, T., Lopez, P., Cetkovich, M., Clark, L., & Manes, F. (2008). Executive functions in pathologic gamblers selected in an ecologic setting. *Cognitive & Behavioral Neurology, 21,* 1–4.

Rollnick, S., Heather, N., & Bell, A. (1992). Negotiating behaviour change in medical settings: The development of brief motivational interviewing. *Journal of Mental Health, 1,* 25–37.

Rollnick, S., Kinnersley, P., & Stott, N. (1993). Methods of helping patients with behavior change. *British Medical Journal, 307,* 188–190.

Rosecrance, J. (1988). *Gambling without guilt: The legitimisation of an American pastime.* California: Brooks/Cole.

Roy, A., Adinoff, B., Roehrich, L., Lamparski, D., Custer, R. L., Lorenz, V. C., Barbaccia, M., Guidotti, A., Costa, E., & Linnoila, M. (1988). Pathological gambling: A psychobiological study. *Archives of General Psychiatry, 45,* 369–373.

Rugle, L. J., & Melamed, L. (1993). Neuropsychological assessment of attention problems in pathological gamblers. *Journal of Nervous & Mental Disease, 181,* 107–112.

Rush, B. R., Bassani, D. G., Urbanoski, K. A., & Castel, S. (2008). Influence of co-occurring mental and substance use disorders on the prevalence of problem gambling in Canada. *Addiction, 103,* 1847–1856.

Russo, A. M., Taber, J. I., McCormick, R. A., & Ramirez, L. F. (1984). An outcome study of an inpatient treatment program for pathological gamblers. *Hospital & Community Psychiatry, 35,* 823–827.

Saiz-Ruiz, J., Blanco, C., Ibáñez, A., Masramon, X., Gómez, M. M., Madrigal, M., & Diez, T. (2005). Sertraline treatment of pathological gambling: A pilot study. *Journal of Clinical Psychiatry, 66,* 28–33.

Saunders, J. B., Aasland, O. G., Babor, T. F.; de la Puente, J. R., & Grant, M. (1993). Development of the Alcohol Use Disorders Screening Test (AUDIT). WHO collaborative project on early detection of persons with harmful alcohol consumption. II. *Addiction, 88,* 791–804.

Scherrer, J. F., Xian, H., Shah, K. R., Volberg, R., Slutske, W. S., & Eisen, S. A. (2005). Effect of genes, environment, and lifetime co-occurring disorders on health-related quality of life in problem and pathological gamblers. *Archives of General Psychiatry, 62,* 677–683.

Schultz, J. H. (1932). Superior degree of autogenic training and raya-yoga. *Zeitschrift Für Die Gesamte Neurologie Und Psychiatrie, 139,* 1–34.

Schwarz, J., & Lindner, A. (1992). Inpatient treatment of male pathological gamblers in Germany. *Journal of Gambling Studies, 8,* 93–109.

Seager, C. P. (1970). Treatment of compulsive gamblers by electrical aversion. *British Journal of Psychiatry, 117,* 545–553.

Shaffer, H. J., Hall, M. N., & Vander Bilt, J. (1997). *Estimating the prevalence of disordered gambling behavior in the United States and Canada: A meta-analysis.* Boston: Harvard University.

Shah, K. R., Eisen, S. A., Xian, H., & Potenza, M. N. (2005). Genetic studies of pathological gambling: A review of methodology and analyses of data from the Vietnam era twin registry. *Journal of Gambling Studies, 21,* 179–203.

Sharpe, L. (1998). Cognitive behavioural treatment of problem gambling. In V. E. Caballo (Ed.). *International handbook of cognitive and behavioural treatments for psychological disorder* (pp. 393–416). Oxford: Pergamon.

Sharpe, L. (2002). A reformulated cognitive-behavioral model of problem gambling: A biopsychosocial perspective. *Clinical Psychology Review, 22,* 1–25.

Sharpe, L., & Tarrier, N. (1993). Towards a Cognitive-Behavioural Theory of Problem Gambling. *British Journal of Psychiatry, 162,* 407–412.

Siever, L. J. (1987). Role of noradrenagic mechanisms in the etiology of the affective disorders. In H. Y. Meltzer (Ed.), *Psychopharmacology: Third generation of progress* (pp. 493–504). New York: Raven Press.

Simmons, J. & Griffiths, R. (2009). *CBT for Beginners.* New York: Sage Publications.

Skinner, B. F. (1953). *Science and human behavior.* New York: Macmillan.

Slutske, W. S., Caspi, A., Moffitt, T. E., & Poulton, R. (2005). Personality and problem gambling: A prospective study of a birth cohort of young adults. *Archives of General Psychiatry, 62,* 769–775.

Smith, J. E., & Meyers, R. J. (2004). *Motivating substance abusers to enter treatment: Working with family members.* New York: Guilford Press.

Smith, M. (1985). *When I say no, I feel guilty.* Toronto: Bantam.

Specker, S. M., Carlson, G. A., Edmonson, K. M., Johnson, P. E., & Marcotte, P. E. (1996). Psychopathology in pathological gamblers seeking treatment. *Journal of Gambling Studies, 12,* 67–81.

Steel, Z., & Blaszczynski, A. P. (1996). The factorial structure of pathological gambling. *Journal of Gambling Studies, 12,* 3–20.

Steel, Z., & Blaszczynski, A. P. (1998). Impulsivity, personality disorders and pathological gambling severity. *Addiction, 93,* 895–905.

Ste-Marie, C., Gupta, R., & Derevensky, J. L. (2006). Anxiety and social stress related to adolescent gambling behavior and substance use. *Journal of Child & Adolescent Substance Abuse, 15,* 55–74.

Stewart, R. M., & Brown, R. I. F. (1988). An outcome study of gamblers anonymous. *British Journal of Psychiatry, 152,* 284–288.

Stinchfield, R., & Winters, K. C. (1996). *Effectiveness of Six State-Supported Compulsive Gambling Treatment Programs in Minnesota.* Saint Paul, MN: Compulsive Gambling Program, Minnesota Department of Human Services.

Stinchfield, R., & Winters, K. C. (2001). Outcome of Minnesota's gambling treatment programs. *Journal of Gambling Studies, 17,* 217–245.

Stucki, S., & Rihs-Middel, M. (2007). Prevalence of adult problem and pathological gambling between 2000 and 2005: An update. *Journal of Gambling Studies, 23,* 245–257.

Sunderwirth, S. G., & Milkman, H. (1991). Behavioral and neurochemical commonalities in addiction. *Contemporary Family Therapy: An International Journal, 13,* 421–433.

Sylvain, C., Ladouceur, R., & Boisvert, J. M. (1997). Cognitive and behavioural treatment of pathological gambling: A controlled study. *Journal of Consulting & Clinical Psychology, 65,* 727–732.

Symes, B. A., & Nicki, R. M. (1997). A preliminary consideration of cue-exposure, response-prevention treatment for pathological gambling behaviour: Two case studies. *Journal of Gambling Studies, 13,* 145–157.

Taber, J. I., McCormick, R. A., Russo, A. M., Adkins, B. J., & Ramirez, L. F. (1987). Follow-up of pathological gamblers after treatment. *American Journal of Psychiatry, 144,* 757–761.

Tannen, D. (1986). *That's not what I meant! How conversational style makes or breaks your relations with others.* New York: William Morrow & Co.

Tavares, H., Zilberman, M. L., & El-Guebaly, N. (2003). Are there cognitive and behavioural approaches specific to the treatment of pathological gambling? *The Canadian Journal of Psychiatry, 48,* 22–27.

Toneatto, T. (1999). Cognitive psychopathology of problem gambling. *Substance Use & Misuse, 34,* 1593–1604.

Toneatto, T., Blitz-Miller, T., Calderwood, K., Dragonetti, R., & Tsanos, A. (1997). Cognitive distortions in heavy gambling. *Journal of Gambling Studies, 13,* 253–266.

Toneatto, T., & Dragonetti, R. (2008). Effectiveness of community-based treatment for problem gambling: A quasi-experimental evaluation of cognitive-behavioral vs. twelve-step therapy. *The American Journal on Addictions, 17,* 298–303.

Toneatto, T., & Ladouceur, R. (2003). Treatment of pathological gambling: A critical review of the literature. *Psychology of Addictive Behaviors, 17,* 284–292.

Toneatto, T., & Millar, G. (2004). Assessing and treating problem gambling: Empirical status and promising trends. *Canadian Journal of Psychiatry, 49,* 517–525.

Toneatto, T., & Sobell, L. C. (1990). Pathological gambling treated with cognitive behavior therapy: A case report. *Addictive Behaviors, 15,* 497–501.

Treatment Protocol Project (1997). *Management of mental disorders* (2nd ed.). Sydney: World Health Organization collaborating centre for mental health and substance Abuse.

Tremblay, N., Boutin, C., & Ladouceur, R. (2008). Improved self-exclusion program: Preliminary results. *Journal of Gambling Studies, 24,* 505–518.

Vachon, J., Vitaro, F., Wanner, B., & Tremblay, R. E. (2004). Adolescent gambling: Relationships with parent gambling and parenting practices. *Psychology of Addictive Behaviors, 18,* 398–401.

Victor, R., & Krug, C. (1967). 'Paradoxical intention' in the treatment of compulsive gambling. *American Journal of Psychotherapy, 21,* 808–814.

Vitaro, F., Brendgen, M., Ladouceur, R., & Tremblay, R. E. (2001). Gambling, delinquency, and drug use during adolescence: Mutual influences and common risk factors. *Journal of Gambling Studies, 17,* 171–190.

Wallisch, L. S. (1998). Determinants of gambling and problem gambling: Three theories. *Dissertation Abstracts International Section A: Humanities & Social Sciences, 58,* 4094. Abstract retrieved April 5, 2008 from PsychInfo database.

Walker, M. B. (1992). Irrational thinking among slot machine players. *Journal of Gambling Studies, 8,* 245–261.

Walker, M. B., Milton, S., & Anjoul, F. (1999). *The assessment of pathological gambling: SOGS, DSM-IV, SCIP and SCID.* Paper presented at the State of Play Conference, Perth, Western Australia.

Walker, M. B., Milton, S., Anjoul, F., Scheftsik, M., Allcock, C. C., Amey, O., & Grant, E. (1999). *Reliability issues in the use of DSM-IV criteria to diagnose pathological gambling.* Paper presented at the Developing Strategic Alliances Conference, Adelaide, South Australia.

Welte, J. W., Barnes, G. M., Wieczorek, W. F., Tidwell, M. O., & Parker, J. (2002). Gambling participation in the U.S. – Results from a national survey. *Journal of Gambling Studies, 18,* 313–337.

Welte, J. W., Wieczorek, W. F., Barnes, G. M., & Tidwell, M. O. (2006). Multiple risk factors for frequent and problem gambling: Individual, social, and ecological. *Journal of Applied Social Psychology, 36,* 1548–1568.

Westphal, J. R., & Johnson, L. J. (2007). Multiple co-occurring behaviours among gamblers in treatment: Implications and assessment. *International Gambling Studies, 7,* 73–99.

Williams, W. A., & Potenza, M. N. (2008). The neurobiology of impulse control disorders. *Revista Brasileira de Psiquiatria, 30*, S24–S30.

Winters, K. C., & Rich, T. (1998). A twin study of adult gambling behavior. *Journal of Gambling Studies, 14*, 213–225.

Witkiewitz, K., & Marlatt, G. A. (2009). *Relapse prevention for alcohol and drug problems: That was zen, this is tao.* Washington, DC: American Psychological Association.

Wolpe, J. (1958). *Psychotherapy by reciprocal inhibition.* Oxford: Stanford University Press.

Wulfert, E., Blanchard, E. B., Freidenberg, B. M., & Martell, R. S. (2006). Retaining pathological gamblers in cognitive behavior therapy through motivational enhancement: A pilot study. *Behavior Modification, 30*, 315–340.

Wulfert, E., Blanchard, E. B., & Martell, R. S. (2003). Conceptualizing and treating pathological gambling: A motivationally enhanced cognitive behavioral approach. *Cognitive & Behavioral Practice, 10*, 61–72.

Xian, H., Scherrer, J. F., Slutske, W. S., Shah, K. R., Volberg, R., & Eisen, S. A. (2007). Genetic and environmental contributions to pathological gambling symptoms in a 10-year follow-up. *Twin Research & Human Genetics, 10*, 174–179.

Yip, P. S. F., Yang, K. C. T., Ip, B. Y. T., Law, Y. W., & Watson, R. (2007). Financial debt and suicide in Hong Kong SAR. *Journal of Applied Social Psychology, 37*, 2788–2799.

Zangeneh, M., Grunfeld, A., & Koenig, S. (2008). Individual factors in the development and maintenance of problem gambling. In M. Zangeneh, A. Blaszczynski, & N. E. Turner (Eds.), *In the pursuit of winning: Problem gambling theory, research and treatment* (pp. 83–94). New York: Springer Science and Business Media.

Zimmerman, M., Breen, R. B., & Posternak, M. A. (2002). An open-label study of Citalopram in the treatment of pathological gambling. *Journal of Clinical Psychiatry, 63*, 44–48.

Zion, M. M., Tracy, E., & Abell, N. (1991). Examining the relationship between spousal involvement in Gam-Anon and relapse behaviors in pathological gamblers. *Journal of Gambling Studies, 7*, 117–131.

Zuckerman, M. (1999). *Vulnerability to psychopathology: A biosocial model.* Washington, DC: American Psychological Association.

Author index

Subject index